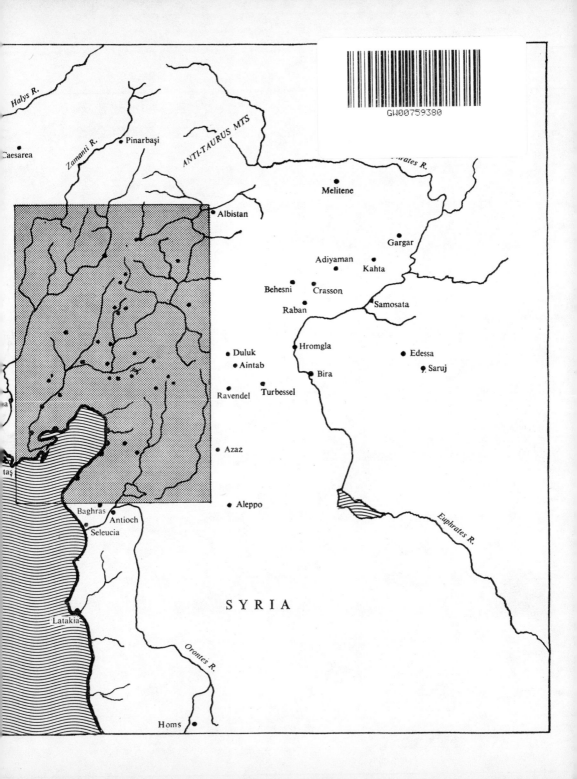

Halys R.

Zamanti R.

Pinarbaşi

Caesarea

ANTI-TAURUS MTS

Euphrates R.

Albistan

Melitene

Gargar

Adiyaman

Kahta

Behesni

Crasson

Samosata

Raban

Hromgla

Edessa

Duluk

Saruj

Aintab

Bira

Ravendel

Turbessel

Azaz

Baghras

Aleppo

Antioch

Seleucia

Euphrates R.

Latakia

S Y R I A

Orontes R.

Homs

THE CILICIAN KINGDOM
OF ARMENIA

THE CILICIAN KINGDOM
OF ARMENIA

T. S. R. BOASE

A. W. LAWRENCE

J. G. DUNBAR & W. W. M. BOAL

J. S. C. RILEY-SMITH

A. T. LUTTRELL

Edited by T. S. R. BOASE

1978

SCOTTISH ACADEMIC PRESS
EDINBURGH & LONDON

Published by
Scottish Academic Press Ltd
33 Montgomery Street, Edinburgh EH7 5JX

SBN 7073 0145 9

Printed in Great Britain by R. & R. Clark Ltd, Edinburgh

PREFACE

From the second half of the eleventh century for some three hundred years Cilicia was under Armenian rulers. In 1198 it became a kingdom; in 1375 the last king was carried away a captive into Egypt. Its history is a stormy one of frontier wars and internal discords, but amidst the turmoil there were writers and artists of distinction and a civilisation as genuine as it was precarious. It is a story that still awaits definitive telling. Father Leonce Alishan published in Venice in 1888 and 1899 two volumes which have been the foundation for later studies, but which have some of the inevitable faults of pioneer work in an obscure and difficult field. More recent accounts, apart from G. G. Micaelian's *Istorya*, untranslated from the Russian, have summarised events in comparatively brief chapters, of which those of Sirapie Der Nersessian in the Wisconsin *History of the Crusades* II and her own volume *The Armenians* are the most authoritative. General histories of the crusades and of the Comnenian emperors have had to deal with Armenian affairs, and in C. Cahen's *La Syrie du Nord* and J. B. Segal's *Edessa* the neighbouring lands, at times under Armenian occupation, have received magisterial treatment. The Armenian kingdom requires, however, fuller consideration in its own right, although there are good reasons why it has not received it. Ideally the narrator requires linguistic knowledge of Armenian, Syriac, Greek, Latin, Arabic, Turkish and Russian. Even more searching are the topographical problems. Much of the territory has never been surveyed for medieval remains; nomenclature has changed bewilderingly, and many important Armenian sites are not yet certainly identified.

Much valuable work is being done and this volume is therefore an interim report which sets down information and theories that in some cases have had long periods of gestation. The castle of Baghras, still an impressive ruin, was the key position in Armenian–Antiochene relations, but has never been published in any detail, and it is more than time that Professor A. W. Lawrence's long acquaintance with it should be made available. Azgit is a fortress with little central place in Armenian frontier policies. The military orders of the Hospital and Temple had at times an important rôle in the Cilician kingdom, and we are fortunate to have historians as well qualified as Dr Luttrell and Dr Riley-Smith to deal with this particular issue. The gazetteer will reveal its own purpose and its own limitations. However incomplete it may be it represents an essential task in Cilician–Armenian studies. Much of it is the result of Professor Lawrence's research (aided by Professor R. B. Serjeant on Arabic sources), but the responsibility for the decisions taken is mine.

In the vexed matter of forms of names, I can claim no consistency, nor I think could I have achieved it. I have used those forms that seem to me most familiar and most likely to be easily identifiable to English readers, and in some places in the gazetteer those used by the authorities to which I refer. Even between the various contributions there is not entire uniformity, and Dr Riley-Smith for instance uses Gaston, the Templars' term, for Baghras.

This book is published with gratefully acknowledged financial assistance from the Calouste Gulbenkian Foundation.

T. S. R. BOASE

PUBLISHER'S NOTE. Dr Boase died before he had finished revising his chapters of the manuscript, and publication, in consequence, was delayed. Professor Lawrence kindly expanded the unfinished captions to the plates. He also provided twenty-five of his own photographs, those of Baghras having particular importance, for the castle has suffered much damage since the photographs were taken.

CONTENTS

ILLUSTRATIONS

Plates

Plates: contd.

Plates: *contd.*

Photographs: Plates 10–12, 14–31, 33, 34, 41, 42, Courtauld Institute (A. W. Lawrence); Plates 4, 35–39, J. Dunbar; Plate 9, Phoebe H. Brown; Plate 5, J. Carslake; Plates 13, 32, M. R. E. Gough; Plates 1–3, 43–47, A. F. Kersting; Plate 6, J. Peck; Plates 40, 44–46, 48, J. Thomson.

Engravings (Plates 7 and 8) after W. H. Bartlett from J. Carne, *Syria* (1838).

Plans

Maps

PLATE I (*frontispiece*)   SILIFKE: from the west

The town is built on the bank of the river Saleph, where there was a bridge from early times and also a ford. The point where a main route from Konya crossed into Cilicia, it was therefore always a place of importance. The castle is on a wooded hill above the town and is one of the major examples of Armenian fortification.

ABBREVIATIONS

AOL	*Archives de l'Orient latin*
AS	*Anatolian Studies*
BSA	*Annual of British School at Athens*
BZ	*Byzantinische Zeitschrift*
CSHB	*Corpus Scriptorum Historiae Byzantinae*
DOP	*Dumbarton Oaks Papers*
ILN	*Illustrated London News*
JA	*Journal Asiatique*
JHS	*Journal of Hellenic Studies*
JRAS	*Journal of the Royal Asiatic Society*
JRGS	*Journal of the Royal Geographical Society*
JRS	*Journal of Roman Studies*
MAMA	*Monumenta Asiae Minoris Antiqua*
MGH	*Monumenta Germaniae Historica*
PG	*Patrologia Graeca*, ed. J. P. Migne
PL	*Patrologia Latina*, ed. J. P. Migne
RA	*Revue Archéologique*
RCAJ	*Royal Central Asian Journal*
REA	*Revue des études arméniennes*

RHC	*Recueil des historiens des Croisades;*
	Arm: Documents arméniens
	Gr: Historiens grecs
	Occ: Historiens occidentaux
	Or: Historiens orientaux
RHGF	*Recueil des historiens des Gaules et de la France*
ROL	*Revue de l'Orient latin*

NOTE: Where short titles are given in the notes, the full title will be found in the bibliography.

I

THE HISTORY OF THE KINGDOM

In the sixth century B.C. the name Armenian came to be applied to a people living in the southern districts of the Caucasus and emerging into some independence with the break up of the Urartian empire. Herodotus thought that they had come from Phrygia, but this remains a debatable statement. They figure in Achaemenid and Parthian history, and with the accession of Tigran the Great in 95 B.C. began a period of expansion which made them a great power in the Near East. This, however, brought Rome against them and in 66 B.C. Tigran was forced to sue for peace. Armenian territories were divided between Rome and Parthia, and later between Byzantium and the Arabs. For long years these lands were in the unhappy position of a buffer state. Constant warfare, however, did not prevent the rise of a national culture. Early in the fourth century Christianity was proclaimed as the state religion of Armenia, probably the first official acceptance as opposed to the mere tolerance laid down by the Constantinian edict of 313. Greek influences were strong and the Greek language much in use, but the Armenian Church soon developed doctrinal and liturgical versions of its own, and this national outlook was much strengthened when in A.D. 406 an Armenian alphabet was adopted, suited to their own linguistic requirements. In the arts, also, there was much activity, and their architecture, in its surviving remains, has often been claimed as the source of new practices.

In the tenth century under the Bagratid dynasty there was a period of relative peace and prosperity. The high tableland that lies between Lake Van and the Caucasus with its mountain passes and deep, narrow valleys, its brief, hot, fertile summers and long obstructive winters, lent itself to parcelling into small communities, hard to hold together; but Gakik I (989–1020), from his capital at Ani, had reduced the various chieftaincies to some measure of unity. Then came renewed intervention from Byzantium, and by 1021 the Emperor Basil II had occupied much of the Armenian territory. In 1045, after strong resistance, Gakik II of Ani was forced to abdicate. Within three years another power was attacking these harassed lands, and the Byzantine dispersion of the Armenian people, a strong fighting stock, left no opposition to stem the advance of the Selchukid Turks. Ani was captured by them in 1064 and shortly afterwards they took Kars. In 1071 the two competing powers met at Manzikert, north of Lake Van; the Byzantine forces were completely defeated, and the emperor, Romanus Diogenes, captured.

Constantine Monomachus (1042–55) had already pressed forward a policy of Armenian resettlement in Cappadocia and Cilicia. Sebastia (Sivas) and Caesarea of Cappadocia (Kayseri) were the two main centres of this dispersion, but in 1042 Ablgharib, of an Armenian family who had long served the Greeks, received the governorship of Tarsus and Mamistra, and Cilicia became another refuge for the displaced Armenians. In the campaign of the Emperor John Zimisces in 975, when he penetrated into northern Syria and the Orontes valley, there was a large contingent of Armenian troops, some of whom may have remained on garrison duty.[1]

Cilicia was a mountain country that could recall something of the earlier Armenian homeland. The great block of the Taurus mountains, a double range at places 100 km. in breadth, includes peaks rising, not as high as the 5,000 m. of Caucasian Mt Ararat, but in some cases nearly to 4,000 m. The mountain barrier, however, cut off a coastal plain, on a southern sea. From Silifke to Mersin this is a comparatively narrow strip, rough and stony on the western half, well earthed and fertile on the eastern. Beyond Mersin it widens out watered by three rivers, the Tarsus Çayi (Cydnus), the Seyhan (Sarus), and the Ceyhan (Pyramus). On the east the plain rounds the Gulf of Alexandretta, where it is bounded by the Amanus mountains, and then it is finally blocked by Mt Cassius projecting into the sea. The main entry from the north through the Taurus mountains was by the Cilician Gates, leading down to Tarsus, and it was on the southern side of this pass that Ablgharib established one of his officers, Oshin the Hetoumid, at the castles of Lampron and Babaron. Beyond the Pass on the northern side the castle of Asgouras was held by another Armenian family, the Nathanaels.

Ablgharib belonged to the Armenian group who had come to terms with Byzantium, taken service there and received imperial appointments. Some of them joined also the Orthodox Church, separated from the Armenian by theological disputes about the nature of Christ and by a different method of calculating the dates of Easter and Christmas. These matters aroused passionate

---

[1] G. Schlumberger, *L'Épopée byzantine à la fin du dixième siècle*, 3 vols. (Paris, 1896), pp. 282–306.

convictions and debates upon them were constantly stimulated by the rival ecclesiastics, so that Armenian quarrelled with Armenian on both political and religious grounds. North of the Cilician Gates, centring on Caesarea, the rule of the Bagratid Gakik II, who had been tricked into surrendering his northern lands, was bitterly hostile to the Greeks. 'He did not cease', Matthew of Edessa wrote of him, 'to nourish in his heart a deep grievance for the loss of the throne of his fathers against this treacherous and perverse race of heretics.' Whenever opportunity occurred he brutally attacked Greek settlements, raping the women and massacring the men. He seized Mark, the Greek metropolitan of Caesarea, and along with his dog, to which he had rashly given the name 'Armenian', tied him up in a sack where the beast slowly devoured his master. Ablgharib began by trying to come to terms with this troublesome neighbour. His daughter was married to Gakik's eldest son, David, but the latter soon found himself a prisoner in the castle of Lampron. Gakik came in 1091 to Tarsus to negotiate his son's release, but on his return, whether or not with Ablgharib's connivance is uncertain, Gakik was seized by some Greeks, sons of a certain Mandale or Pantaleon, murdered in their castle of Cybistra and his body hung out in ignominy on the castle walls. It was a deed that was long to be remembered, but for the time being Gakik's forces, little more than a brigand band, seem to have dispersed, and one of his officers, Rupen, occupied a fortress at Gobidara, probably in the hills north of Sis. Rupen's son, Constantine, in 1091 seized the castle of Vahka, commanding a route through the Taurus leading down to Adana. This marks the introduction to Cilicia of the family that was to play the leading part there in the establishment of an Armenian state.

In the chaos following Manzikert little Byzantine control could be exercised and everywhere more or less independent chieftaincies were set up. At Antioch Philaretus Brachamius, another of the Armenian–Byzantine officers, gradually extended his power over northern Syria. In Antioch Vasak, an Armenian of distinguished ancestry, held rule till his assassination about 1080 by some Greek soldiers. Philaretus exacted vengeance for the act, and himself occupied Antioch. At the same period Vasil, whose father Abu-Kab had for a time ruled in Edessa, seized that town, where he died some four years later leaving a reputation for good government, 'a pious man', Matthew of Edessa calls him 'and merciful to widows'. After a brief period of disputes Edessa was brutally occupied by one of Philaretus' adherents. Cruelty and treachery characterised all Philaretus' acts and the Armenian chroniclers have little good to say of him. An Orthodox by faith, he became according to Matthew of Edessa a renegade to Islam, but his career outlined the possibility of a new Armenian state bounded by the Amanus mountains on the west, the upper reaches of the Euphrates on the north-east, and then extending beyond the great river to include Edessa. Marash, Albistan, Melitene, Kesoun (Crasson) and Gargar were all in his power. His vision, however, had little reality. By the time of his death in 1085 Selchukid pressure was breaking up his territories.[2] Antioch was lost in 1084 and for the next six years the strong government of the sultan of Baghdad, Malik Shah, controlled the whole area. On Malik's death in 1092 and the internal Selchukid disputes that followed, Armenian leaders, with the extra-ordinary resilience of their race, once more came to the fore. Two of Philaretus' captains Gabriel, or Khoril, and Thoros, succeeded in establishing themselves at Melitene and Edessa respectively. Both of them Orthodox like their master, they were in this respect suspect to many of their compatriots. At Marash another Armenian, Tatoul, held rule. All these had received confirmation from Alexius Comnenus as he gradually restored order to the empire, and Thoros had received the title of *curopalates*. East of Marash at Kesoun and Raban a more genuine Armenian, Kogh Vasil (Basil the Robber), held several castles, and was to pass on his lands to his adopted son, Dgha Vasil. Kesoun under them became the main rallying point for the Armenian people. It was a brother of Kogh Vasil, Bagrat or Pancrace, who made contact with the crusading forces at Nicaea in 1097 and accompanied them on their march across Asia Minor, forming a close alliance with one of their leaders, Baldwin of Boulogne.

The coming of the first crusade changed the whole position for these struggling and scattered Armenian groups. The main body of the Franks took the route along the northern slopes of the Taurus from Heraclea (Eregli) to Tyana, Augustopolis (Niğde) and Caesarea. Here their main opponents were the Danishmendid Turks, who under their able ruler Malik-Ghazi Gumushtigin had established themselves in eastern Anatolia, with their chief town at Sebastia. Sometimes in enmity with Kilij-Arslan, the Selchukid sultan of Roum, some-times with Byzantine support, they were gradually absorbing the strongholds of southern Cappadocia, and Gabriel of Melitene was hard pressed by them at the time of the crusaders' arrival. The Danishmendids had attempted an attack on the Franks at Heraclea, but had been driven off, and to the Armenians the crusaders at first appeared as heaven-sent deliverers. Godfrey of Bouillon and the main body advanced to Coxon (Göksun) and from there by a terrible

[2] J. Laurent, 'Byzance et Antioche sous le curopalate Philarète', *Revue des études arméniennes* IX (1929), pp. 61–72; J. B. Segal, *Edessa, the Blessed City* (Oxford, 1970), pp. 192–257.

autumn crossing of the Anti-Taurus, 'the diabolical mountains', came to Marash, where they made no attempt to dispossess the Armenian Tatoul. Thence the crusaders had an easy march down to the plain of Antioch, and the nine months siege of that town.

Before this, however, two parties had detached themselves from the main body. From Heraclea Tancred, a Norman from southern Italy, having strongly opposed the Caesarea–Marash route, had crossed by the Cilician Gates into the coastal plain and laid siege to the Turkish garrison in Tarsus. The Christian population at once made contact with him, but before the town could be occupied another and larger crusading force under Baldwin of Boulogne with his cousin, Baldwin of Le Bourg, appeared, and the Turks fled by night. They did not, however, move to any great distance. A further Norman detachment, seeking Tancred who had moved eastward, were excluded from Tarsus by Baldwin and fell victims to a surprise attack by the Turks. In revenge for this defeat, attributed to Baldwin's callous refusal of entrance into Tarsus, the Normans, under Richard of the Principate, Tancred's harsh and impolitic cousin, attacked Baldwin when the latter caught up with Tancred outside Mamistra. The leaders soon came to their senses and made terms, but it was the first time that crusader had fought crusader and it can have little edified the local Christians, however used they may have been to their own civil broils. Their chroniclers in fact give little space to this first crusading raid and, though Tancred cleared the Turks from Adana and Mamistra, there was as yet no serious attempt at permanent Frankish occupation. Contact was made with both Oshin of Lampron and the Rupenian, Constantine of Vahka, each of whom was ready to play the Franks off against the other. To the Armenian chroniclers, it was Baldwin's next move, the occupation of Edessa, that was of importance.

Between Marash and the Euphrates lay the lands of Kogh Vasil, the brother of Baldwin's Armenian adviser, Bagrat, and from Edessa itself there were appeals for assistance from the Armenian governor, Thoros. Frankish mercenaries had fought under Philaretus and it was no new expedient to seek their support. With Armenian help, for he had only a force of 100 horsemen, Baldwin in the winter of 1097–8 occupied Ravendel (Ruwandan) and Turbessel (Tel-Bashir). From here he began to negotiate with Thoros as to the position to be given him in Edessa. His Armenian allies, very rightly, became suspicious of his aims and in particular Bagrat, who had been entrusted with Ravendel, was accused of plotting against Baldwin and was seized and tortured. He escaped to join his brother, but from then on Kogh Vasil must have been wary of Frankish help.

B

The story of Baldwin's adoption by Thoros, the plot of which another Armenian, Constantine of Gargar, seems to have been the main organiser, the resulting assassination of Thoros, and Baldwin's acceptance as lord of Edessa, have been told in detail by Matthew of Edessa, who in all probability was as a young man eyewitness of these events. Thoros, son-in-law of Gabriel of Melitene, belonged to the group of Orthodox Armenians, formerly Byzantine officers, who were suspect alike to the Armenians and the Syrians. It was this that made Baldwin's path easy. Doctrinally the Latins were as much at variance with the local churches as were the Greeks, but they were newcomers with no tradition of hostility and persecution.[3]

Baldwin's next moves were in relation to his Moslem neighbours. Balduk, the Turkish emir of Samosata, was the nearest danger, against which Baldwin had already led a raid before Thoros was deposed. The emir now recognised his authority and unwisely came to reside in Edessa, where Baldwin soon found an excuse for disposing of him. Saruj, a Moslem town to the south-east of Edessa, was occupied, and when in May 1098 the great army of Kerboga of Mosul, with detachments from the sultanates of Iraq and Persia, marched to the relief of Antioch, Edessa resisted him during a three weeks' siege, a respite of infinite value to the wearied main army of the crusaders. Baldwin was now ruler of an Armenian and a Moslem state, and already was exercising a policy curiously at variance in its religious tolerance with the propaganda of the Council of Clermont. He encouraged intermarriage between the Franks and the Armenians, and himself married an Armenian, Arda, niece of Constantine of Vahka. Then in 1100 Baldwin was called to take over the Kingdom of Jerusalem and ceded the County of Edessa to his cousin, Baldwin of Le Bourg.

In 1102 Constantine of Vahka died. He had aided the crusading forces at Antioch by sending supplies and had been recognised by them as an ally. He left two sons, Thoros and Leon, the former of whom was in later Armenian historiography to be known as Thoros I and who till his death in 1129 held some form of rule based on the fortresses of Vahka and Partzapert. The crusaders in Antioch, however, left him little opportunity for extending his rule. Bohemond, the Norman ruler of this city, had early made an unsuccessful attempt to oust Tatoul from Marash. Then in 1100 he and Richard of the Principate, answering an appeal from Gabriel of Melitene, fell into a Danishmendid ambush and were carried prisoners to Kharput. It was news that spread alarm among the Christian populations of the region, but it was seen as a judgment on the sins of the Franks, who had left the true way and had no care of the Lord's

[3] J. Laurent, 'Des Grecs aux Croisés', *Byzantion* I (1924), pp. 387–449.

teaching. 'That which they defended', wrote Matthew of Edessa, 'was that which they coveted.' Notwithstanding, it was the Armenian, Kogh-Vasil, lord of Behesni and Kesoun, who played the largest part, both as negotiator and contributor, in ransoming Bohemond. The latter when released soon abandoned Antioch in order to resume the traditional Norman policy of attacking Byzantium across the Adriatic, but on his departure for the West he left as his regent the ruthless and able Tancred, who directed his attacks against the Greek garrisons of the Cilician coastal plain. It was an area where Byzantium was gradually reoccupying its former territory, but one in which, since his first raid there, Tancred had been interested. Now he brought Mamistra, Adana and Tarsus under Antiochene control.

Baldwin II, following the first Baldwin's example, had married an Armenian, Morfia, the daughter of Gabriel of Melitene and sister-in-law of the murdered Thoros; but this alliance was to prove of little value, for in 1103 Malik-Ghazi of Danishmend captured Melitene, and Gabriel, betrayed it seems by some of his own people, was put to death. This brought a new threat to Baldwin's northern frontier, and he occupied Marash, turning out Tatoul, who still nominally held the place from Byzantium. Then between 1104 and 1108 Baldwin of Le Bourg in his turn was a prisoner in Moslem hands, eventually those of Chavli of Mosul, who released him and took him as an ally against Sharaf-ad-Din Maudud of Mosul, commissioned by the sultan from Baghdad to restore order amongst the warring Moslem states of northern Syria. During Baldwin's captivity Tancred ruled Edessa through his cousin Richard of the Principate, whose tyranny soon alienated his Armenian subjects: 'the rule of the Franks,' wrote Matthew of Edessa, 'had passed into inferior hands'. In particular the town of Albistan where the route from Marash joined that from Coxon to Melitene was handed over to the Moslems by its Armenian inhabitants and the Frankish garrison of three hundred men were massacred. Matthew has a telling phrase describing the precarious balance sought by the Franks, a minority among strange peoples and faiths: 'they destroyed affection and joy among friends, treason and hate were everywhere'. And not only between Franks and indigenes, for on Baldwin's release, Tancred held to these territories, and four years of civil war followed in which neither side hesitated to employ Moslem allies. Tancred died in 1112 and the heir to Antioch was an absent child, Bohemond II. The same year Kogh Vasil died and his lands passed to his young adopted son, Dgha Vasil, who sought to strengthen his position by marrying in 1116 the daughter of Leon, brother of Thoros I. The latter's suspicions seem to have been aroused by this union for he seized Vasil and

PLATE 2

SILIFKE

Southern exterior of the Castle

As the Frontispiece shows, the castle stretches along the top of a steep-sided ridge, from which, however, it was isolated by a flattened strip of rock 10 to 15 m. wide, bordered by a low wall. Outside this was a ditch, twice as wide, around most of the circuit though not towards the east or north-east, where the ground falls more steeply; here a ramp ascends to the entrance which was near one end of the ditch, and there is a postern at the other. Several parts of the circuit were lined internally with very long buildings attached to the wall; some of these were evidently two-storeyed. The ground-floor rooms would, in general, have best been used for storage; the castle must, of course, have been provisioned to withstand a siege, and its cisterns could keep an ample reserve of rain-water. A building of immense length was entered through five doorways in a row though only one partition is visible, separating a room less than 7 m. square from one that extends 48 m. along the back of the circuit. Holes along the crown of its vault held, no doubt, the fittings for chains by which lamps were suspended. Probably this building was the Hall; another of similar width but only half as long may have been the chapel, since it is nearly 7 m. high. Both should perhaps be ascribed to the Hospitallers.

A. W. L.

handed him over to Baldwin of Edessa. Put to the torture, the young man ceded his estates and, now less dangerous, was allowed to rejoin his father-in-law in Cilicia. It was an incident in a fierce period of Armenian deprivation. Baldwin seized Bira from its Armenian lord, Ablgharib, assigning it to his cousin, Galeran of Le Puiset, and marrying him to Ablgharib's daughter. Constantine of Gargar, the leader of the plot that had established the first Baldwin, was in 1118 imprisoned in the citadel of Samosata. In an earthquake the tower fell and amongst the tumbled masonry was found the corpse of Constantine, still chained to a pillar. Bagrat, another early ally, had been driven from his lands at Ravendel. In 1114 a more terrible earthquake had destroyed this area. Its centre seems to have been at Marash, where Matthew of Edessa estimates that 40,000 persons perished, 'for it was a very populous city'. But the devastation was experienced as far as Sis, and along the Euphrates towns and fortresses crumbled. It is little wonder that Baldwin could occupy or re-occupy so much of this ruined country and that there was an element of desperation in the brutality with which he did it.

In 1118 Baldwin I of Jerusalem died without an heir. He had repudiated his childless and uncongenial Armenian wife, but his second marriage with Adelaide of Sicily, in itself of doubtful legality, for the Armenian lady was still alive, proved no more successful. The barons of the Kingdom called upon Baldwin of Le Bourg to succeed him. The prime mover in this was Joscelin of Courtenay. He was by his mother a first cousin of the second Baldwin, who, when he succeeded to Edessa in 1100, had enfeoffed Joscelin with the fortress of Turbessel and the land west of the Euphrates. Joscelin had then married, according to the policy of the time, a daughter of Constantine of Vahka, sister of Thoros and Leon. He had shared Baldwin's captivity in 1104 to 1108, but later there had been friction between them. Now, however, he secured his cousin's accession to Jerusalem and in return received the County of Edessa. He was a doughty warrior and strong ruler, allied with Antioch through his second wife, Maria of Salerno, the sister of Roger, Tancred's nephew and successor, until the coming of age of the young Bohemond. But in 1119 Roger perished in the fatal battle of the 'field of blood', warring against Ilghazi of Mardin and three years later Joscelin and Galeran of Bira were both captured. Baldwin II a year later, seeking to defend these northern territories, shared the same fate and was sent to join the other prisoners at Kharput. From there Joscelin, aided by Armenians who paid sorely for doing so, made a daring escape, but it was not till June 1124 that Baldwin was able to ransom himself. His Armenian wife, Morfia, busied herself with raising the necessary funds.

Thoros from his mountains seems to have watched these events without seeking to join in them. His only conquest was Anavarza, where an inscription still recalls his refortification of 'this second Troy'. To the Armenian chroniclers he is above all the avenger of the murder of Gakik. Matthew of Edessa tells the story in detail: the three sons of Pantaleon still held the castle of Cybistra, and rashly came on an embassy to Thoros to negotiate a possible handing over of the place; the negotiations broke down, and Thoros led his forces to attack and, somewhat surprisingly, for it seems to have been strong, to take the castle. There they found the sword and robes of Gakik, which they received with tears. Thoros then put the brothers to torture to disclose their treasure. One of them flung himself from the battlements, another threatened Thoros: 'You, an Armenian, what reply will you give to our sovereign for having maltreated Romans?' 'Who were you', replied Thoros, 'when you assassinated a hero, the king of Armenia, consecrated by the Holy Unction, and for that you must answer to the Armenian nation', and he fell on him and battered him to death. Then with the third brother and the rich treasures of the castle, he withdrew to Vahka.

In 1118 Thoros sent a contingent of troops under his brother Leon to aid Roger of Antioch in the capture of Azaz, but this was his main contact with the Latins. Leon succeeded him in 1129. In the same year Baldwin II of Jerusalem died. His heiress Melisend was on her mother's side of Armenian blood, and frequently showed her awareness of it. A powerful husband had been sought for her and she was married to Fulk, Count of Anjou. The personalities were changing. Bohemond II had in 1126 at last arrived to claim his heritage, and had been married to one of Baldwin II's daughters, Alice, a difficult woman much given to intrigue. But Bohemond's rule was brief. Four years later he was killed leading a raid into Cilicia where he clashed with a Danishmendid force on a similar errand, and perished in this chance encounter. Both expeditions were probably provoked by marauding raids from the Armenian highlands. The weakness of Antioch tempted Leon, who had his northern frontier protected by a Danishmendid alliance, and between 1132 and 1135 he occupied Mamistra, Adana, Tarsus and Sarvantikar. This brought him into contact with a new enemy. Galeran of Bira had been killed in captivity, sawn asunder it was said. A new county of Marash had been formed out of his lands and those formerly held by Kogh Vasil and assigned to a Baldwin, whom the Armenian chroniclers describe as a brother of Raymond of Poitiers, the ruler of Antioch since his marriage in 1136 with the princess, Constance, Bohemond II's daughter. Western sources know nothing of this relationship and little of Baldwin, but

William IX of Aquitaine could well have provided illegitimate as well as an uncertain number of legitimate progeny. To the Armenians, Baldwin was a familiar figure, and we have a long funeral oration about him written by his friend and chaplain Basil. It is not uncritical: accusations of arrogance, cruelty and desire for plunder are made against him, but he is notwithstanding Basil's 'well beloved Baldwin'. Gregory the Preacher, who came from Kesoun and knew this area, tells us in his chronicle that Baldwin preferred Armenians to Latins, spoke Armenian fluently and was 'a fine young man, a victorious and intrepid warrior, perspicacious, wise and prudent'.[4] Such a man was likely to react quickly against Leon's expansion of his frontiers, particularly as Leon in 1135 had captured the fortress of Sarvantikar, which had been in Antiochine control. Leon was lured into a visit and then treacherously captured, but he was released within two months, when it was known that the Emperor John Comnenus was leading an expedition southwards that might be as dangerous to Antioch as it was to Cilicia.

Leon's brief captivity gave scope to the ferocity of his people. His sons, a markedly difficult set of young men, quarrelled amongst themselves, and one of them, Constantine, was blinded by his brothers. While they were thus engaged, the Danishmendids, despite the truce, raided the Cilician plain and also laid siege to Marash. The arrival of the Byzantine army in 1137 led by the emperor forced the Danishmendids to withdraw, but also brought a new and greater danger to Cilicia. John Comnenus seems to have made Antalya the base for his campaign and to have advanced along the coastal route. Here several of the towns still had Greek garrisons, and the Hetoumids from their castles of Lampron and Babaron supported him against Thoros. On the eastern Armenian boundary, Baldwin of Marash entered into negotiation with the emperor. Tarsus, Adana and Mamistra surrendered, and Anavarza, after a resolute defence that lasted thirty-seven days, was taken. John Comnenus proceeded to Antioch, capturing Til Hamdun and leaving a force to besiege Vahka, Leon's northern retreat, which eventually fell. Leon was captured in the mountains and with two of his sons, Rupen and Thoros, was sent a prisoner to Constantinople. Rupen was killed there and Leon died in captivity. Two others of his sons, Mleh and Stephen, had taken refuge with Joscelin of Edessa, their cousin, who had supported Leon against Antioch and Baldwin of Marash.

The Byzantine conquest of Cilicia was completed in the winter of 1137–8

---

[4] The date at which Baldwin took over his county is uncertain. It would seem most probable that he was given it by Raymond, as a buffer state between Antioch and Edessa, in which case the date would be 1136.

and for the next seven years the country was at unusual peace under Byzantine rule. Even the death of John Comnenus, wounded by a poisoned arrow while hunting in Cilicia, did not immediately lead to a slackening of control. How the wound occurred, whether accident or assassination, remains a mystery. At first it was regarded as a trifling matter. But poisoning set in, and on 8 April 1143, having nominated his second son Manuel as his successor, the emperor died in his camp near Anavarza.

Armenian resistance recovered with the escape from Constantinople, probably in 1145, of Leon's son, Thoros. Reaching Cilicia, probably by sea, he received help from the Jacobite patriarch, Athanasius, who gave him a small guard of twelve men and admitted him into the castle of Amouda, two miles south of Anavarza. Thoros occupied the latter in 1148 and also the old Rupenid stronghold of Vahka. In 1151 he took Til Hamdun and Mamistra. Antioch at this period was preoccupied with the capture of Edessa by Zengi in 1144; Byzantium with the passage of the second crusade, an expedition that the loss of Edessa had provoked. When eventually in 1152 a Byzantine force under Andronicus Comnenus, the future emperor, was sent against him, Thoros defeated him, and in the battle Sempad of Babaron was killed, fighting for the Greeks, and Oshin II of Lampron was captured. Thoros took the opportunity to arrange a marriage between Oshin's son Hetoum and one of his own daughters, a diplomatic move, though the bride was later to be repudiated. He himself had strengthened his alliance with Joscelin of Edessa by marrying the daughter of one of Joscelin's vassals, Simon of Raban.

The fall of Edessa resulted in the collapse of the Frankish hold on the County. When Joscelin II attempted in 1146 to regain the town, he was defeated by Nur-ad-Din, and Baldwin of Marash, here fighting on Joscelin's side, was killed in the field, winning, as his Armenian supporters claimed, the crown of martyrdom, though he had died unshriven. William of Tyre reports his death as that of a distinguished leader, but clearly knows little of him. Four years later Joscelin II was taken prisoner and, unmourned, for he was of little worth, passed to his death in captivity. His valiant wife, Beatrice of Saône, stoutly defended Turbessel, but it was impossible to hold. Surprisingly the Emperor Manuel offered to purchase it from her, along with the remaining fortresses of Ravendel, Samosata, Aintab, Duluk and Bira. Byzantine garrisons occupied but could not keep them. Manuel's purchase had presumably been made with some future Syrian campaign in view, but he made no effort to defend his acquisition and Nur-ad-Din rapidly reduced this group of fortresses. The Armenian population of the district were, under the careful direction of King Baldwin III, safely evacuated to Antioch. The Frankish–Armenian Counties of Edessa and Marash were at an end. One stronghold had not been ceded to Byzantium. Beatrice handed over Hromgla (Rum Qalat) to the Armenian patriarch for his head-quarters, and there somewhat surprisingly the patriarchate remained for over a hundred years, despite the fact that it must normally, in these shifting frontiers, have been deep in Moslem territory. Marash was taken by Masud, son of Kilij-Arslan, in 1148 and shortly afterwards Behesni, Kesoun and Raban were in his hands. Stephen of Armenia, Thoros' brother, for a time raided and dis-turbed the territory from his fastness of Pertounk, bringing severe persecution on the people of Marash and Kesoun from their Moslem overlords. But from now on this area was to be in dispute between Kilij Arslan II and Nur-ad-Din and neither Armenia nor Antioch was to have much say in its destiny.

Meanwhile in Cilicia Thoros had been creating something that began to look like a state. Manuel had tried to dislodge him, first by persuading Masud of Iconium to attack him and then, when the Selchukid forces were driven back by Thoros' brother, Stephen and a Templar force from Baghras, by hiring Reginald of Châtillon, recently married to the widowed Constance of Antioch, to invade Cilicia. It was an inconclusive business. Manuel did not send the promised money; Reginald and Thoros came to terms and recouped them-selves by a peculiarly brutal raid on Cyprus. Retaliation was bound to follow, but when Manuel and the Byzantine army in 1158 marched through Cilicia and encamped at Mamistra, Thoros, largely thanks to the skilful mediation of Baldwin III, made his peace with the emperor, coming to his camp in penitential garb and receiving some recognition of his position in Armenia, though Byzan-tine governors were left in the main townships.

The relations of Thoros with the Latins remained friendly. He visited King Amalric in Jerusalem, and is said to have offered to send 30,000 Armenian settlers to the Kingdom, a scheme that broke down owing to problems of Latin ecclesiastical taxation. According to Bar Hebraeus it was an intervention by Thoros that secured the rule of Bohemond III of Antioch against the claims of his mother, Constance. Certainly in 1164 Thoros participated with Bohemond, Raymond of Tripoli and the Greek commander at Tarsus, Constantine Colo-man, in an attack on Nur-ad-Din. At first successful, the allies found them-selves threatened by a considerable muster of the enemy. Thoros counselled a withdrawal and took off his contingent. The others rashly pressed on and the Frankish leaders were all taken prisoner. Thoros obtained the release of Bohe-mond and Coloman, both under Byzantine protection, by threatening to burn alive all his own captives.

Cilicia, however, remained secure. Benjamin of Tudela, visiting it shortly
before 1167, describes it as the land of Thoros, ruler of the mountains and king
of Armenia, and gives its western frontier as beginning at Corycus.[5] 'King' was
only a courtesy term; no kingship had yet been established, but its use shows
the position accorded to Thoros. His main problem in the concluding years of
his reign was control of his brothers. Stephen, for a time imprisoned when
Thoros was warned against him, carried on ceaseless and exacerbating raids
against the Greek posts and finally in 1164 was lured by the Greek garrison into
the castle of Hamus and murdered, reputedly by being boiled alive. This fierce
act roused the Armenians to a massacre of the Greeks, who were then defended
by the Hetoumids, reopening the ancient Armenian feud. The youngest brother,
Mleh, was an even more turbulent spirit and Thoros banished him from the
Kingdom. He had at one time been admitted to the order of the Temple, but
had left or been expelled; he now took refuge with Nur-ad-Din, and it was with
Moslem troops that he entered Cilicia on Thoros' death in 1168, drove out the
regent, Thomas, Thoros' and his own nephew, and soon disposed of Thoros'
young son, Rupen II. Fierce and unscrupulous, he rapidly gained ground with
Turkish help, besieged, unsuccessfully, the Hetoumid castle of Lampron, drove
the Antiochenes and the Templars from the Amanus mountains, and defeated
and captured the Byzantine governor Constantine Coloman, handing him over
to Nur-ad-Din, who in return ceded Marash to him. But Mleh's dependence
on Moslem aid roused popular feeling against him; the Armenian barons rose
and killed him on Nur-ad-Din's death in 1174. The two sons of the murdered
Stephen, Rupen and Leon, had been taken by their mother Rita, daughter of
the Sempad killed in Thoros' victory of 1152, a woman of remarkable character
and longevity, to the safety of her brother's castle at Babaron, and the elder,
Rupen, was now summoned as Mleh's successor. His immediate task was to
clear the raiding Turkoman bands, who under Mleh's pro-Islamic policy had
been penetrating Cilicia. Rupen III sought a Frankish alliance and married
Isabel, daughter of Humphrey of Toron, going to Jerusalem for the ceremony,
and thereby forming a link with the leading Palestinian families. By 1183 his
position seemed sufficiently established for him to resume that traditional
activity of his house, the siege of Lampron. From their mountain castles the
Hetoumids constantly raided the coastal plain, carrying off cattle and women.
It was a problem that had to be ended, despite the protection the Hetoumid
family had given to Rupen in his boyhood. Hetoum of Lampron, however,

[5] See J. Prawer, *Histoire du Royaume Latin de Jérusalem*, trs. G. Nahon (Paris,
1969), I, p. 571. *Benjamin of Tudela*, trs. M. N. Adler, p. 15.

appealed to Bohemond III of Antioch, who invited Rupen to an interview (one chronicler says he went to Antioch for orgies with evil women) and then seized him, holding him prisoner for a year and only releasing him for a ransom of 1,000 *tategans*[6] and the surrender of Sarvantikar, Til Hamdun, Mamistra and Adana, sites which, if ever handed over, were quickly regained. Rupen's captivity had given an opportunity to his younger brother Leon to show his mettle, and it was to him that in 1187 Rupen surrendered his office, withdrawing to the monastery of Trazarg, outside Sis, where he died in the same year.

Leon II was fortunate in the time at which he came to power. Saladin's defeat of the crusading kingdom and his campaign of 1188 against Antioch left Armenia in a new position as representative of Christendom. The death of Manuel Comnenus in 1180 had led to a period of confused rivalries in Constantinople, and in 1187 imperial power was in the uncertain hands of Isaac Angelus. The long rule of Kilij-Arslan II in Iconium was nearing its end amid the disputes of his sons as to the succession. Leon was quick to seize his opportunities. Commerical privileges were given to the Venetians and Genoese to draw their trade to Ayas (Lajazzo) which for a time became the chief entrepôt of the eastern Mediterranean. Baronial independence was curbed by the gradual infiltration of theories of western feudalism and the giving of western titles to office holders. The pope was placated by professions of devotion which skilfully hid the lack of any doctrinal change in the Armenian Church. Impregnable Lampron was acquired by the familiar ruse of luring the Hetoumids to a festival and then arresting them. Leon gave it in charge to his mother Rita and came to terms with the Hetoumids by betrothing his younger niece, Philippa, to Oshin of Lampron. Another of the Hetoumids, Shahenshah, took at this time on Leon's behalf the fortress of Loulon on the northern approach to the Cilician Gates, and Leon led raids beyond the Taurus mountains penetrating as far as Caesarea.

The Hetoumids as a family had played a large part in the religious and cultural life of the Kingdom. Hetoum III after the loss of Lampron retired to a monastery, eventually becoming Abbot of Trazarg and one of Leon's trusted councillors. An even more remarkable man was his brother, Nerses of Lampron, archbishop of Tarsus. Born in 1153, he was brought up at the court of Manuel Comnenus, who would have kept him in his employment, but Nerses remained firm in the religious vocation to which his parents had devoted him. He returned to the family monastery of Skevra and was ordained by his great-uncle, the

[6] The Armenian *tategan* approximately equalled the Arab *dinar*.

PLATE 3

SIS

View of round tower of castle from the south

Scarcely anything remains of the Armenian capital except the castle, which stood high above the town, stretching for some 900 m. along a ridge of jagged rock interrupted by clefts and descending laterally in shelves. The height and width of the summit vary all the way; the enclosing walls are therefore far apart in some places where the space between them is divided into separately fortified wards, in which were residential buildings, now ruined. Outer wards also exist; wherever it would have been easy to climb the hillside a wall was built across the slope. At the south end, however, the ridge narrows to a point which is filled with the single tower illustrated. No photograph taken from the ground can show more than a small fraction of the site; only a set of views from a helicopter could do justice to its complexity.   A. W. L.

Catholicos, Nerses Schnorhali (the Gracious). It was the monastic life that drew him, and he spent some time in one of the houses of the Black Mountain and at Saghrou in the Taurus. Knowing Greek, Latin and Syriac, as well as his own Armenian, he represents a point of contact of various cultures. Nerses Schnorhali had since 1170 been engaged in negotiations with the Greek Church. His successor, the Catholicos Gregory Dgha (1172–89), was anxious to use the younger Nerses's abilities and persuaded him, unwillingly, to become archbishop of Tarsus in 1176. At a synod held at Hromgla in 1179 he spoke in favour of a compromise with Byzantium. Here the outstanding questions were the recognition of the two natures in Christ as interpreted by the Fourth Council, that of Chalcedon; the celebration of Christmas on 25 December, instead of the Armenian custom of combining it with the Epiphany on 6 January; the computations for fixing the date of Easter; the use of fermented bread in the mass; and the disuse of the Armenian formula 'Holy God, who has been crucified' at the close of the liturgical hymn of the trisagion (thrice holy). The Jacobite Church was also involved in these problems, but the Jacobite patriarch of Antioch, Michael, the chronicler of these events, had stated his view: 'It is not seemly at the eleventh hour and in hope of gain to change beliefs out of human consideration'. Between the Armenian Church, less extreme than the Jacobite, and Byzantium there was perhaps no great gap on the central theological problem, but there was a long history of persecution behind the debate, and a deep feeling of the part that the Church had played, amid constant civil disputes, in preserving the national awareness of the Armenian people.

Nothing came of those schemes of reunion. In relation to the Latin Church, political considerations had prime consideration. Leon was prepared to make promises to the papacy and then plead the impossibility of enforcing them against national feeling. From ancient Armenia, a Church in the hands of the infidel, uncompromising in its stand and fortified by the heroism of a sometimes persecuted minority, there was constant criticism of Cilician readiness to placate the papacy, and in particular Nerses of Lampron was singled out for attack. Leon warned him that he must cease from some of his innovations, such as his use of vestments on the Latin model and his removal of the curtain separating the mass from the people. In his reply we have a document of singular tolerance and enlightenment, a striking picture of the times and a reminder that amid these ambushes, treacheries and murders, there were men of noble thought and well-informed judgment. 'If now', he wrote, 'I declare myself the partisan of one nation, how can I be in communion with other Christians?' He admired much in the Latins, particularly their church building and the seemliness of their robes and rites, as opposed to the rugged asceticism of the Caucasian Armenians, who had to conduct most of their services in secret. 'Marash, this great and rich city, which under the Armenians had neither an episcopal see nor a church, when it fell to the Franks was provided with a large church.' The Armenians had only copied the freedom and licence of the Latins, not the fervour of their piety. 'When an Armenian enters a church with a Frank, the Frank bursts into tears as he prays, the Armenian stands beside him as a beast without reason.' In the cathedral of St Sophia at Tarsus the Gospel was read in Greek, Latin and Armenian, and the decision as to which language to use was a matter for the bishop to decide. If Leon agreed to give up his Frankish customs and Frankish clothes, then Nerses would consider amending his ritual. He was equally aware, however, of native Armenian culture and he encouraged the Armenian skill in illumination. Several handsome manuscripts still survive inscribed as having been commissioned by him.[7] He himself was an author and on one journey he was plundered by a roving Turkish band and lost the manuscript of his *Reflections on the Institution of the Church*. Five years later it turned up in a township of the Ceyhan district, and any author can sympathise with his pleasure at its recovery.

This was the man whom in 1190 Leon selected to head his embassy to meet the Emperor Frederick Barbarossa as he approached Cilicia. Nerses had been taking final counsel with the Catholicos at Hromgla, and the situation required some diplomatic thought, for the Catholicos had been safeguarding the position by correspondence with Saladin. He reached the imperial army on the western borders of Cilicia, and obtained from Barbarossa a promise that Armenia should be converted into a kingship. The army was at Silifke preparing to cross the Saleph, even in summer a broad and fast-flowing river. There, seeking for a ford that might supplement the bridge crossing, the emperor on 10 June 1190 was drowned. His death in Armenian territory made a deep impression on Leon and his people and destroyed immediate hopes of the royal crown, for the German leaders, distraught by the loss of the emperor, were not prepared to negotiate further.

Leon sent down an Armenian contingent to the crusading camp at Acre and himself joined Cœur-de-Lion in the conquest of Cyprus, but it was Antioch that soon claimed his attention. After Saladin in 1188 had destroyed Baghras, Leon had occupied and rebuilt it. This at once raised issues with Bohemond III and

---

[7] Matenadaran No. 1568 (a volume of sacred poems by the eleventh-century poet Gregory Narekatsi), dated 1173; Mekhitharist Library, Venice, No. 1635, Gospels of 1193.

the Templars, and Leon invited Bohemond to an interview to discuss them. It is strange how trustingly invitations were accepted, and this one was no exception to the dangers involved. Bohemond was seized and held to ransom, and only released when Henry of Champagne, the new king-consort of Jerusalem, 'a man friend of peace and good',[8] came to Sis to negotiate a settlement. Leon retained Baghras, but gave the elder of Rupen II's daughters, Alice, as a bride to Bohemond's eldest son Raymond.[9]

Then on 6 January 1198[10] in the presence of the Imperial chancellor, Conrad of Hildesheim, and the papal legate, Conrad of Mainz, Leon was crowned king by the Armenian Catholicos, Gregory Abirad, in the cathedral at Tarsus. This marked the recognition of Armenia as an independent state. The coronation was witnessed by bishops and barons, the leading men of the realm.[10a]

In the previous year Leon's nephew by marriage, Raymond, the heir to Antioch, had died, and his Rupenid wife Alice had borne him a posthumous son, Raymond-Rupen. To ensure his great-nephew's accession to Antioch, uniting thereby, as he had no son, Armenia and Antioch, now became the corner-stone of Leon's policy. This strategically and politically admirable plan was endorsed by the papal legate and the Antiochene barons swore to recognise the child's rights, but when in 1201 Bohemond III died, Raymond-Rupen was only three years old. Bohemond le Borgne of Tripoli, Bohemond III's second son, claimed the succession, strongly supported by the Templars who resented the loss of Baghras. Anti-Armenian feeling was easily roused and intermittent warfare went on with varying balance of success for some twenty years. Both sides appealed to the papacy and this obscure struggle, in which neither side hesitated to call in Moslem allies, was to be a main preoccupation of the over-burdened Innocent III. There were raids, battles, legatine visits, excommunications. The patriarch of Antioch was starved to death in a dungeon for supporting Rupen's cause. The son of Bohemond le Borgne was in 1213 struck down by an

---

[8] Michael the Syrian, *RHC.Arm.* I, p. 405.

[9] Rupen's two daughters, Alice and Philippa (the latter having been betrothed as a child to Oshin of Lampron), had both been married in 1189 to two princes of the Sassounian house of ancient Armenia, Hetoum and Shahnshah, who were respectively given the lordships of Mamistra and Silifke. They were, however, both assassinated in 1193. On their mother's side they were nephews of the Catholicos Gregory Dgha, and it was after his death that they were mysteriously removed, whether or not on Leon's orders remains uncertain.

[10] For discussion of the date see *A History of the Crusades* ed. K. M. Setton, II, p. 648, n. 23.

[10a] Sempad *RHC.Arm.* I, p. 634.

PLATE 4

VAHKA

From the south-west

In the hills north of Sis, its position was chosen probably for its inaccessibility, rather than for any strategic purpose. Steep paths ran through the hillside, but the main route was further east. It was a strong point from which a garrison could in security keep some watch on raiding bands and store its own booty. Originally a Byzantine fortress, it was occupied by Constantine around 1090, and was the main base of the Rupenid family in their early days. Taken by John Comnenus in 1137, and two years later by the Danishmendids, it returned to Armenian control under Thoros II, and the present buildings are probably largely from his time. As with many Armenian castles, its plan is largely determined by the site on which it is placed and the walls on the line of the rock face.

Assassin at the porch of the cathedral of Tortosa, and rumour accused the Hospitallers of having instigated the deed. Leon had in 1207 and again in 1210 through Raymond-Rupen granted Gibel and the Château de la Veille, on the borders of Tripoli and Antioch, to the Hospital; acts well calculated to foster local animosities.[11] Events swung now one way, now another, but in 1216 Leon seemed to have gained the upper hand. Raymond-Rupen was crowned prince in Antioch. Then three years later a conspiracy admitted Bohemond into the city, and Raymond-Rupen driven out hastened to the crusading forces at Damietta to appeal to the papal legate.

While these border disturbances continued, Leon had problems nearer home. Leon's relations with the Catholicos had always been troubled. In 1193 he had secured the election of Gregory V, hoping to find in him a conciliatory influence amongst the disputing factions. Instead he soon showed himself to be an authoritarian and uncompromising ruler, and Leon sent John, archbishop of Sis, to fetch him from Hromgla. Gregory was imprisoned at Gobidara, and fell to his death in an attempted escape from the castle. John of Sis replaced him. He was a member of the Hetoumid family and one of Leon's closest advisers. Here too, however, a quarrel arose. The cause is obscure. In 1205 John had denounced the queen for adultery, and Leon had imprisoned her at Vahka. His rage was directed against his wife, not the Catholicos, but it may well have led to embittered relations. Then in 1207 Leon imprisoned, on what charges is not known, two of John's cousins, John's brother-in-law Henry, lord of Norpert and Camardias, and his son Constantine, lord of Silifke. The protests of the Catholicos led to a complete breach. Leon declared him deposed, and John melted down the church plate for money to fortify Hromgla. For some five years the discord lasted, until in the end Hetoum of Lampron, the abbot of Trazarg, induced the king and the Catholicos to come to terms.

The adulterous queen was now dead, and Leon took a second wife, Sybilla of Lusignan, daughter of Aimery of Cyprus and sister of Melisend, wife of Bohemond IV; by her he had a daughter, Zabel. His daughter Rita by his first wife was married to John of Brienne and had by him a son. The possible heirs to the throne were therefore this child, Raymond-Rupen as grandson of Rupen III, and Zabel, though no woman had as yet succeeded to the throne in Cilicia. In the end, wearied by the business of Antioch, Leon nominated Zabel as his heir, betrothing her to the son of Andrew of Hungary. Within a year Rita, the wife of John of Brienne, and her child were both dead. Then in May 1219,

---

[11] See Riley-Smith, *Knights of St. John*, p. 155. For the Antiochene dispute see Cahen, *Syrie du Nord*, pp. 579–636.

C

having reigned for thirty-two years, Leon himself died.

He had some real claim to the epithet 'the Great' which his subjects accorded to him. Some unity and peace had been secured, and some control exercised over his unruly baronage. The use of western titles, baron, constable, chancellor, seneschal, bailiff and so forth, corresponded to a new feudal relationship with the Crown. The royal state, borrowing here from Byzantium, was enhanced by elaborate robes and etiquette. The Genoese and Venetian treaties brought not only transit trade, but new outlets for local produce from the fertile coastal plain; timber from the Taurus forests was in much demand, though already the goat, prime enemy of trees, had become a rival in the country's economy, and goatskins and goathair cloth were a main export. Despite its timber, Cilicia had not produced in any number a fleet or merchant vessels of its own, and the treaties with the Italian merchant cities were therefore of prime importance. The great timber market was in fact Alexandria, for Egypt could not provide material for her own navy, but this trade was much frowned upon, not least by the Hospitallers once they were installed in Rhodes, and if Cilicia almost certainly practised it, prohibitions and interruptions were frequent. Leon celebrated his coronation by issuing golden coinage, but to judge by survivals, gold coins were never numerous, and the bulk of the Armenian money was silver or copper. The Armenian *tategan* was an equivalent of the *dinar* and was coined in both gold and silver. Not least of their trading advantages was the widespread dispersion of the Armenian people, so that their colonies, from Italy to China, formed a link with the homelands and showed both national trading acumen and persistent devotion to the national Church.

The dispute over Antioch had involved Leon in attacks from Bohemond's Moslem allies, for a time encouraged by the Catholicos, John, in particular Az-Zahir of Aleppo and Kai-Khusrau I of Iconium. In 1208–9 Leon had lost to the latter the fortress of Pertounk, fifteen miles to the north-west of Marash. In 1216 Kai-Khusrau's successor, Izz-ad-Din Kai-Kaus, attacked the fortress of Gaban and defeated an Armenian force sent to relieve it, taking prisoner several of the leading Armenian nobles. Leon then took the field in person, and succeeded in relieving the castle, but the prisoners were not ransomed for some time, and then only by the surrender of the fortresses of Loulon and Lauzada. Amongst these prisoners had been Constantine, lord of Babaron and Partzapert, Leon's first cousin, together with Adam of Baghras. Married to a daughter of the main Hetoumid line, a man who Michael the Syrian states 'professed the Greek religion', Adam had been appointed *bailli* for Zabel, but in 1221 he was struck down in the streets of Sis, by an Assassin it was said, although not without suspicion of complicity by Constantine, whose ambition for his own advancement was becoming all too evident. His immediate obstacle was Raymond-Rupen who, now married to a Lusignan, a half-sister of his father's widow, had arrived to enforce his claim and had been welcomed at Tarsus. The town, however, was treacherously opened to Constantine, and Raymond-Rupen speedily ended his days in prison. He had been a young man of promise, precipitated early into a high but disputed position, but his arrogance had alienated his great-uncle's affections. Zabel meanwhile had been repudiated by Andrew of Hungary on her father's death and a husband had to be found for her. Constantine decided in favour of Philip of Antioch, the fourth son of Bohemond IV. The move was a recognition of Bohemond's position as prince and put an end to schemes of Armenian–Antiochene union in favour of peace between the states. It was stipulated, however, that Philip must join the Armenian Church. Leon's westernising policy was unpopular, both with the baronage and with the Armenian ecclesiastics, and it had failed in its main object of consolidating a new Christian power by the union with Antioch. Philip, happy in his marriage, unfortunately had little political sense; Latins were given important posts and part of the royal treasure was sent to Antioch. In 1225 after three years of rule, he was seized by night in Zabel's room, hurried to prison and soon poisoned there despite appeals from his father. On 14 June 1226, Zabel, much against her will, was married to Constantine's son, Hetoum, and the two rival houses were at last united on the throne of Armenia.

Hetoum's immediate problems, under his father's guidance (for Constantine lived till 1263), were on his western frontier. The Latin conquest of Constantinople had left the more outlying parts of Byzantium defenceless. Kai-Khusrau I, the Selchukid sultan of Roum, in 1207 had occupied Antalya and opened up the southern gulf to Selchukid trade. In 1221 his son Ala'ud-din Kai-Qobad extended his control by capturing Kalonoros from the Armenians. Kai-Qobad rebuilt the town on its great rocky promontory, renaming it after himself as Ala'iya – now Alanya. His rule, 1220–37, was one of the most prosperous in the history of the sultanate and his buildings in Antalya, Alanya and Anamur still testify to its splendour. He invaded Armenia in 1233, exacting tribute, but on the whole he was a peaceful neighbour, ready to further trading relations. His reign, however, ended the Armenian control on the eastern coast of the bay of Antalya. Under Leon a row of fortresses had been occupied along that rugged sea front, and the inland route from Anamur to Laranda had also been in Armenian control. When Leon in 1218 surrendered the fortresses of Loulon and Lauzada, the Armenian expansion on the Cappadocian side of the

PLATE 5   THE INCREDULITY OF ST THOMAS

From Armenian Psalter of 1272, St James
Jerusalem, MS. 2563 f. 368

This is from a Gospel Book illustrated in Cilicia in 1272 for Keran, wife of Leon III (MS. 2563, Church of St James, Jerusalem). It is a work that shows the fullest development of Armenian illumination. The name of the artist is not known. He was certainly influenced by Thoros Roslin, but brings a new sense of movement to his figures.

Taurus had been ended. Now, with Kai-Qobad's fortification of Anamur, their western frontier was driven back to the lower reaches of the Saleph river and the fortresses of Bragana, Norpert, Camardias and Silifke. This was the area where Leon in 1207 had faced revolt from the relatives of the Catholicos, John, and he had in 1210 transferred Norpert, Camardias and Silifke to the Hospitallers.[12] This last however they had sold back to Constantine in 1226 to extricate themselves from a delicate position when Zabel had taken refuge there from her forced marriage with Hetoum.

In 1243 a new danger threatened. The Selchukid army, under Kai-Qobad's successor Kai-Khusrau II, was completely routed by the Mongols in a battle near Siwas, where Georgians and Armenians were fighting in the Mongol army and 2,000 Frankish mercenaries in that of Roum.[13] Anatolia was overrun by the victors. Kai Khusrau's wife and daughter had fled for refuge to Hetoum, who now, when summoned to do so by the Mongols, handed them over. This act was regarded at the time as a breach of the code of hospitality and some of the Armenian nobles joined with the Selchukids in an attack on Hetoum, occupying a few Armenian fortresses. But Hetoum was clear as to his policy, to come to terms with these new invaders. More shrewdly than anyone he recognised the strength of the Mongols and the possibility of obtaining protection from them. He sent his brother, Sempad the Constable, on an embassy to their capital at Karakorum. Sempad left Armenia in 1247 and returned in 1250 with terms pledging that the Mongols would respect and protect the Armenian kingdom. In 1253 Hetoum himself went to visit the Great Khan and was absent for three years from his kingdom, returning through Greater Armenia, the homeland which no Cilician ruler had visited. He came now with assurances of Mongol readiness to protect the Christian Churches in their dominions and himself became the protagonist of schemes of Mongol–Christian alliance to regain the Holy Land. Armenian troops fought in the Mongol armies, and Hetoum occupied Marash and restored the Armenian sphere of influence to an extent that recalled the days of Philaretus in the eleventh century. Antioch too was now practically an Armenian dependency. Through the mediation of Louis IX the young Bohemond VI of Tripoli and Antioch had in 1254 married Hetoum's daughter, Sybilla, and peace had been made between them. But

---

[12] Earlier, before 1149, the Hospitallers had some holdings round Til Hamdoun, Mamistra and Harunia, possibly ceded to them by Antioch, which do not seem to have survived the conquest of these areas by Thoros II. They had also interests in the area round Turbessel and Behesni. See Cahen, *Syrie*, pp. 514, 525.

[13] Howorth, *History of the Mongols* I, pp. 166–7.

Bohemond's headquarters were in Tripoli, and even when Latakia was once more reoccupied with Mongol help, Antioch remained under Armenian rather than Tripolitan control. With the army of Hulagu, the Mongol conqueror of Baghdad, Hetoum entered Aleppo, that untaken city, and in March 1260 he and Bohemond rode with the Mongol general Kitbogha through the streets of Damascus. It was a moment of triumph, but it was not to last. In the widespread Mongol empire there were always revolts stirring, disputed successions distracting the Great Khan and shifting the sphere of urgency. In September 1260, the Mongol force, an inadequate one, under Kitbogha was completely destroyed by a Mamluk army from Egypt, and when reinforcements arrived they only temporarily stemmed the advance of the Mamluks under their new and powerful leader, Baybars. Hetoum, however, was able not only to hold his own, but even to expand his territories. In 1262 he seized the fortified town of Behesni, pushing his territories beyond Marash to the Euphrates boundary. The following year, on his western frontier, he repulsed a Turkoman band, the Karamanids, who, displaced by Mongol pressure, had established themselves round the Antalyan gulf. Their leader, Karaman, was killed in the conflict. Well might the scribe and illuminator Thoros Roslin in a colophon of a gospel book written for Prince Leon, call Hetoum 'the holy king who repulsed the hordes of the progeny of Hagar and the generations of the infidel'.[14]

But steadily Baybars was advancing through Syria. Caesarea, Haifa, Arsuf, Tibnin, Safad fell in 1265 and 1266, and he then turned on Armenia, the chief Mongol ally. Hetoum hurried to Tabriz to seek Mongol help. In his absence the Mamluks crossed the Amanus mountains and entered Cilicia. The Constable Sempad with the two young princes, Thoros and Leon, led the Armenian forces against him, but were hopelessly outnumbered and routed. Thoros was killed; Leon and Sempad's son Vasil captured. For twenty days the enemy pillaged the coastal plain unopposed. 'Sis and its chief church were given to the flames, the tombs of the kings and princes violated, and their bones torn from this last resting place, burned, and scattered as ashes to the winds.'[15] Hetoum returned to find in his country a devastation from which it never recovered.

Two years later, on 12 May 1268, the Mamluks stormed Antioch, with a terrible massacre and destruction. Simon the Constable and other refugees escaped to Armenia. It was with this new threat, with the terrible tales of the atrocities in the city that had long been so close to Armenian affairs, that Hetoum,

---

[14] The Four Gospels (1262), Armenian Patriarchate Jerusalem MS. 2660.
[15] Chronology of Hetoum, *RHC.Arm.* I, p. 487.

having secured the release of his son, Leon, from Egypt, abdicated in his favour, and withdrew to spend the remaining years of his life in a monastery. He was a far-sighted man, capable of decision, and understanding the circumstances in which he lived. Under him the arts had flourished, and if ruin has left little trace of his buildings, the illuminations of Thoros Roslin give splendour to his reign. Here was an artist who could create a fusion of artistic impulses from East and West and claim a high place by any standard.[16] Others such as the Master of the Frere Gospel, painted for Vasak, the son of Hetoum I, and the Master of the Gospels of 1272 (Plate 5),[17] painted for Leon III's wife, could rival him in iconographic inventiveness, and it is little wonder that there was in Armenia a touching pride in the products of their scriptoria. Manuscripts pillaged by the Moslems were frequently bought back, and in one instance a famous example, found thrown away in the crevice of a river bank, had miraculous powers attributed to it.[18] Metal-work also flourished, and from the monastery of Skevra, though nothing remains of its buildings, a silver-gilt reliquary survives, now in the Hermitage Museum at Leningrad; it was made in 1293 for Hetoum II and shows him kneeling beneath the figure of the Virgin.

One figure, that of his elder brother, the Constable Sempad, stands out through Hetoum's reign as an example of integrity, loyalty and practical sense. Hetoum had obtained the crown by marriage with Zabel. The rôle of an elder brother, thus superseded, would never have been an easy one, and Cilician history is full of fraternal disputes and fratricides. The Constable was ever his brother's soundest adviser and supporter. His account of his embassy to the Tartars written to his brother-in-law, Henry I of Cyprus, is an observant, percipient appreciation of this new factor in Eastern affairs, and Sempad's advice must have underlain Hetoum's pro-Mongol policy. He wrote a history of the Cilician kingdom which is the most judicious survey that we have of its troubled events. Much of the earlier part was based on Matthew of Edessa, but he also used, he tells us, 'Frank historians'.[19] In the field of law, he revised the Armenian Law Book of Mkhit'ar Gosh (1184), or possibly composed a new work from similar sources; and he translated, to meet the problems of Leon II's

[16] The signed MSS. date from 1256–68/9. If the attribution to him of the great lectionary in Matenadaran (MS. 979) is correct his career extended to 1288.

[17] Armenian Patriarchate, Jerusalem, MS. 2563. For a recent appraisal of these illuminations see J. Beckwith, *Early Christian and Byzantine Art* (Harmondsworth, 1970), pp. 138–9. [18] Sanjian, *Colophons*, pp. 78, 98, 100.

[19] S. der Nersessian, 'The Armenian Chronicle of the Constable Sempad', *DOP* XIII (1959), pp. 143–68.

westernising reforms, the Assizes of Antioch. He had received them from Simon, Constable of Antioch, probably the man in command in the final siege, and it is the Armenian translation that has preserved our knowledge of the code. In 1276 this remarkable man, at the age of sixty-eight, died when his horse bolted and dashed him against a tree.

When Leon III succeeded Hetoum his one hope was in the Mongol alliance, but at first little assistance came from it. In 1275 the Mamluks once more raided the coastal plain with comparative immunity. Then in 1281 a Mongol army invaded Syria and the Armenian forces joined it. The Mamluks, now under the Sultan Kalavun, met this allied force near Homs and completely routed it. Leon was left defenceless, and in 1285 had to purchase a peace with Cairo at the crippling cost of an annual tribute of one million dirhams, and with a pledge that the Armenians would build no more castles.[20]

In 1291 with the fall of Acre, the long agony of the crusading states ended. Ayas was once more, as a hundred years earlier, the only important Christian port on the mainland of the Levant. The trading cities still had their privileges there and Leon gave a new and extended charter to the Genoese,[21] but the raising of the customs dues was almost the only means of finding the tribute for Egypt and Leon was caught in a dilemma by which he could only decrease the advantages gained by the lack of rivals. Cilicia, however, was still prosperous. Marco Polo describes it in the later thirteenth century as having 'great abundance of everything', though the climate was unhealthy, and the men, once warriors 'worth five of any other race', were now 'slavish and mean, given to gluttony and drinking. They have abundance of red and white wine, and drink it much.' Lajazzo was the port to which all came who wished to travel into the interior. Marco Polo must have known it, and it was probably there, in 1296, in a sea battle between the Genoese and the Venetians, that he was captured and taken to prison in Genoa.[22]

In 1289, at the age of fifty-three, Leon died worn out by his problems. He had received much affection from his people. Stories of his captivity and his constancy to the Christian faith were made into ballads. 'He was a prince inclined by nature to piety, resolute in adversity and without pride in prosperity. He followed the will of the Lord.'[23]

The new king, Hetoum II, carried on his father's policy, visiting the Mon-

---

[20] Canard, 'Le Royaume d'Arménie-Cilicie', *REA*. n.s. IV (1967), pp. 216–59.
[21] *RHC.Or.* I, pp. 745–58.
[22] See A. C. Moule and P. Pelliot, *Marco Polo* (London, 1938), pp. 31 and 94.
[23] *RHC.Arm.* I, p. 531.

gols, marrying one sister to Aimery, brother of Henry II of Cyprus, and another to Michael IX Palaeologus. But, with a heedless disregard of pressing dangers, he was destroyed from within his own territories. His brother Sempad seized power while Hetoum was absent in Constantinople, and on his return the king was arrested and blinded, inefficiently, for some sight was left. He had already once abdicated (1292) in favour of his brother Thoros, whom Sempad now strangled. Yet with the help of another brother, Constantine, Hetoum was once more in 1298 back on the throne. Both his brothers were very sensibly despatched for safe-keeping to his brother-in-law in Constantinople, and he himself aided three more Mongol expeditions into Syria and for a brief moment was entrusted with the control of Jerusalem. Then in 1304 the Grand Khan, Ghazan, declared for Islam as the official faith of his dominions. It was a blow to all Christian hopes, even if the Mongols for a time remained tolerant in religious matters. Ghazan was no persecutor, and his death was 'a great grief among our suffering Christian nations'. His successor, a son of Arghun, Kharbanda, was a very different character, who ordered that all Christians throughout his dominions must wear 'a mark of opprobrium', a black linen strip over the shoulder.[24] In 1307 Hetoum and his nephew, Thoros' son, now king as Leon IV, visiting the Mongol emir Bilarghu at Anavarza, were murdered with all their followers. The Il-Khan avenged their deaths, but their assassination was indicative of the changed position of the Christian communities.

Hetoum II unfortunately was a vacillating character, constantly seeking a refuge in the Church, either at a monastery he built at Mamistra, or later by becoming a Franciscan friar. Such personal indulgences were little suited to the times. We have an account of them in the writings of another Hetoum, lord of Corycus, probably, for there is no certainty, son of Oshin of Corycus, brother of Hetoum I. This Hetoum had certainly played some part in the embassies to the Tartars and also in the campaign of 1303 against the Mamluks. In 1305 he left Armenia, whether voluntarily or not is again uncertain, for the abbey of Bella Pais in Cyprus, where he intended, like others of his family, to end his days in the monastic life. By 1307 however he was at Poitiers, where he presented to Pope Clement V his *Fleurs des histoires de la terre d'Orient*, an account of the Mongols, interspersed with some contemporary Armenian history, and ending with a scheme for a new crusade, which would have Armenia as its base. In 1308 he returned to Cyprus, bringing a letter from Pope Clement V to Aimery, the usurping ruler, married to Hetoum II's sister, on the subject

[24] Sanjian, *Colophons*, pp. 48, 56.

of the Templars. From there it seems likely that he went to Cilicia, where he died shortly afterwards. His literary activities, his restless longing for the monastic life, and his Roman, rather than Armenian, bias are characteristic of this ambiguous civilisation, where the national traditions were disturbed, sometimes distorted, by the overpowering influence of the West, and where men became more and more articulate as all hopes of stability lessened.

On the murder of Hetoum II and Leon IV, neither of them leaving any offspring, the throne passed to a brother of Hetoum's, Oshin, married to a daughter of Hetoum the Historian. He died in 1320, poisoned it was thought by his cousin and brother-in-law, another Oshin, lord of Corycus, who claimed to act as regent for the young heir, Leon V, and married him to his daughter Alice. Isabella, King Oshin's sister, the widow of Aimery of Cyprus, and two of her sons, who unfortunately were at hand, were imprisoned and murdered to avoid possible claimants. Then in 1329, having reached the age of nineteen, the king asserted himself, and had his wife and his stepfather both disposed of. He took as his second wife Constance of Aragon, the widow of Henry II of Cyprus, a pro-Latin move which did little to enhance his popularity, and shut himself up in the citadel of Sis, waiting and appealing for Western aid, till in 1341 the barons rose against him and he too was murdered.

Such doings hardly served to create a favourable image of Armenia in the West. In the *Directorium ad passagium faciendum*, a pamphlet addressed to Philip VI in 1332 by a Dominican who had visited Cilicia, the writer warns the king of Armenian unreliability. When hard pressed by the Turks they appeal to Rome but 'the leopard cannot change his spots, nor the Ethiopian his skin: they partake of every error known in the East. . . . Their king (Leon III) had nine children, and all, sons and daughters alike, have come to a violent end, except one daughter and no one knows what her end will be. One brother killed another with the sword; another poisoned his brother; another strangled his brother in prison, so that they all murdered one another till only the last was left and he was poisoned and died miserably.' The truth was not so black, but the family feuds were bloody enough to make it a not surprising picture.

The barons now offered the crown to John of Lusignan, one of the surviving sons of Isabel and Aimery of Cyprus, but he had an elder brother Guy, who had been making a name for himself in the service of the Greek emperor. John wrote to him urging him to come and take the Armenian crown, an invitation which, perhaps not surprisingly, Guy was loth to accept. In the end however he agreed and in 1342 came to Armenia. He was a vigorous and determined man, but deeply committed to the Latin cause. His younger brother, Bemon, was sent to Rome to seek for help, but these were negotiations that were bound to rouse resentment in Armenia and in 1344 both Guy and Bemon were killed in a rising, and power was seized by another Constantine, whose father Baldwin had been Marshal of Armenia and belonged to a younger Hetoumid line. Constantine abandoned Guy's vigorous policy for a series of treaties with Egypt, ceding Tarsus and Adana to the sultan. He also aimed at removing all claimants of the Lusignan branch. John of Lusignan, Guy's brother, had died shortly before the latter's murder, but his wife, Soldane, was living with two young sons, Bemon aged five and Leon aged two. They were imprisoned at Corycus and orders given for their murder, but the lady managed to escape in time with her sons from the castle and take refuge in Cyprus. The usurper Constantine reigned for nineteen years, dying, most unusually, a natural death in 1363. His two sons had predeceased him. He was succeeded by his cousin Constantine, the sixth of the name, for in Armenian reckoning Guy of Lusignan is given the less foreign name of Constantine IV. Hard pressed by the Karamanids on his western borders he took the bold step of calling in Peter I of Cyprus to his assistance by offering him the port and castle of Corycus, and possibly the reversion of the kingdom. From Corycus Peter, aided by the Hospitallers from Rhodes, surprised and captured Antalya in August 1360.

The occupation of Antalya offered some chance for a revival of Cilician trade. During the disturbed reigns of the first half of the century, little protection had been available against Egyptian inroads. Ayas had been sacked in 1322 and left defenceless. As long as its twin fortresses protected its sheltered bay it was an important asset both politically and economically in Armenian affairs. After 1322 the sea castle was never rebuilt. In 1336 the people of Ayas murdered two of the Mamluk officials, bringing vengeance on themselves and on Armenians in Jerusalem. 'I copied this', wrote a scribe in Jerusalem, 'under much anguish and fear and day in and day out we expected to be tortured and killed.'[25] In 1337, after another raid, the townspeople of Ayas were only spared a general massacre on terms that involved razing the fortifications. From then on, with a brief interlude in 1367, Ayas was in Moslem hands. Antalya, however, was the last Cilician gain. Peter's further activity was directed towards a great raid on Alexandria, which left enduring hatred between Mamluk Egypt and Cyprus and which was to be terribly avenged.

On the murder of Peter in 1369 Constantine VI, who seems to have been a realist in politics, sought a treaty with the sultan of Cairo and was thought by

[25] Sanjian, *Colophons*, p. 95.

the Armenians to be prepared to hand over the kingdom to him, a humane alternative to bloody conquest that the barons were not prepared to tolerate. In 1373 Constantine in his turn was murdered, and Leon, son of John of Lusignan and the much tried Soldane, was called to the throne.

This at least is how it is chronicled by Jean Dardel, Leon VI's chaplain, when he was a prisoner in Cairo, whose *Chronique d'Arménie* must represent Leon's recollections of his early youth and reign and is our authority for the confused and sordid history with which we have been dealing. Unfortunately there is some reason to think that Leon's views of events were hardly accurate. The lady Soldane, if that is in fact her name, seems to have been John of Lusignan's Armenian mistress not his wife, and Leon was illegitimate. This certainly was the way it appeared in Rome, and in Cyprus his claims to the estates of his grandmother, the murdered Isabella, were entirely rejected. The Genoese, now dominant in Cyprus, in fact suspected Leon of being involved in King Peter's murder and it was only grudgingly that he was allowed to depart to Cilicia.

In Armenia also there seem to have been doubts. On the death of Constantine IV without heirs, there was a year's regency under a lady whose career summarises much of the disturbed period in which she lived. Marie, 'the old queen', was the daughter of Oshin of Corycus and the widow of Constantine V. Her mother, Jeanne of Anjou, had been married first to another Oshin, the king of Armenia who died in 1320. It was Oshin of Corycus who had brought the royal bride from Naples, and something of the old tale of Tristan and Iseult seems to have been re-enacted, for on King Oshin's death his namesake of Corycus married the widowed queen, a step which was thought dangerous by the ruling house, and he was assassinated in 1329. Jeanne had predeceased him. It was their daughter who now briefly held the regency. That, however, was not woman's work, and, whatever the doubts about his birth, Leon became king as Leon VI in 1374, and he and his wife, Margaret of Soissons, were crowned at Sis on 14 September 1374; but it was soon apparent that there was little hope of uniting the Armenians for any effort and that treachery was at work. Achot, a Hetoumid by birth, had fled to Cairo and become a Moslem, but many Armenians remained in contact with him and put him forward as pretender to the throne. When the Egyptian forces arrived before Sis Leon for a time held out in the citadel, but the city was completely sacked. 'Who can recount', wrote a scribe on a copy of the *Assizes of Antioch*, 'the tragedy that my eyes witnessed, for I saw the bright sun, the stars and the moon fall down.' Leon escaped from the citadel to Gaban, but was captured, and with his wife

PLATE 6   LAMPRON

Apartments at end of inner ward

In the rivalries of the Rupenids and Hetoumids, this castle played a great part. The building on the summit is palatial in scale. It consists of five rooms, one of which presents a curved end to the precipice while another is polygonal externally (as can be seen on the left) though it, too, is rounded within, forming the apse of the hall. Here, as so often, it is the outline of the plateau that determines the plan of the fortress. It remained impregnable and Leon II only secured it by treachery.   A. W. L.

and 'the old queen' taken prisoner to Cairo. Released from there, he visited the western capitals seeking, more and more hopelessly, for help to regain his insecure kingdom. He died in 1393 in Paris and this last, if somewhat dubious, Cilician king was buried in St-Denis, where his monument ironically has survived the iconoclasm that has obliterated greater names and can still be seen, a strangely placed reminder of the dynasties that for three hundred years ruled, or sought to rule, this southern stretch of the Turkish coast. James I of Cyprus added on Leon's death the title of king of Armenia to his equally empty title of king of Jerusalem, and eventually through his great-granddaughter Carlotta it passed improbably to the house of Savoy.

The Mamluk conquest was of short duration. After Timur's victory over the Turks at Angora in 1402, the Tartars swept over Asia Minor and Syria. That also was a brief occupation. When in 1453 the Ottomans took Constantinople, Cilicia passed under their control. The Armenian population still for a time looked to the West for aid and continued negotiations with the papacy, but Cilicia rapidly declined into a minor Ottoman province, where its Christian inhabitants were always exposed to outbursts of Moslem fervour. They survived, however, with some religious freedom, till in 1895 and 1896 large-scale massacres were let loose on the area. The resistance of the Armenians of Zeytin, in the mountains near Marash, showed that the spirit of their race had not declined, and when again in 1915 Adana and Antioch became the scenes of terrible butchery, the Armenians defended themselves in a camp on the Jebel Musa, till rescued by a French cruiser. The toll in slaughter and dispersal had been a heavy one. Only gradually and uncertainly have Armenians recovered in numbers and security. Their churches have been destroyed, and their place-names forgotten; their history can only be traced through many obliterations of its records and monuments.

THE CASTLE OF BAGHRAS

Preface

Although it was one of the larger castles of the Knights Templar and has the additional interest of being in part built by the kingdom of Armenia, Baghras has not previously received serious attention. Yet its ruins, as regards the complexity of the defences, can bear comparison with any others of the Latin East (Krak des Chevaliers excepted), and its history is among the most diversified. For it owed its importance to that very fact which has caused its neglect by modern travellers and archaeologists: its remoteness from the great centres of the crusader states. It was a frontier post, situated in a region which belongs by nature neither to Syria nor to Asia Minor and has constantly suffered changes of ownership. The two latest have occurred in quick succession, since the beginning of this study. Baghras at that time belonged to Syria, as it lay in the Sanjack of Alexandretta, which for a few months became the autonomous state of Hatay and subsequently was incorporated into Turkey in 1939.

The survey upon which this account is based was made during the summer of 1938. The plans are the work of Miss Phoebe H. Brown, A.B. (Bryn Mawr), graduate of the architecture school of the University of California. The project was greatly facilitated by arrangements made by Dr E. H. R. Altounyan, M.C., and Miss Bridget Altounyan. The Turkoman villagers of Baghras were constantly helpful.

A first draft of the text was completed in 1939. In 1950 Mr M. R. E. Gough kindly went to Baghras and checked a number of specific points. In August 1951 I spent a day there, comparing the written description with the ruins. Much destruction (largely due to an earthquake) had occurred since my previous visit, but some more features had been exposed by erosion or human activities.

A. W. L.

2

THE CASTLE OF BAGHRAS

SITUATION

There are two routes from Asia Minor to Syria inland of the Amanus range – a relatively unimportant road down the Kara Su valley into the east end of the Antioch plain, and the railway route to Aleppo. Travellers bound for the regions south of Aleppo must always have preferred the far more direct route beside the Gulf of Alexandretta and over the Amanus range – *viam difficilem sed cunctarum ad Syros directissimam*, as the crusaders found.[1] In classical times and in the Middle Ages, while Antioch flourished, the route from the pass led through Baghras, whereas the modern road avoids it, heading for Aleppo. On the north slope the old track climbs along the steep side of the valley past Beylan (now Belen), after which it winds for a couple of hours across ridges and through small ravines down to Baghras. There it turns eastward down an easy valley with a small but constant river (the Karamurt), descending gently for an hour's walk before entering the plain, 26 km. from Antioch and 4 km. from the junction of the Alexandretta and Aleppo motor-roads at the foot of the Beylan Pass. The ruined Han Karamurt, an enormous caravan station built some four centuries ago, stands in the valley, a kilometre from its mouth.[2]

The Turkoman village of Baghras lies beside the river, at the mouth of the side valley by which the old track descends from the Beylan Pass.[3] A quarter of a mile away, upstream, is the greatest castle of the Amanus region, on a hill which slopes fairly gently to the village at its eastern foot, but is precipitous

[1] Ralph of Caen, *RHC.Occ.* III, p. 639.
[2] For the former importance of the route see Dussaud, *Topographie*, pp. 433–52.
[3] The best account of the route is by Hartmann, *Zeitschrift der Gesellschaft für Erdkunde* XXIX (1894), pp. 170, 171, 176, but it is marred by an error, for he cannot have ridden from the Han to Baghras village in half an hour, unless he galloped, and his map was drawn to correspond with the abbreviated record.

PLATE 7   CALENDRIA IN 1838

Drawn by W. H. Bartlett for John Carne's
Syria, the Holy Land and Asia Minor

In the far west of Cilicia the mountains reach the coast, which is generally rocky; only an occasional narrow valley can support a few inhabitants, living on their own produce, though in the Roman period some communities grew rich enough from seafaring to build enduring tombs. The most extensive and ostentatious necropolis arose at Calendris, a place that has ever since retained its name almost unchanged; a relatively large population must have flourished there, owing to the superiority of the harbour. Beaufort, who charted these waters in 1811, observed it as 'a snug but very small port, from whence the couriers from Constantinople to Cyprus embark.' Nearness to Cyprus was, of course, a greater asset under the Armenian kingdom, when coastwise shipping also must often have put in (as it apparently still did when Leonardo da Vinci wrote a highly-coloured account of an earthquake in this region).

Several accounts mention the hexagonal tower defending the port but today there are no remains of these extensive fortifications, some of which were probably Armenian work.

A. W. L.

on the other sides. The isolated hill apparently originated through a movement of the earth's crust, whereby this enormous mass of limestone slipped apart from the larger hill on the north, leaving a gorge through which the river flows; its banks are rough as a result of successive minor landslides, but above rise precipices of bare rock on either side. Upstream the valley is several hundred yards wide and would seem therefore to antedate the arrival of the castle hill to block its eastern end.[4] Half a mile above the castle is a group of a dozen springs[5] at which the river rises in summer. Above this point, the mountains close from north and west upon the course of the winter torrent. On the south the rock is bordered by a long high ridge which gradually descends to the plain of Antioch, while smaller encroaching hills advance to the river. Although the view from the castle is extensive, especially eastwards, it is interrupted by hills of greater or less elevation in every direction. The motor-road from Alexandretta to Antioch comes in sight of the castle for two short stretches only, one on a bend towards the foot of the pass, the other in the plain near the mouth of the Baghras valley. The old track from the pass to the village comes within sight of the castle only for the first half of the last mile, and even then the view is mostly blocked by trees or by a rise in the foreground.

In situation Baghras differs sharply from the other castles of the Amanus, which occupy very prominent positions and were well placed to control all traffic along the few practicable routes in this mountainous area. Baghras is more comparable to Cursat, which was as vital to the defence of Antioch on the south as Baghras on the north. Of Cursat (Qalat Qusair, now locally called Qalat az Zaw) there is no view obtainable except in its immediate neighbourhood, and it lies at two hours' journey from any road now in use or likely to have possessed importance in the past; the site is a piece of plateau, isolated by deep river valleys and by an artificial cutting. These two castles were especially valuable as bases from which strong garrisons could annoy forces either advancing towards or besieging Antioch. Their area was accordingly much greater and

[4] The construction of the Great Rift valley, at the north end of which Baghras lies, occurred ages after the formation of the rock of which the hill consists; Prof. C. E. Tilley very kindly examined a specimen (from the talus of the castle's south-west corner) and found it to be a fossiliferous limestone of Lower Tertiary age. The district is still a seismic area and a comparatively recent earthquake could have been responsible for the separation of the hill, which is not explicable by collapse of caves.

[5] Presumably identical with the *Fons Gustonis* which belonged to the Abbey of St Paul before the Armenian occupation (Raynaldus, *Annales Ecclesiastici* on 1205; in Baronius, vol. XX, p. 221, Bar-le-Duc/Paris, 1864–82) and the *Fontaine de Gaston* where in 1194 Leon of Armenia met the Prince of Antioch (*RHC.Occ.* II, pp. 207, 214).

D

their defences, especially those of Baghras, more skilful and elaborate than those of other strongholds.

We noticed no old pottery in the neighbourhood of the modern village of Baghras, although bare earth is exposed in the gardens around the houses and in vineyards to the south. The valley south of the castle hill is very narrow – apparently an old bed of the river – and the adjoining slopes are mostly too steep and arid to have been chosen for habitation, but a more desirable side valley comes in opposite the first stretch of the gallery of the castle, causing a widening to nearly 300 m. of the flatground. At its mouth stand some ruins called Kizlar Kalesi, 'Girls' Castle', and there is much pottery of medieval and somewhat later times. Farther up the hill across which runs the aqueduct many remains of walls can be seen, but little pottery.

The only recognisable building[6] at Kizlar Kalesi, a small bath-house, is perhaps that built in 1552 by the Turkish Sultan Sulaiman 'in an agreeable and picturesque spot'.[7] The site most favoured for habitation lies slightly north and west, in the wide valley between the aqueduct hill and the river, especially at a distance of 91–183 m. west of the castle. Here the ground over a wide area is studded with pottery, more often of the Roman and medieval than of later periods,[8] and many fragments of roof tiles testify to Roman or Byzantine settlement. Here too we picked up a flint – a flake not later than the beginning of the Bronze Age.

HISTORY

The name of Baghras has existed for at least two thousand years and perhaps its local pronunciation remained unchanged, but the Turkish government has imposed the spelling Bakras.[9] It first appears in Strabo (XVI 751) as Pagrai, a feminine plural; but in late popular Greek the accusative form Pagras would

[6] I failed to recognise a culvert (*ponceau*) mentioned by Jacquot, *Antioche* II, p. 197.

[7] *Chèref-Nâmeh*, trs. Charmoy I, 1, p. 273.

[8] Mr C. N. Johns and Mr J. H. Iliffe kindly examined specimens of pottery and gave them as exact dates as is now feasible.

[9] Hartmann (*Zeitschrift der Gesellschaft für Erdkunde* XXIX, p. 170) heard local people say Bughras, and this form occurs in editions of Imad-ad-Din and Ibn Batuta. I have also seen Baqraṣ and Baqras in the Chèref-Nâmeh (ed. Charmoy I, 1, pp. 80, 285) and Abu-l-Fida (cited ibid., p. 793). In medieval Armenian the name is spelt Paghras but in the western dialect P is sounded as B.

be used in place of the nominative and the initial letter would be given the sound of B, so that no alteration can since have been made except a substitution of the oriental *gh* for *gamma*. There is however no reason to suppose that the name is Greek by origin and it is more likely to be Semitic. In that event the *gamma* would stand for *gh*, a sound not represented in the Greek alphabet.

Pliny mentions Pagrae (or rather Pagras, for he uses the accusative), and Ptolemy names Pagrai, among the towns of Pieria. Lesser authors vary the spelling: we find Pagaris, Padas, Pagris and Pangrios.

In the fifth century Pagrai is described as a *stathmos* or station,[10] and it would seem that no fortifications existed there at the Arab conquest in 638. The first Moslem owner of Baghras, the distinguished Maslamah ibn Abd al Malik, 'gave it as an inalienable legacy (*waqf*) to be used in the cause of righteousness'. Its situation at the frontier and on the main route to Cilicia made it the regular base for summer and winter raids into the Byzantine territory across the Amanus. Presumably as a safeguard against counter-raids, the Umaiyad caliph Hisham (724–43) is recorded as having 'established a garrison of 50 men and built a fort for it' at Baghras.[11] The military importance of Baghras must have declined, but its commerce increased as the frontier was pushed northwards. Traffic across the Pass must have been stimulated when Harun-ar-Rashid in 786 gave security to the Gulf of Alexandretta by fortifying a line of towns to the north. There are some grounds for supposing the fortifications to have been strengthened, if not extended, by 968, as a defence against the Byzantines, for in the campaign of that year Pagras or Pagra (both forms are neuter singulars) is included among the 'largest and most notable fortresses' taken by Nicephorus Phocas in Cilicia and Syria.

Yahya of Antioch, a Christian Arab who completed his chronicle about the year 1015, omits Baghras in this context, but asserts that Nicephorus Phocas, on his return from Syria, 'had the fortress of Baghras built opposite Antioch, at the entrance to the mountain pass, and put Michael Bourtzes there as commander', leaving him at first with 1,000 men and later sending reinforcements. Michael stayed there till shortly before the capture of Antioch in October 969.[12] Other authors confirm Nicephorus' building of a fortress in the Antioch district, but do not state its name. Leo Diaconus has the fullest account: in order to set an example, the emperor himself walked up the hill carrying the first stone, and his army completed the building in three days.[13]

---

[10] Sozomen, *Historia Ecclesiastica*, *PG*. LXVII, col. 1518.
[11] Baladhuri, trs. Hitti, pp. 228, 253–6, 258, 268–9.
[12] *Patrologia Orientalis* XVIII, pp. 816, 822.   [13] *PG*. CXVII, col. 768.

PLATE 8   BAGHRAS IN 1838

Drawn by W. H. Bartlett for John Carne's Syria, the Holy Land and Asia Minor: seen from the east, showing, not very accurately, bossed tower of lower enceinte and above the inner enceinte the hall on right and open end of chapel on left.

The view is undoubtedly romanticised, but more of the lower *enceinte* was then standing, and Bartlett's drawing shows how impressive the castle appeared. He did not go up to the ruins, and could not see from a distance how some parts related to others or realise the significance of details such as the dark patch that should mark the entrance; he has misplaced it alongside of instead at the centre of the gatehouse, which is correctly shown at the right end of the outer wall. The landscape is drawn with reasonable accuracy, especially in the nearer portions. The road in the foreground, coming from Antioch, actually turns in front of the castle hill to a ford over the Karamurt; the old route from the village to Beylan (and eventually through Alexandretta to Cilicia) leads up to the right of the houses between a low ridge and the great hill behind. This was the hill that Saladin climbed to observe the castle from the lip of the gorge in order to decide his plan of assault. The stream flowing through the gorge rises at a copious spring known to the Crusaders as the Fountain of Gaston, some 300 metres beyond the castle.   A. W. L.

Once the Byzantines had captured Antioch and its southern approaches they had no reason to maintain either a large camp or a strong fort at Baghras – although it is true that the Arabs twice attempted to regain the lost city. In the following century Byzantine possession became precarious and finally nominal. After Antioch had paid tribute to Mosul for several years, the Armenian Philaretus incorporated it in a principality owing vague allegiance to Constantinople, but the Persian governor he appointed soon delivered the city to the Selchukid Turks. Baghras must have changed hands simultaneously in 1084.

In the First Crusade Tancred is stated to have destroyed certain 'Turkish mountain-strongholds garrisoned by fine soldiers' including the *Castrum Adolescentium* called *de Bakelers* or (in another manuscript) *des Bachelers* – a corruption of Baghras having apparently been taken as the French word for a novice in arms by Albert of Aix, writing after 1120.[14] Kamal-ad-Din merely records that the Franks camped at Baghras on 12 September 1097 and used it as a base for raids on the territory of Antioch before laying siege to the city.[15] A third account of the campaign is likewise silent about the resistance offered by the garrison, alluding only to the route of Tancred's army across the mountains which separate Alexandretta and the 'small fort' of Baghras – *Alexandriolam Guastonemque oppidulum*.[16]

The crusaders habitually refer to Baghras under this name of Guaston, Gaston, Gastrin, Gastin, Gastim, or Gastun; the identification admits of no reasonable doubt, as may be seen by examination of the references collected here. Dussaud has suggested that the first syllable of the crusader name represents an attempt to render the oriental sound – *ghras*. This is the more probable because the *Ba-* is very lightly sounded in modern speech – whether Arabic, Armenian or Turkish – whereas the remainder of the word is strongly accented. The source of the Frankish termination has not yet been clearly explained. A parallel might be found perhaps in the Latin transliteration of a place-name in Cilicia as either Amuda or Amudain – both forms occur in one official document of the Armenian kingdom, the *-in* being added in the Latin version to reproduce the reading of the Armenian text which must have ended with a demonstrative suffix, which in the modern language has become the article.[17]

[14] *RHC.Occ.* IV, p. 357.
[15] *RHC.Or.* III, p. 578.   [16] *RHC.Occ.* III, p. 639.
[17] I owe this information to Prof. H. W. Bailey. I may add that Amuda is usual in Arabic, but Nuwairi speaks of the ford of Amudain or Amudein; the vowels are not indicated. If the latter form was meant it could be interpreted as a dual, applying to settlements on both banks of the river; the *-ain* is an Arabic plural ending which could scarcely have been intended in that sense but would be a reproduction of the Armenian.

A Byzantine Golden Bull includes the *strategaton Pagras* among the places held by the emperor's new vassal-state, the principality of Antioch.[18] Its history under crusading rule is obscure. It is rarely mentioned in the first fifty years and then always in connection with movements of hostile troops, to which the castle obviously formed no impediment.

A Moslem army sent to relieve Antioch encamped near there till its defeat in February 1098.[19] In 1115 the Turks returned in strength to the *civitates Gallorum* of Gastum and Harim, but were driven out by Franks and Armenians.[20] In July and September 1132 the Byzantine Emperor John Comnenus went past on his way to subdue Antioch and on the return journey. In 1137 another Byzantine army is recorded to have withdrawn from Antioch to Ba'rin[20a] – a name otherwise unknown in that district and perhaps a mistake for Baghras, for the change is easily made in Arabic script. In 1142 John camped before the *oppidum* or *chastel* of Gastun, intending again to besiege Antioch.[21]

Though the emperor's death frustrated this project, Byzantine aggression had resulted in the Franks losing a number of fortresses 'on the confines of Antioch', and Baghras may have been one of them.[22] But a new power was growing up in Cilicia, where Armenian refugees had formed a Byzantine vassal-state after the Moslem conquest of their home-lands near Ararat. Thoros, the ruler of Cilician Armenia, took possession of the fortresses in question. The prince of Antioch and the Templars demanded their return, and a battle was fought near Alexandretta during the year beginning October 1156. When peace was made Thoros surrendered the castles while the Templars swore to give aid to Armenia in future. It has been inferred that Baghras was one of these Templar possessions because another battle at the Portal (Jonah's Pillar), just north of Alexandretta, was fought either that same year or earlier between Turks from Konya and a mixed force containing some Armenians in addition to 'brothers, warrior-friends of Christ'.[23] These knights may safely be identified as Templars, but it is clear that the Order did not hold Baghras continuously from this date, for in the winter of 1160–1 the fief was in the gift of the prince of Antioch. He conferred it upon Gerard, formerly of Sidon, who had been exiled for piracy

[18] Anna Comnena, *RHC.Gr.* I, p. 181.
[19] Bar Hebraeus, *Chronography*, p. 235.
[20] *RHC.Occ.* IV, p. 701.
[20a] Qalanisi, *Damascus Chronicle*, trans. Gibb, p. 244.
[21] William of Tyre, *RHC.Occ.* I, p. 689.
[22] In 1149 Nur-ad-Din defeated the crusaders at a place written variously as Busra, Yaghra or Baghras; only the mouth of the valley could be meant.
[23] Gregory the Priest, *RHC.Arm.* I, p. 171.

and almost immediately recommenced depredations by both land and sea. He was therefore driven out by the prince of Antioch and became a renegade. (He was eventually captured by Baldwin III and burned alive at Jerusalem.) The Templars themselves declared (in 1209) that they owed possession of Gaston to Pope Alexander III, 1159–81. But it had also once belonged, so Armenia claimed in 1199, to Thoros' villainous brother, Mleh. When Thoros died, leaving an infant heir, Mleh became a brigand-leader and received Moslem aid; he had formerly been a Templar and a Catholic. He is said to have taken from the Templars all that they possessed in Armenia. Probably these conquests do not date from 1168, his year of dependence on Aleppo, but were made during his usurpation of all Armenia, which he held 1169–75. He is recorded to have established himself by 'taking possession of castles and towns all over the country'.[24] The Templars therefore may conceivably have held Baghras for brief periods in the first half and in the middle of the twelfth century, but are not likely to have occupied it continuously before 1175.

Baghras became the Order's northern headquarters, to judge from the story of how a renegade 'sent messages to the Temple to the castle of Gaston', stipulating for a safe return as reward for kidnapping Saladin's nephew.[25] They lost it again in 1188. After the capitulation of Darbsak on 13 September Saladin proceeded to Baghras, which surrendered on the 26th, with the permission of the government of Antioch, which was prevented by an Arab detachment from sending to its relief.[26] The castle was 'well provisioned and possessed great means of defence and a large garrison', according to Imad ad-Din.[27] But Bar Hebraeus contradicts this statement, explaining the capitulation on the ground that 'there were not in it sufficient soldiers to fight', which is credible, for the Templars' numbers must have been depleted by their losses at Hattin a couple of months earlier. Another contemporary account is given by Baha ad Din. Saladin, writes the eyewitness Imad ad-Din, 'put mangonels all round Baghras on the heights . . . for weeks each of our mangonels shot a torrent of

[24] Michael the Syrian, *RHC.Arm.* I, pp. 354, 362; Innocent III, *Epistolae* XII, pp. 45, 259; William of Tyre, *RHC.Occ.* I, 2, p. 991: see also Grousset, *Histoire des Croisades* II, p. 568.

[25] *RHC.Occ.* II, p. 72.

[26] He took Gaston and Darbsak according to Ansbert and to *Eracles* (*RHC.Occ.* II, p. 72), while an Armenian elegy alludes to Baghras in this connection as Sara (*RHC.Arm.* I, p. 303). As a further confirmation of the identification of Gaston, it may be remarked that Jamal ad Din knows Baghras as a Templar fortress (note by Quatremère to Maqrizi, *Hist. des Sultanes Mamlouks* I, 2, p. 266).

[27] *RHC.Or.* IV, p. 378.

stones on the place'. But the 'mangonels produced no effect on the walls, because of their great height'.[28] 'We were finding the struggle very long', continues Al Imad, 'and it seemed to us that its fatigues were never going to end, when we saw the door of the castle open and give passage to a man who came to ask mercy for the occupants in exchange for the place and all the goods it contained. We made a rough count of the stock of grain that remained and it amounted to 12,000 sacks. The sultan gave Baghras and Darbsak (Trapessac) to the lord of Azaz, Alam ad Din Suleiman ibn Jandar . . . I said to myself . . . "As he is poor he will sell all the goods to satisfy his thirst for wealth and then give orders to destroy the place instead of applying himself to govern it, on the pretext that if we kept it it would prove a trap and that its defence would involve the Moslems in perils of every kind." This happened some years later as I had foreseen; the place was evacuated, but to the detriment of the true believers.'

The Moslems abandoned the castle on the approach of the main body of the German crusade of 1190, after the garrison 'numbering but a few men' had successfully attacked the first isolated division on its way to Antioch. Next year, when Saladin was engaged on the siege of Acre, he 'sent certain horsemen to go and empty the fortress of Baghras of provisions and to destroy it. And when they had gone and had destroyed a little of it they heard that Leon, the ruler of Cilicia, was ready to capture them, and they left it and fled. And the men of Antioch heard of their flight, and they came to Baghras, and they found in it twelve thousand measures of wheat. And they carried them to Antioch. And after some days Leon came, and he gained the mastery over the Franks and took Baghras from them.'[29] Several other accounts agree that the place was damaged by the Arabs and rebuilt by the Armenians.[30] For instance, Ibn al Athir writes: 'Saladin ordered its demolition, which was done. But it was a great cause of harm to the Moslems, for the son of Leon, prince of the Armenians, marched on this place which was near his land. He rebuilt Baghras with much care and placed there a detachment of his army to make incursions on the neighbouring territory. Baghras is still in the hands of the Armenians and the cultivated country round Aleppo suffers greatly from their incursions.' Perhaps Leon did not go in person to Baghras, as is implied in a rhymed chronicle, for according to *L'Estoire de Eracles*, 'Fouques de Bouillon, cousin germane of the

[28] *RHC.Or.* III, p. 117 and *RHC.Or.* I, p. 732.

[29] Bar Hebraeus, *Chronography*, p. 336.

[30] Abu-l-Fida says that it was rebuilt by the Franks (*Annales Muslemici* tr. J. J. Reiske and J. G. C. Adler, IV (Copenhagen, 1792), p. 421; V (1794), p. 23).

aforesaid Leon, hearing that the Saracens had slighted the aforesaid castle, entered into the castle and seized it and held it twenty years'.[31] The length of Fulk's tenure is however uncertain. His mother was a daughter of Leon I, and his father is described as 'of Antioch', so that he was a man of some standing. It must have been while he held the castle that Leon treacherously lured Bohemond of Antioch there 'to see the place', probably in 1194. But from 1198 to 1215 Adam, who later was *bailli* for the princess Zabel, is referred to as lord of Baghras or of Gaston, and also as seneschal from 1207 to 1215.[32]

The only medieval description of the castle dates from the Armenian occupation. Wilbrand of Oldenburg, who went there in 1211, describes Gaston as 'a very strong castle, with three very strong towered walls round it, situated in the last mountains of Armenia. It diligently watches the entrances and paths of that land, to the king of which it belongs, that is to say the king of Armenia. The Templars complain that they are despoiled by his possession of it. Antioch is overlooked from it direct and from the neighbourhood; it is four leagues away.'[33] It is not known whether the earthquake of the following year had any effect; it caused damage at Antioch and Damascus.

The quarrel with the Templars proceeded for many years. The Pope asked Leon in 1199 to give the castle back, and in a letter, which apparently dates from 1207, Leon even promised to do so.[34] In a peace-treaty which Leon signed in the Moslem year corresponding to July 1208–9, the sultans of Konya and Aleppo insisted on the cession of Baghras to the Templars, with the object of weakening Armenia. The pope tried excommunication, which also proved a failure. Finally, Armenian territory was devastated by raiders from Antioch, including fifty other knights in addition to the Templars, until Leon surrendered the castle. This happened not earlier than the autumn of 1211 and probably in the following year, for the excommunication was not lifted till the beginning of 1213.[35] The Templars seem to have held only the castle itself, while the land in the vicinity remained for several years the property of its secular lord. For on 15 March 1215 the right to levy custom dues is reserved to Adam of Gaston, in a Golden Bull of privileges granted by Leon to the Genoese.

[31] *RHC.Or* I, p. 732, *Arm.* I, p. 512, *Occ.* I, p. 136.

[32] For Fulk and Adam see Rüdt-Collenberg, *The Rupenides, Hethumides and Lusignans*, pp. 51, 60.

[33] *Peregrinatores*, ed. Laurent, p. 174.

[34] cf. Röhricht, *Geschichte des Königreichs Jerusalem*, p. 711. Raynaldus, *Annales Eccles.* on 1205, in Baronius, vol. XX, p. 221, with note by Mansi.

[35] Innocent III, *Ep.* XVI, no. 7; there is no mention of Gaston in letter no. 2 of February, which complains of many other actions of Leon's. *RHC.Occ.* II, p. 317.

The Order would have been specially amenable at that time, if Leon had already occupied Antioch, as may have been the case; the sources are at variance. According to Ibn Wasil he delivered Baghras to the Templars on his departure in 1216.[36]

The second Templar occupation lasted till the collapse of the Principality of Antioch before Baybars in 1268.[37] In 1226 'the sultan of Aleppo came with a large force of cavalry and attacked Bagras, without success'. In a second siege in the autumn of 1236 'it would have fallen into the hands of the Aleppines, if the truce just concluded with the Prince of Antioch had not forced them to retire'. Finally on 27 May 1268, Baybars' forces occupied Baghras, 'the garrison of which had retired in great haste upon the capture of Antioch' leaving one old woman and a large quantity of provisions and weapons of war.[38]

On Baybars' capture of the castle 'he filled it with men and war material' (so Abu-l-Fida reports), for the Arabs needed it as a safeguard against Armenia. The frontier now ran through the range behind the castle, but as Armenia proved unable to take the offensive its military value diminished. Baghras had in fact reverted to its old position of a frontier post and a base for incursions across the Amanus into Christian territory – only this now belonged to Armenia instead of to the Byzantine empire, and the expeditions were more serious, aiming at actual conquest. This was achieved by the Arab annexation of the entire Gulf of Alexandretta in 1347 and of the last remnant of the Armenian kingdom in 1375. Subsequently the castle would not have been worth the cost of upkeep. The town on the other hand must already have waned with the commercial disuse of the Beylan Pass consequent on the decay of Antioch, which set in after 1268, and the hostile relations which prevailed between it and Armenia. A mild revival might have resulted from Arab annexation first of eastern and then of western Cilicia.

For administrative purposes the place was the departmental capital of the Qinnasrin, or Aleppo Province, as in the early days of Islam.[39] But for a few

---

[36] Quoted W. B. Stevenson, *Crusaders in the East* (Cambridge, 1907), p. 299 n. 1.

[37] *RHC.Arm.* I, p. 648; Grousset (*Histoire* III, p. 364) declares that the Armenians did not resign themselves to the cession of Baghras and that it was as a protest that they flayed alive a few Templars in (?) 1233 (*RHC.Occ.* III, p. 363). The chronicler does not explain the motive for this action and I suspect Grousset of having inferred it without much justification. The king and the baron who lost Baghras were both dead, and more active causes of friction had had time to develop between Armenia and the Order.

[38] *RHC.Or.* I, pp. 112, 152: Maqrizi, *Histoire* I, 2, p. 56.

[39] The Government of Baghras is included in the Arab domains in two treaties of 1283 and 1285 (Maqrizi II, 1, p. 226, 205).

years around 1300 Baghras and the district of which it remained the capital
were held by the Mongols of Persia, then in alliance with the Armenians.[40]
The first appearance of the Mongols was in 1280, when their khan organised a
raid; his army took Aintab on 18 October, Baghras, Darbsak, and, on 20 October
Aleppo, but there is nothing to indicate that the castle at Baghras was attacked.
At least four Arab expeditions passed through, in the years 1283, 1298 (when
there were two campaigns) and 1302. In 1324 Marino Sanudo notes the *castrum*
of Baghras, the name of Gaston having by now perished. A visitor of 1326
declares: 'it is a quite impregnable castle, and no one thinks of attacking it'.[41]
But neglect was now beginning, and it is unlikely that serious repairs were
undertaken. Damage may have been caused by an earthquake of 1344, which
shook Constantinople, Syria and Egypt, and by another in 1402 which devastated
the Aegean; and perhaps there were others of which I know no record. When
Bertrandon de la Broquière crossed the Amanus from Antioch to Alexandretta,
in 1432, the castles he saw were all 'apparently destroyed'; he would have
passed Baghras castle at a distance of a quarter of a mile. In 1477 the sultan
Qaitbay inspected the castle at Baghras 'otherwise called Bab el Muluk' (the
Gate of the Kings)[42] – the kingdom of Armenia had been extinguished by the
Arabs a century before, but its place had been taken by the Ottoman empire.
In the wars between the Ottoman and the Arab empires the possession of the
pass of Baghras was again contested,[43] and even the Turkish conquest in 1516
failed to establish a lasting peace, for it was broken by rebellions[44] as well as
by chronic brigandage in the mountains above the castle. When Sultan Sulaiman
founded a caravan station in the middle of the range, in 1563, it quickly grew
into a town, but Baghras did not immediately decline, if one may trust the

[40] See Howorth, *Hist. of Mongols* III, p. 444.   [41] Ibn Battuta I, p. 163.
[42] Translated by Mrs Devonshire, in *Bulletin de l'Institut français d'archéologie
orientale* XX, p. 12; cf. notes by Dussaud, in *La Syrie antique et médiévale illustrée*, II
(Paris, 1931), p. 262 and *Topographie historique*, p. 435. The passages on Antioch,
Baghras and Darbsak are muddled together. On p. 13, after the account of the road
leading from Baghras, there follows a sentence apparently describing the Antioch river-
side, with its hydraulic wheels and stalls – though the ruins of one mill do exist a few
miles below Baghras. The citadels between which the sultan climbed are presumably
not those at Baghras and Darbsak but two parts of Baghras. The governor of Aleppo
was appointed in charge of the castle, which now controlled only a small district with
no trade.
[43] There was fighting between the Turks and the Egyptians here in 1489 (J. von
Hammer-Purgstall, *Gesch. d. osman. Reiches*, II (Pest, 1828), p. 299).
[44] A rebel held the pass in 1607 (ibid., IV, p. 403), and a battle took place two
centuries later between the Turks and Ibrahim's Egyptians.

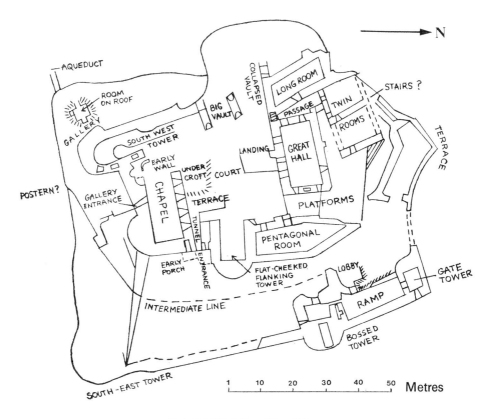

BAGHRAS *Key Plan*

Plate 9 (opposite)   BAGHRAS

Drawing of plan and section by Phoebe H. Brown, 1938

Walls on the summit are shown in solid black if still weight-bearing, in fairly dark tints if the base alone is well-preserved, in paler tints if it is barely traceable. Buildings on the slopes of the hill, and the natural surroundings of the castle, are shown tinted, darkening as the level descends.

NORTH

SECTION

SECTION

SECTION

PLAN

SECTION
VERTICAL DIMENSIONS APPROXIMATED

BAGHRAS

SCALE

FEET

MEASURED AUGUST 1938

oriental geographers. They habitually borrow information from their pre-decessors and some of their facts about Baghras must have been out of date; for example they continue to mention the hospice built there by Zubayda, wife of Harun ar-Rashid, although an eighth-century foundation could hardly have survived the crusades. The khan and the cathedral mosque were probably kept up, also the municipal Court of Justice, which had been founded in the early Islamic period and refounded in 1326. The baths, built by Sulaiman in 1552, probably remained also.[45] But all these amenities have long ceased to function; only the ruined bath may be identifiable, at Kizlar Kalesi, outside the castle. As Antioch dwindled in importance traffic from the north deserted the old road, turning aside at Beylan towards Aleppo, and Baghras became a little village of Turkomans, in a dead-end valley.

DESCRIPTION AND DATING

To avoid repetition, I preface my description by a statement of facts which are of fairly general application throughout the ruins. The sole building material now visible is stone. As a rule it was shaped only by hammer point and had to be packed with smaller lumps or chips of stone in the joints; unless otherwise stated, the masonry is of this type, which I describe as 'rough-trim' and con-sisting of 'stones', reserving the word 'blocks' for chisel-dressed masonry and 'rubble' for the worst quality building. All covered spaces, apart from one possible instance of a wooden ceiling due to an alteration, were vaulted – generally barrel-vaulted; when I speak simply of 'a room' it should be under-stood as having a barrel-vault, either round or very slightly pointed. The defensive walls were in most places backed by a line of such rooms; their vaults sprang off the inner face of the external wall and so made a very wide rampart walk, presumably lined by a battlemented parapet of which nothing remains. I use the term 'curtain' for any stretch of defensive wall other than a tower, regardless of whether or not a room stood behind it. A 'doorway' is distinguished from an 'archway' by the presence of a small rear-arch and reveals or other provision for fitting a door.

[45] *Chèref-Nâmeh*, trs. Charmoy, I, 1, p. 272. The account in Haji Khalfa's *Jihan Numa* of 1648 (under the Aleppo Province of Syria) seems to be entirely borrowed from older sources. A notice of a River Baghras – so called after a neighbouring village which was inhabited by Christians – appears in both the *Chèref-Nâmeh* (p. 286, and note, p. 793) and *Jihan Numa*, but Abu-l-Fida gives the name more plausibly as Yaghra. See in general, Gaudefroy-Demombynes, *La Syrie à l'époque des Mamelouks*, p. 88.

The condition of the castle in 1938 is described throughout in the present tense; later information [printed in *italic* type within square brackets] shows how fast the ruins are now crumbling.

1. *The Entrance System*

The Exterior. The hill on which the castle stands descends gradually towards the east in a ridge about 400 m. long, which is bounded on the north by a precipice but can be reached all along the south side with little difficulty (though much effort), up slopes broken by occasional outcrops of rock. On the top of the ridge the natural contours have evidently been altered by considerable quarrying; stone from here is, in fact, to be seen in various parts of the castle. [*Practically the whole of the ridge was brought under cultivation between 1938 and 1951, with the result that the remainder of this paragraph is no longer verifiable.*] Near the castle there are slight indications of two walls which originally terraced the slope. Of the outer there remains a short stretch, roughly parallel with the entrance ramp from which it is about 90 m. distant. The other wall, only about 18 m. outside the entrance, runs in the same general direction but an angle in its course suggests that at this point it probably supported a road zigzagging up a slope of rock. A steep-fronted shelf of rock has been cut like a berm along the foot of the lower enceinte but smoothes out as it approaches the gateway, so that a masonry barrier might have been desirable here.

The castle was entered at its north-east corner. On a platform of rock, projecting over an abyss on the north, stands a gate-tower, formerly of two storeys. A simple round arch, rising from ground level, forms the outer doorway and occupies practically the entire east wall; this wall has lost its external facing on the ground-floor and no longer exists above, but it does not seem to have projected appreciably from the adjoining curtain. [*Müller-Wiener's plan suggests that it has been removed by a landslip.*]

The stretch of curtain to the south, which forms the exterior of the entrance ramp, has been altered in a rather unsightly manner. The lower part consists of small rough-trim stones packed with great quantities of chips; the horizontal mortar-joints are thus exceptionally thick compared with most work throughout the castle, though analogous to those of the gallery. Higher up, rows of larger dressed blocks of a darker colour are sandwiched between courses of small stones laid in narrow joints; the dark patching comprises almost the entire height of the wall near the gate-tower and then slants upwards at roughly 45 degrees till it levels off as a band occupying about one-third of the total height, and so meets the rounded tower to the south. The masonry below changes, just before the tower is reached, to drafted bossed blocks, varying considerably in size but rarely less than twice as large as those of the curtain base to the north; the whole face of the tower consists of this bossed masonry, which at the outset extends for two or three blocks in each course up to half the height of the curtain, and then is overlaid by the usual small stones. Unquestionably the large-block work is later than the rest of the curtain base, because it ceases to break joint regularly north of the tower, in order to lessen the difficulty of joining its unequal but invariably taller courses with those of the comparatively uniform rough-trim; here alone the joints of superimposed blocks are sometimes in vertical line.

The exterior of the tower is unlike any other portion of the castle, but the bossed masonry merely faces a rubble core. The large blocks, set wide apart in very hard mortar, are mostly drafted at the edges, leaving an irregular boss projecting in the middle, though some are dressed practically flat (like almost all in the adjoining piece of curtain). In all the rest of the castle only one bossed block is noticeable, embedded in a fallen lump of otherwise nondescript masonry upon a terrace of the north slope. Local examples of the style remain at a tower inside the fort of Sariseki and another at Darbsak (Trapesac) which is possibly a late gateway, for it stands apart from, and below, the main line of wall half-way down the slope. In the south of the crusader country such masonry is not uncommon; at Sidon it occurs in work associated with St Louis. In the present instance it may be ascribed to a similar period, because the room inside contains capitals plainly of late crusader origin and is presumably contemporary with the facing. In a joint of the external masonry was embedded a sherd of the green-glazed ware associated with the Mamluk period. An arched opening in the face of the tower, high at its centre, is the enlarged relic of an arrow-slit, approached from within through a special passage. An upper storey, shown in Bartlett's engraving of 1838, has entirely perished (Pl. 8).

On the south the bossed masonry terminates at the very beginning of another curtain, which is homogeneous for its entire height. It consists of stones rather smaller than those composing the base of the northward curtain, very roughly squared and set with less packing, especially in the horizontal joints. The whole exterior seems to have been plastered. The nature of the junction indicates that the curtain and tower are not contemporary. The curtain is probably the older; the last few stones in each course may have had to be replaced by the builders of the tower and consequently became liable to fall. The curtain is very thick, as befits its height and some incorporation of native rock, the scarped upright face of which has been exposed in places by the fall of blocks from the single layer that covered it. In fact, therefore, an irregular slope was cut back to make a shelf on which the wall stands.

To the south the dilapidated top of the curtain drops lower, rises again and finally breaks off at a point where the inner half of its thickness is occupied by the southward spring of an arch, which may have covered an embrasure. The whole curtain is shown intact on Bartlett's view of 1838, but a gap now extends all the way to the south-east corner, where a tall remnant of a tower rises abruptly. The attachment of the curtain can be seen in the straight flank, just before the exterior of the enceinte begins to curve; a northward arch-spring probably belonged to an embrasure at the junction. Another wall diverges inward from the back of the tower-flank at an acute angle, and breaks after containing the arch of an embrasure that commanded a terrace behind the south outer wall of the castle.

The Interior. The ground floor of the gate-tower forms a small room built of roughly trimmed stones. Extremely poor rubble, incorporating stones of very uneven sizes, composes the east wall, which contains the entrance arch, and is probably a late repair. At the north corner of the west wall a low and narrow archway had been carefully blocked [*but was open in* 1951, *disclosing a vaulted cell,* 75 *cm. wide by* 2.40 *m. long and* 1.35*m. high*; *this, of course, is not shown on the* 1938 *plan. The only portion of the gate-tower on Müller-Wiener's plan is the back wall of the cell, and presumably an encroachment by the precipice had removed the rest.*]

The inner exit from the gate-tower is a round arch situated at right angles to persons entering the castle, at the west end of the south wall. The archway, which rests on large ashlar on the outward as well as the inward side, faces up a gently sloping ramp. The northern half of the ramp has been covered by cross-vaults, beginning from the arch, but in 1938 only one complete span remained out of the four, together with three of the requisite four separate piers – two on the west practically free-standing, one on the east engaged in the curtain. [*By 1951 there remained only the rubble core of one, and a scrap of vaulting attached to the gate-tower.*] The fourth pier vanished many centuries ago, for it must have been engaged in a piece of curtain that needed reconstruction, which has given the wall an uninterrupted face; there is no means of knowing whether the vaulting was then shored up or left tattered. The three extant piers are square in section. The thick, squared piers – three of the original four – are faced with great smooth blocks and filled with cemented rubble; the actual vaults were built of long narrow pieces of stone, carelessly shaped, in the usual way. The roof over the vaulting stood low for defence of the curtain but commanded the open south half of the ramp; perhaps the most advantageous effect of the vaulting was to darken the room inside the gate-tower so that anybody entering it from sunlight was temporarily blinded.

The west wall is of shoddy rubble and seems to be of later date. It supports a terrace behind the ramp. The east wall is better built, and crudely bonded to the vault piers. A rectangular opening in the south wall of the gate-tower, close to the curtain, overlooked the roof of the vaulting; it might have been a window or a small doorway. This is coigned with smooth blocks and covered by a lintel, relieved above by an arch which has partly subsided. The frame was built with a disregard for quality which makes it very unseemly on the inward face and has resulted towards the ramp in the loss of the lower part of the eastern jamb. The sill lies not more than one course above the crown of one of the vault-springs, the edge of which was shaped to fit into the haunch of the archway below, while its base rested on a bed of smooth blocks considerably larger than the rough-trimmed stones of the usual courses. A corresponding scrap of cross-vaulting survives over the other haunch, proving contemporaneity with the lower part of the tower wall.

The southern half of the ramp seems never to have been roofed. It contained a staircase, carried on an arch applied against the face of the east wall close to the last vault, to the roof of which it must have led. The top of this wall [*which fell between 1938 and 1951*] is an obvious repair, both on the inner side and externally; it retains no remnant of the wall-walk, which is likely to have been corbelled out.

The ramp was commanded at the south end by the side wall of the bossed tower, in front of which the road into the castle turned off to the right. There was direct communication between the ramp and the tower by a passage, entered through a narrower doorway with a slightly pointed arch of big wide voussoirs, the smooth surface of which contrasts with its surround of rough-trim, amply packed; the vault over the passage is almost flat and ends at the back with rubble voussoirs in a similar rough-trim face. The passage branches in the middle of its thickness, behind the holes for a draw-bar which secured the door; here a narrower passage diverges eastwards into the embrasure of an arrow-slit, which permitted a line of fire down the whole length of the ramp.

The room inside the bossed tower was cross-vaulted, on piers slightly projecting from its corners. The capitals from which the vaults spring are 23 cm. high with a moulding beneath a plain abacus. They form the only piece of pure decoration in the whole castle except for the even simpler mouldings in the entrance tunnel of the upper enceinte. Poor as they are, these capitals must be

E

of European design, and there can be little doubt that they belong to the thirteenth century period of crusader occupation. The vaulting cannot have been inserted into pre-existing walls unless they were re-faced.

Three walls of the room are homogeneous. The east wall, however, is placed crooked, resting against a corner of the capital instead of being, like the others, set behind the centre of the side, and it consists of smaller stones than the others, laid dry. At the north end is an arched recess centred on the exterior of the tower, containing a doorway with draw-holes on the nearer side; the bar that moved in them controlled entry to a tiny room beyond, which ended at what must have been an arrow-slit, though it has degenerated into a jagged but still arched hole at the centre of the tower. The masonry in the recess is unlike that of the room, being really part of the rubble core of the outer wall. [*By 1951 half of the east wall had fallen.*]

Large pointed arches, with finely cut voussoirs, led from the tower into rooms south and west. [*By 1951 the whole south wall had fallen.*] To the south there was apparently a flat space large enough for two such rooms, but the general destruction in that area and the deep consequent accumulation of rubbish makes their extent uncertain. The one room on the west was of the same width as that within the tower. Attached to it on the north was a lobby, reached from the head of the ramp by a large doorway [*mostly destroyed between 1938 and 1951*], which enforced a turn at right angles – the second after entering the castle. The door opened westwards; a draw-bar secured it against intrusion from the ramp. The style of the arch suggests contemporaneity with the doorways inside the tower, though the construction is stronger, as befitted a position of greater danger. The lobby formed an inner gatehouse; the roof, though well below the level of the tower-vault, was high enough to overlook that of the ramp vaulting. The barrel-vault is complete except at the far end where it has fallen, together with the archway which must have occupied almost the entire west wall. [*By 1951 the whole vault had fallen.*]

The ground behind the lobby rises steeply to a broken cliff which forms the base of the inner enceinte. The occupants of the castle probably had the choice of turning at a right angle, either to left or right – for a minor path may be assumed to have led on the right behind the ramp to the back of the gate-tower, and onwards to the north slope. The main route, however, could only have turned left, past the room behind the tower, and then have slanted again towards the left, commanded from the roofs of rooms backing on the curtain, till it passed below the D-shaped tower of the upper enceinte; here it must have swung to the right to climb to the south-east corner of the upper enceinte.

Dating. The earliest remains in this area must have been built after the Armenian seizure of Baghras in 1191 and before 1211. This is made clear by comparison of the two eyewitness reports of 1187 and 1211. At the earlier date the castle was out of effective range of mangonels; since that could not have been true of this section, only the present upper enceinte can have existed at first, whereas in 1211 there were already 'three lines of wall' (the inner wall of the ramp being counted as an intermediate line). The ramp with its cross-vaulting fits well into the latter period; the monumental Hospitaller parallel at Krak des Chevaliers seems to date from about 1200, while the vaulted passage at Ajlun, which is Arab, belongs to a series of improvements to which an inscription of 1214–15 refers.

Some correlations of building are fairly clear. The gate-tower must be contemporary with the cross-vaulting of the ramp, because the doorway between them is integrated, on the ramp side, with piers supporting the vaults. The present inner wall of the ramp is an insertion; at the north end it is aligned with the vault-piers, against which it abuts without bonding, and their preservation implies that the vaulting was still complete at the time. The whole of this wall seems of one build; the bend brings the south end into line with the lobby frontage, which adjoins the bossed tower and should be contemporary therewith, i.e. crusader work of the middle rather than the early thirteenth century. The sequences are best expressed in tabular form:

External	*Internal*
I Ramp curtain to two-thirds height at south, base only at north; curtain south of bossed tower.	I Ramp curtain as preserved beside midway vault-pier; cross-vaulting of ramp; gate-tower except for outer doorway.
II Bossed tower.	II Inner wall of ramp; room in bossed tower; lobby.
III Repair of ramp curtain, by patching at top of south end and almost complete rebuilding at north end.	III Top of ramp curtain at south end; demolition of cross-vaulting at north end of ramp, and rebuilding of curtain there.

These stages can be related to the recorded history in only one plausible manner:

    I. Original outer enceinte, Armenian, *c.* 1200.

    II. Templar repairs and improvements after the Aleppine siege of 1236.

    III. Arab repairs (at earliest, after the Templars had set fire to the buildings in 1283).

On that hypothesis the Aleppines in 1236 would have breached the site of the bossed tower (where there ought already to have been a tower to provide flanking for the bend in the curtain); they would then have proceeded to damage the inner wall and exit of the ramp. The outer gateway, too, may have required rebuilding after the siege, but some later date is equally plausible.

There may also be a relic of a period intermediate between I and II. [*The collapse by 1951 of the south-east corner of the ramp curtain showed that the tower began externally slightly northward of its north wall, as though that wall had followed a course determined at an earlier period than the actual tower.*] The exceptional thickness of the wall between the ramp and tower would be compatible with reconstruction to retain the cross-vaulting of the tower, while the doorway in this wall is stylistically so incongruous with the two others that gave access to the tower that it can scarcely be contemporaneous with them; it may be older than the rubble in which it is set, just as very similar voussoirs can be seen where the aqueduct enters the castle to be obviously later than the surrounding masonry, which must surely be Armenian. Whatever its date the doorway certainly marked the end of the ramp of its period, because it gives too little clearance for a main route; it may have led into a previous tower, replaced after the siege of 1236.

2. *The Outer Defences on south and west*

The south-eastern walls. Of the south-east corner-tower there remains the tall stump, already mentioned, above a rounded base of the exterior, which may be a true revetment or merely a lining to a rock platform; the actual facing has perished except for the lowest courses. The eastern half of the south wall, from this point to past the beginning of the gallery, survives only as the masonry revetment of a terrace that presumably consists largely, if not entirely, of rock. It may be assumed that a natural slope was cut back to make a cliff that is hidden behind the upright revetment, leaving an almost level floor of rock at the foot, now covered by stones which have fallen from the revetment and the parapet, if not also from free-standing courses. The terrace slopes gently upwards towards the west while the ground outside rises more steeply, so that the height of the revetment decreases; its facing is preserved for a length of some 21 m. from the junction with the tower, and along this stretch the height decreases from roughly nine to six metres. Beyond that, the facing has been destroyed by the fall of free-standing masonry from above, where there are still some scanty remains half-buried in rubbish; one wall of a lost room runs southward from the revetment for 4.5 metres.

The revetment keeps on the same axis throughout, converging upon the much higher wall of the gallery, which it reaches as a tapering shelf, blunted at the apex, some three metres above the sloping ground outside; its outline here is distinguishable alternately by masonry and by scarped rock. The shelf was almost doubled in height by a low vault built upon it. At the eastern end, part of the spring of the vault remains in the frontage of the gallery, where it seems to have started a third of a metre or so above the level at the west. But for most of its length, which was about 12 m., the vault has completely pulled away, leaving only a horizontal slit in the gallery wall and taking the facing off the revetment in its fall. The western end, immediately above the junction of the revetment and gallery frontage, was formed by a cross-wall which turns out at right angles from the gallery frontage for over one metre. The span of the vault cannot be ascertained at any point but must have been very narrow, especially at the west end, where the rock at the foot of the revetment is irregularly cut and gives no indication that any masonry projected beyond the general line of the façade. Consequently it is barely conceivable that the vault enclosed the corridor to a postern, which would have been out of reach from the ground without steps or a ladder. Since a room so long and narrow would not have been built for its own sake, obviously had no retaining effect and apparently dipped from east to west, this part is likely to have been a conduit to drain the run-off after storms. The situation would have fitted that purpose. The slit begins, on the east, in the face of the massive end of the tall upper frontage which continues this far past the mouth of the gallery; from that point, a retaining-wall runs on almost the same axis, across the slope that descends from the chapel and the gateway of the upper enceinte. Fallen blocks and other refuse now leave the top of the retaining-wall exposed almost halfway to the east curtain, but conceal its further course. The wall must have supported a path, and possibly a water tank; nowhere else in the castle could there have been an open reservoir of the size the crusaders favoured.

The Exterior of the Gallery. The exterior of the gallery is now visible from roof to base for its entire length, though for a distance of over 12 m. from its eastern end the lower part was formerly concealed by the vault attached to the revetment. For a distance of several metres westward of the end of the revetment the wall rests on a scarped face of rock which may always have been exposed, but elsewhere the rock was covered by a talus of masonry. The talus now begins where the upright wall makes a bend inwards – the corner being buttressed by maintaining the previous line in the lower portion only, up to the height of some 7·5 metres. The steeply sloping talus runs continuously from this point to the far end of the gallery, midway along the west side of the castle. Apart from minor patches on the west side, the talus consists uniformly of very rough blocks, varying considerably in size and shape but larger as a rule than the characteristic rough-trim stones of Baghras; they are set into and smoothed over with such excellent mortar that pieces as big as a cart have bounded down the slope without disintegrating. The wide joints contain small stones and fragments of tiles embedded in the mortar. The material here is the bluish-grey rock of the castle hill, whereas the free-standing wall of the gallery above is of a warmer colour, appearing in the mass as buff. The bluish-grey fossiliferous limestone of the talus is compact and granular, as is some of the buff, while the softer, yellower stone has an uneven lenticular structure and contains many narrow cavities, sometimes ten or more centimetres long; its worst qualities were used indoors for choice. Neither rock breaks naturally into blocks suitable for building. The gallery wall consists of the usual rough-trim stones laid in mortar and packed with small scraps in almost every horizontal joint and many of the vertical. This wall too remains practically homogeneous for the entire length of the gallery, in spite of a vertical joint extending from the top to almost its full depth where it passes the south-west corner of the upper enceinte; here much of the masonry has fallen.

Shortly after the beginning of the gallery the wall is pierced by two well-preserved arrow-slits at quite different levels. The lower one is the first of a series opening at irregular intervals just above the gallery floor but now, with this exception, manifest externally as jagged holes; because of the great elevation, each provided an unusually wide field of fire, while the slope of the talus reduced the extent of dead ground. The upper arrow-slit, which retains a flat stone across the head, is no longer accessible and must have lit a passage inside the roof of the gallery.

At the castle's south-west corner an aqueduct enters on a culvert, the upper part of which is of similar style to the wall, while the lower is comparable with the talus though smaller stones are used. In spite of having lost a number of courses from the top, the culvert stands perhaps as high as 15 m. above the bed of the little gulley at the foot of the wall and crosses it by a coigned archway flush with each rough-trim face; plain flat imposts of slight projection, set at what was probably half the original total height, carry an almost round, pointed arch. [*This tall portion with the arch collapsed before Müller-Wiener examined the castle; he mistook the debris for the remains of a wall.*] The next surviving stretch of the culvert is at some distance up the slope to the west and there may have been another archway in the gap. Isolated stretches higher up

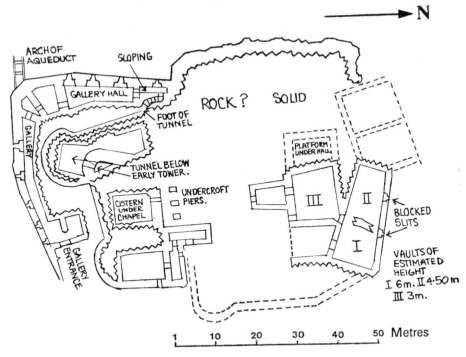

BAGHRAS   *Plan of substructures*

Walls of unknown thickness are shown toothed on the hidden side. The
unsurveyed rock-cut course of the tunnel is omitted.

show that the same direction was maintained almost to the summit of the ridge,
into which the water channel must have been sunk. Dr Kennedy, who was for
many years the missionary of the Reformed Presbyterian Church of Ireland in
the Alexandretta district, informed me that he once traced the aqueduct to its
source, a spring a couple of miles away in the hills.

Overlooking the aqueduct, but sunk nearly to the ceiling into the roof of
the gallery, is a square vaulted room which seems to have been about three or
four metres high. It is built mainly of long smooth blocks with no rubble
filling. Except for walls inside the gallery underneath this room the style is
unique at Baghras, but far better masonry of the same style links the interiors
of the two great towers at Kuseyr Kale (Cursat), south of Antioch, which are

believed to be due to the beneficence of St Louis. An arched niche of rough-trim in the back (east) wall seems always to have been blocked, and contains a relieving arch near the floor, eccentrically placed – no doubt to cover the aqueduct channel. Blind double niches, also of rough-trim, interrupt the north and south walls. A deeper niche on the west had already lost its exterior by 1938 [*and by 1951 the entire wall had perished*] and may have terminated in an embrasure rather than a doorway. The room may have been accessible through the floor alone; a flight of steps led up towards it from the interior of the gallery, but this is choked too low down for the destination to be certain.

The uniform design of the gallery has been slightly affected on the west side by later modifications. Just north of the aqueduct is a walled-up aperture, at a slightly higher level than the other arrow-slits on this side, and at several places beyond this point the talus has been repaired, to judge by patches of unusually large buff stones. The gallery ends abruptly at the middle of the west side, half-way up the southern face of a great cliff which runs along the remainder of the west side (and turns a corner to the north). The cliff-face was revetted in continuation of the upper enceinte; from the roof of the gallery one can climb up to an aperture in the revetment, now blocked, where there seems to have been an arrow-slit to command the gallery roof; it must have opened off some chamber or passage which is no longer accessible.

The Interior of the Gallery. A little open court outside the gallery is bounded on the south by the prolongation of the frontage, on the north by the slope at the base of the chapel. On the west, the front of the gallery stands high; it consists of a cross-wall, supporting a terrace between the frontage and the actual base of the chapel, and includes, at ground level, a wide round arch, with long voussoirs of somewhat irregular shape packed in places with chips of stone.

The archway gives on to a large vaulted space, perhaps six metres high, partitioned in line with the north jamb to form a passage straight ahead and a guard-room off to the north. The partial collapse of the partition has revealed two water-pipes of coarse earthenware running horizontally along it towards the north side of the archway. The passage, which is the gallery proper, averages about two metres wide while the height may be some 4.5 metres above the floor. The walls rise almost without inward inclination to a short way below the slightly pointed vault. Holes were left at this level for the centering scaffold. They cannot have supported a loft, because in most places it would scarcely have been high enough for a short man to stand upright, even at the middle. A series of arrow-slits rises practically at ground level, each in an embrasure with a slightly pointed vault. For the whole length of the south side the masonry is homogeneous; the rough-trim stones measure about 25 by 20 cm., and into the mortar of almost every horizontal joint and many vertical joints small scraps are packed. This is the identical style used in the original curtain of the ramp.

A narrow staircase rose in the north wall, opposite the south-west corner of the upper enceinte, but it is choked with fallen earth and stones. Just beyond it, the gallery is crossed by a wall, beside which the water pipes are again exposed (on the north side). A low arch through the cross wall leads into a room that turns the corner of the castle. Its vault must be about 5.5 metres above the floor; it is lined (except on the inner east side) with great smooth yellowish blocks, comparable to the best in the room superimposed upon it. The room is lit only by an arrow-slit, in an embrasure reached by a doorway which penetrates the lining that thickens the south wall. The north wall of the gallery is prolonged across the room by a partition which carries the water-channel of the aqueduct, maintaining approximately the same angle as the external culvert. The partition is faced with large ashlar blocks, and stands about two metres high; an arch, necessarily with low head-room, allows passage through it to the north end of the room, which is almost dark because it receives only indirect lighting, from the arrow-slit on the other side of the aqueduct partition and from a big archway in the north wall. But the frame of a former arrow-slit is visible externally, opposite this wall, the construction of which presumably covered its embrasure. Like the partition, the wall is faced on both sides with large ashlar but has been crudely repaired. The round arch through it evidently began to spread, becoming somewhat pointed in the process, as can be seen on its northern face. A patch of medium sized stones with coarse packing was then put over the haunch of the arch and across to the east wall; to the west of the arch-crown there is a little coarse packing in white mortar over the voussoirs, which had sunk out of alignment, and smaller patches indicate that the entire wall west of the arch had subsided a trifle. The abutment on the external wall to the west had been weakened by a wide crack, which likewise is filled with white mortar.

This wall forms the south end of a long hall, extremely irregular in shape and constructed of diverse styles of masonry. The lop-sided, slightly pointed vault (with local inequalities enhancing its lack of symmetry) curves down to the floor at either side. The walls consist of rough-trim stones (about 25 by 15 cm. on the average), abundantly packed with rough chips or even water-worn pebbles. The stones in the northern portion are larger though equally rough, less packing is used, and the surface has been well plastered, whereas in the southern portion traces of plaster survive only near the top; probably this part of the wall was built later and therefore has not been plastered so often. The wall along the remainder of the west side is exceptionally thick and so could afford to be of poorer work than the southern portion. It consists of low, uneven courses of stones which vary greatly in length, so much so that they give an incorrect impression of being headers and stretchers. It changes direction slightly on either side of three large embrasures with pointed vaults that penetrate the main vault; each is contracted by a pointed rear-arch which must have included an arrow-slit, but every frontage has fallen. A platform, 60 cm. high extends along the whole of the west side to a varying width, averaging under two metres. Its inward edge runs parallel with the first 2 m. of the east wall but on coming opposite the first embrasure changes direction to an axis not shared with any wall, and gradually narrows northwards.

The north wall resembles the northern part of the east wall so closely that it must be contemporaneous. At its centre is an archway, placed with its threshold beside the east edge of the extrados of another, which opens just above floor level. The upper archway is choked; it must have led into the thickness of the roof where a tunnel presumably existed and may have communicated with an aperture, now blocked, that overlooked the gallery from the revetted cliff on the north. The lower archway [*which was completely buried by 1951*] gives on a short corridor, the vault and floor of which both slope steeply downwards; it ends northward with a masonry lining to the cliff. The west wall contains an embrasure, partly walled up; the arrow-slit is visible externally. Opposite, in the east wall, stands a doorway with a pointed arch (of better masonry than the surrounding very rough stones), behind which rises a steep flight of steps, less than one metre wide, beneath a sloping barrel-vault, The sides are lined with rough-trim masonry, except on the left wall beside the first few steps, where the native rock has always been exposed. The passage winds continually till near the top, where it rises less steeply, with an inclined floor instead of steps. It ends at a doorway, again with a pointed arch, which leads into a little vault half choked with fallen stones. They come from a jagged hole at the edge of the ceiling, an enlargement of the original exit, through which is reached the floor of a room sunk beneath a little vault of its own; this rises in the centre of the basement floor under the south-west tower of the upper enceinte. [*This upper exit had become choked by 1950, though it remained visible.*] The basement itself is otherwise accessible only through an enlarged hole (probably for a trap-door) in the floor of the room above, which seems a late addition to the tower.

Dating. The talus must have been designed in preparation for the gallery, of which it secures the foundations. There need be no hesitation in ascribing both to the Armenians of *c.* 1200; the gallery and the ramp must belong to the same building programme, for defensive reasons, and the masonry of the gallery is of the type used in the original ramp curtain. The aqueduct can be regarded as almost an integral part of the gallery and there is no reason to separate it chronologically, so far as the exterior is concerned. An unmistakably later programme of reconstruction is responsible for the ashlar: the aqueduct conduit inside the gallery, the lining of the room around the conduit, the wall between it and the gallery hall, and the room on the gallery roof. In these the masonry, with broad voussoirs, is definitely of crusader style. Since a partial rebuilding of the gallery hall was apparently undertaken simultaneously, together perhaps with the neighbouring repairs to the talus which utilised large blocks, the siege of 1236 may have occasioned the whole programme, as it did the second programme at the entrance, where, however, the broad voussoirs may be slightly earlier. An earthquake that struck Antioch in 1212 is, perhaps, the more likely cause. A final period is represented only by repairs after subsidence inside the gallery; as in the case of reconstruction around the entrance to the outer enceinte, this slovenly work is probably Arab.

The underground passage should be contemporary with the gallery because its function was clearly to maintain contact with the upper enceinte in case the enemy broke into the lower. In that event, the defenders of the south-eastern area would retreat into the gallery. The existence of the passage then enabled the commander to choose, unhurriedly, between ordering the evacuation of the gallery and holding it as a base for sallies; he could send and withdraw reinforcements without the knowledge of the enemy.

3. *The North Ledge*

Along the north of the castle, the hill rises steadily westwards; the entire side consists of cliff. Landslides have diversified the face with bulging or overhanging masses of rock, and screes mask the lower half or third of its height. The occupants of the castle had nothing to fear and much to gain from a ledge which starts behind the gate-tower and reaches almost to the summit of the hill, near the north-west corner, where there seems to have been a stair to the upper enceinte; the intervening cliff is everywhere too steep for any other means of access. The ledge formed a short-cut between the summit and the ramp. It would have been useful if reinforcements were urgently required to defend the entrance, and absolutely essential if the enemy broke through the outer enceinte and so gained control over the devious main route upwards; the defenders of the entrance could still retreat in safety up the ledge. The rock just below it has evidently been scarped in places, to obviate any risk of surprise attack from the gorge; either contemporaneously or at a rather later date, the ledge was made impregnable for its entire length, in one part by a wall along the verge, in others by tall vaulted corridors which could not be bypassed.

A landslide behind the gate-tower has cut away the outset of the ledge, which must have risen steeply there; the gap is some 12 m. long. A cross-wall then descends from the rock base of the upper enceinte to meet the curtain, and forms the end of a long room attached thereto. The broken end of the curtain which joins it from the east seems to have been coigned, and externally the masonry of the upper room looks of better quality than usual, for the stones appear to have been approximately squared, although close investigation is impossible. The site certainly called for a high standard of work; it also gave opportunity for a more leisurely schedule than could have been afforded in areas of greater military danger. The curtain follows the shape of the hillside past a projecting corner, so that the room bends sharply. It is complete to the far end, at which there is a gap in the roof at the junction with a shorter vaulted room communicating with it. A doorway at the west end of the shorter room opens on a little triangle of open ground, at the foot of the twin north rooms of the upper enceinte, where the vertical interval to the floor of the eastern room is 7.5 m. but the ledge rises to within 3.5 m. of the western – possibly only 3 m. but fallen refuse prevents measurement. The triangle is bordered on the left by a talus under the rooms; on the right a terrifying precipice, well over 33 m. deep, slants inwards [*and by 1951 the apex of the triangle had fallen down it*]. After making an indentation at the north-west corner, the sheer cliff turns again along the western side of the hill under high walls which stand on the actual verge, while isolated patches of talus cover any hollows in the rock beneath which might have given a foothold. [*Erosion between 1938 and 1951 uncovered on the triangle what seemed to be a relic of the means of communication between the ledge and the twin rooms, a very thick wall continuing the inward wall of the short room on the ledge, though on a different axis; it stands parallel with and beside the talus. Probably it supported a stair which would have been approached by making a half-circle turn from the door of the short room and could have ended at either or both of the twin rooms.*]

Dating. If the Armenians built the lower enceinte, they would have felt obliged to make the ledge defensible in some fashion. But the vaulted rooms upon it should probably be attributed to their Templar successors, the builders of the twin rooms.

4. *The north half of the Upper Enceinte*

Buildings along the exterior. Throughout this part of the castle the design is primarily domestic; the mere height of the buildings along the edge was sufficient defence. The cliff on the west, scarped and revetted, formed a more than adequate safeguard along the northern half of that side. Its foot is heaped with fallen masonry, and on the summit there remain only disconnected traces of the buildings that must have stood there; the rock slopes towards the verge, and such stones as did not roll to it when each wall collapsed have doubtless been pushed over by village boys, who seem tireless in that respect. At the north end there was a short narrow room, entered by a doorway on the south. It contains a low arched recess, approximately 1.50 m. square, in the base of a thickened portion of the east wall, close to the north end; this could have been an oven. The vault sprang off the back wall of an intact, abnormally long, room on the east and probably extended its roof-platform. Their joint south wall runs aslant in conformity with the axis of the hall, to which it is joined by an arch across a little service court. The long room was entered only from this court, by two archways which thicken upwards because the wall itself curves from just above floor level to the centre of a pointed vault. They admitted enough light to the windowless interior; three rectangular traps along the centre of the vault are more efficient as ventilators than for lighting, but their presence coupled with the fact that there are two doorways through the opposite wall of the hall, identify the room as the kitchen, although the vault shows scarcely a trace of smoke. The southern archway, with a plain round arch intersecting the vault, is integral to the wall, but the northern is faced with ashlar, which splays both outwards and inwards; the blocks of the sides match the courses of the surrounding rough-trim stones but are about twice as long, while the voussoirs are equally long but thin.

Into the face of the kitchen is bonded the south wall of one of twin rooms, which continues its roof platform and shares the north part of its east wall, but the kitchen extends farther towards the north over a projection of the cliff; the north end stands actually on the edge. Patches of talus beneath fill hollows in the cliff face. The talus becomes almost continuous after turning the corner, as substructure beneath lost walls of the twin rooms; beyond them it runs inwards to merge in an upright wall, supporting a terrace which extends to the north-east corner.

The free-standing north wall of both the twin rooms has perished except for a scrap of the base at the west end; it breaks off 1.35 m. short of their dividing wall. At this spot a voussoir, rising eastwards, could be seen, just below the floor level. [*By 1951 it had vanished and the space from here to the dividing wall had washed out to a depth of half a metre, leaving a straight edge on the west. In the east wall another voussoir had been revealed, rising westwards as though an arch had covered the present gap in the north wall, below the floor-level of the west part of the room.*] The east wall breaks off just beyond, where a voussoir springs northwards at the same underfloor level, beginning an arch that could have received the stair assumed to have been built from the ledge. Over most of the western half of the room very uneven rock is exposed at higher levels than the threshold of an unusually tall and wide doorway which stands at the west end of the south wall, while at the east end of the same wall is a smaller archway with the bottom of its keystone only 10 cm higher than the threshold of the other; its own threshold is buried, but is likely to lie at roughly the level of the arch which formerly opened through the north wall, immediately opposite. A depression along the east wall must therefore have sloped and may have formed a ramp to the presumed stairhead above the ledge.

The larger doorway is covered by a flattish, very slightly pointed, arch of excellent construction. It rises 2.50 m. above the rock floor inside the room; a keystone on the outside corresponds to a vertical joint within at the apex. Both jambs bear masons' marks N, L, V and, less distinctively, I; even without this use of the Latin alphabet the work is recognisably crusader. Against the south side of each jamb, but not bonded, stands a pillar composed of a single large block in each course; neither pillar is preserved more than halfway up but they must have propped the stair arch that crossed beside the top of this doorway. The smaller doorway, placed lower in the same wall, is round-arched. There are no indications of a partition between the two doorways, nor is there any support for flooring over the lower; probably steps led down to it. Both were needed because of an external obstruction between them, an arch across the junction of the service court and a passage that separates the twin rooms from the hall.

The arch is of the extremely massive construction the crusaders habitually used to carry stairs, as was evidently its function. Its base emerges from the north-west corner of the hall at a discordant angle which brings the highest voussoir practically square against the wall of the twin room, beside the east jamb of the larger doorway; it is bonded in. The actual stair must have started in the service-court close to the northern doorway of the hall, and have gained a height of roughly a metre before it reached the arch, when it widened to 1.09 m.; eventually it may have continued to rise over the arch till a last step made the roof of the twin room accessible, but the original design provided for a second flight to the roof of the kitchen. The remains of an upper arch, 1.29 cm. wide, spring at right angles from a height of 81 cm. over the crown of the intrados; the left edge stands directly above the jamb of the lower arch while the right was applied against the wall of the twin room. Consequently the doorway was covered as though by a hood, to which the pillars were, no doubt, prolonged upwards for support. But only the three lowest courses of the upper arch survived till 1938, and the rest had been demolished long ago; it would have met the kitchen at a spot where rough patching has been inserted. Both arches were built of huge, coarsely chiselled blocks, with a cemented fill of rough stones about 25 cm. square (like those composing the walls of the hall). The voussoirs are 30 cm. high and vary in width at the foot between 20 and 33 cm.; a keystone was used, at least, in the lower arch. In 1938 even a person of medium height had to stoop uncomfortably to go through this arch, but it might have given enough headroom for a tall man if steps led down through it to the lower level required by the smaller doorway. [*By 1951 no vestige of either arch remained apart from the impost at the corner of the hall.*]

A slightly pointed vault of undressed stones (at the top, long and thin), covers the western twin room, the west and south walls of which are of rough-trim stones measuring about 25 × 23 cm. This type of masonry occurs in the east wall too but only in four courses, the rest consisting of small oblong un-dressed stones, probably because the room beyond stands so much lower that the vault begins to curve at that level. The wall which separates the twin rooms is pierced by a hatch, just across the corner from the small doorway but higher up; it measures 53 cm. wide by 59 cm. high. It slopes steeply downwards in the thickness of the wall, dropping about 90 cm. to the eastward room; its top there is lower than the base on the other side, which is approximately level with the middle of the small doorway. The eastward room retains much of its vault, which is pierced by a trap; the roof, like the floor, is lower than that of its twin by several feet. The whole of the north wall has fallen and practically all the south wall. The only entrance now visible is an archway on the east, so near the south corner that its sides splay into the room. It was obviously intended for easy access to the hall, into which a similar splayed doorway opens almost at right angles to the threshold. The east wall breaks off northward at the spring of an arch. [*The interior of the room, which in 1938 was largely choked, had been almost cleared of fallen stones by 1951, exposing recesses in both surviving walls. Two round-arched niches on the west and one on the east are about 90 cm. high and some 50 cm. wide. In the base of the east wall is*

PLATES 10–34 BAGHRAS

As the castle suffered much destruction between the author's visits of 1938 and 1951, each photograph is dated.

PLATE 10. *From the north* (1938).
Saladin planned his attack from this viewpoint across the gorge. The arrow points to vegetation concealing the stretch of outer enceinte from gate-tower to bossed tower. The north ledge ascends from behind the gate-tower to below the vaults of twin rooms; beyond them are the side and grassed roofs of, first, the hall and then the chapel, with the taller south-west tower to its right. Below is the arch of the aqueduct; along the slope, the shadowed face of another scrap of aqueduct.

PLATE 11. *From the east* (1951).
From left to right, above: upper enceinte with chapel, D-shaped tower, hall; below: outer enceinte with stump of south-east tower, east curtains separated by bossed tower, gatehouse (with entrance in shadow).

PLATE 12. *Outer enceinte from the east, with bossed tower at centre* (1938).

PLATE 13. *From the south-east* (1950).
From left to right, above: upper enceinte with south-west tower, chapel (showing pair of niches at broken end), D-shaped tower; below: aqueduct on arch, exterior of gallery.

PLATE 14. *Interior of gate-tower* (1951).
Left: entrance (figure beside modern blockage). Right: archway to ramp.

PLATE 15. *Ramp, looking up from interior of gate-tower* (1938).

PLATE 16. *Gate-tower from ramp* (1938).
Above: wall of upper storey with window. Below, from left to right: remains of vaulting, archway to entrance room, attachment of lost vault, back of curtain.

PLATE 10   BAGHRAS   *From the north*

PLATE 11   BAGHRAS   *From the east*

PLATE 12   BAGHRAS   *Outer enceinte from the east*

PLATE 13   BAGHRAS   *From the south-east*

PLATE 14 (left)

BAGHRAS

Interior of gate-tower

PLATE 15 (below) BAGHRAS *Ramp*

PLATE 16   BAGHRAS

Gate-tower from ramp

PLATE 17   BAGHRAS

Bossed tower from the north

PLATE 18 (opposite)   BAGHRAS   *Interior of bossed tower*

PLATE 19 (left)

BAGHRAS

Room over gallery

PLATE 20 (below)

BAGHRAS

From the west

PLATE 21 (left)

BAGHRAS

Mouth of gallery

PLATE 22 (right)

BAGHRAS

Gallery

PLATE 23   BAGHRAS

Gallery hall from the north

PLATE 24

BAGHRAS   *Hall and platform from the south-east*

PLATE 25   BAGHRAS   *View to Plain of Antioch*

PLATE 26   BAGHRAS

Interior of hall from the east

PLATE 27

BAGHRAS

*Niches and doorway
in hall*

PLATE 28

BAGHRAS

Service Court

PLATE 29   BAGHRAS

North end of Service Court

PLATE 30   BAGHRAS

Vault of chapel

PLATE 31   BAGHRAS

Chapel and south-west tower

PLATE 32   BAGHRAS   *Window in chapel*

PLATE 33 (left)

BAGHRAS

Undercroft

PLATE 34 (below)

BAGHRAS

Basement of south-west tower

PLATE 17. *Bossed tower from the north* (1938).
Doorway from ramp in foreground.

PLATE 18. *Interior of bossed tower from south-east corner* (1938).
At centre: capital. On right: doorway to ramp.

PLATE 19. *Room over gallery* (1938).
Niche in east wall with relieving arch.

PLATE 20. *From the west* (1938).
Above: remnants of fallen rooms. Below, from left to right: cliff, exterior of
gallery hall (with embrasures), aqueduct (seen end-on) and (above it) opened
end of room over gallery, south exterior of gallery.

PLATE 21. *Mouth of gallery* (1938).
On left, below: archway into gallery. On right, above: east face of south-west
tower.

PLATE 22. *Gallery* (1938).
Looking from mouth through guardroom. Embrasures in outward wall.

PLATE 23. *Gallery hall from the north* (1938).
On right: platform leading to embrasures. At far end: archway to aqueduct
support.

PLATE 24. *Hall and platform from the south-east* (1938).
From left to right: doorway to hall from landing, archway to room under hall,
arch supporting platform beside east end of hall.

PLATE 25. *View to Plain of Antioch from central court* (1938).
From left to right: spring of lost vault on south exterior of hall, two doorways
to hall from landing, remains of pentagonal room, vault of D-shaped tower.

PLATE 26. *Interior of hall from the east* (1938).
Doorway on left edge is shown also in Plate 27.

PLATE 27. *Niches and doorway in hall* (1951).
East part of south wall with south-east corner, washbasin niche, smoke-blackened
niche, doorway to landing above central court.

F

PLATE 28. *Service court* (1938).
Looking through larger doorway of western twin room, past stair-arches and west exterior of hall, to arch joining roofs of kitchen and hall.

PLATE 29. *North end of service court* (1938).
From left to right: south exterior of kitchen, larger doorway of western twin room, stair-arches.

PLATE 30. *Vault of chapel* (1938).
From west, showing heads of windows; hall in left background.

PLATE 31. *Chapel and south-west tower from central court* (1938).
On left: chapel. Right foreground: side of large vault with wall on haunch. Right background: south-west tower broken open and (above it) bisecting wall.

PLATE 32. *Window in chapel, looking through to hall* (1950).

PLATE 33. *Undercroft from the east* (1938).
On left edge: archway through base of chapel to cistern.

PLATE 34. *Basement of south-west tower* (1951).
Above, from left to right: inner face of final west wall, breach to room under north part of tower, curved wall of earlier tower with original doorway. Below, at left of foreground: hole leading down to room where tunnel debouches.

A. W. L.

a vaulted recess, roughly 1.50 m. square, entered through an arch, the intrados of which stands approximately level with the niche floors; these are likely to have stood roughly a metre above ground. The presence of the niches and larger recess suggests that the room was a pantry or store, from which food and wine could be passed through the hatch to the other twin room, the buttery proper.]

Opposite the middle of the ruined south wall of the store, a solitary voussoir projects towards it from the hall, resting on an impost block which is bonded flush and descends to the present ground level. The width, 60 cm., is insufficient for a stair-support; the arch was probably built to hold a door, which enabled the passage to be closed – maybe against pilferers.

The enceinte evidently – though only the base remains – turned sharply inwards beside half the length of the east wall of the store, and then bent at an obtuse angle to form the frontage of a vault under the terrace that extends to the north-east corner. The terrace could be defended only from its own level, with the aid of a thin and presumably low parapet. Two windows pierce the external wall underneath, but merely light the vaulted room that supports the terrace; their pointed arches rise to 1.50 cm. above the sill, and their greatest width is 90 cm. The room is exceptionally tall. Its rock floor slopes from west to east and the height is correspondingly increased from an estimated $4\frac{1}{2}$ to six metres. A central partition, built at a slight slant, is apparently a later insertion to give additional support to the terrace; it stops short of the north wall to avoid obstructing the more easterly of the lights, and perhaps a gap between the other end and the south wall is likewise intentional. At the west side of the gap a deeply recessed archway leads to a small room underneath the east end of the hall, and that in turn communicates with another, which projects into the central court and can be entered therefrom.

The room beneath the terrace is also entered by an archway at the back of a great open-fronted arch which springs from the east end of the hall to a room behind the first curtain of the east side. The arch supported a platform along the south edge of the terrace but almost one metre lower; its chief function may have been to buttress the hall. The terrace now rises prominently over the first stretch of curtain on the east side, but only because that has partly fallen, together with the roof over the pointed end of a pentagonal room along the curtain; the roof preserved over the broader part of the room is approximately level with the terrace. The curtain stands on a shelf of rock, the face of which may have been scarped. The masonry consists of roughly squared stones, with the joints lavishly packed, till the south half of the room, where there is a gap over a metre wide from top to bottom of the facing. Rubble then ensues, and continues round the adjoining tower; the stones are much smaller, scarcely shaped at all, and set in mortar which shows little packing. Because the tower is much higher, the pentagonal room has its own party wall which runs at an angle to that of the tower and is thin at the inner end but gradually thickens until it reaches the curtain. The builders of the room appear to have adopted the economical expedient of leaning their vault against the side of the tower while preserving enough of the old curtain to maintain a secure bond with the tower; the rest of the curtain they rebuilt, possibly in order to add the vault behind it.

The inward, west wall of the pentagonal room contains three archways. The most northerly is beneath the open-fronted arch. The middle one opens under a massive arch of large blocks [*demolished between 1938 and 1951*], upon which a stair ascended to the platform. The strange proportions of the room and the provision of three entrances (two from the central court), incline me to identify it as a stable.

Buildings on the north side of the court. The chronological sequence of construction appears more clearly if the hall is approached along the central court from the west. The south wall of the kitchen is connected with the corner of the hall by an arch, 2.18 m. thick, which crosses the end of the service court, there 2.33 m. wide, and is bonded at each end. The roof of the hall stands high above that of the kitchen but the masonry over the arch rose correspondingly; it was probably stepped, but is still easily climbed to the hall roof. Off the south wall of the kitchen, well below roof level, sprang a vault which was obviously a later addition; it can barely have spanned half the space that now intervenes between the kitchen and a large vault to the south. Nor did the low vault extend as far as the arch closing the service court, outside which there was another vault of the same height, forming a corridor between it and a somewhat higher vault which sprang off the hall, from the corner to midway along the south wall. This, too, must be an addition; it is aligned inwards of the original frontage of the hall, which was cut back to a depth of at least three courses to receive the crown of the vault, which was merely applied, with the result that it is now pulling away.

The great hall, because of its Gothic design, must be Templar work of the thirteenth century. Properly termed the Refectory, in speech it was more often called the Palace; so, at least, may be inferred from the Order's bilingual Rule, which ordains that the common meal be taken in a *palais, et meaus seroit apeles refroiter – in quidem palatio sed melius dicitur refectorio.*[46]

[46] H. de Curzon, *La Règle du temple* (1886), p. 23.

Easily the most distinguished building at Baghras, the hall matches the chapel in size but is far better preserved. The plastered interior is finely proportioned and of impressive simplicity. The end-walls are upright; the side walls rise vertically to about one-third of the total height, then curve into a slightly pointed vault, 8·60 m. above the floor. Three rectangular traps are most unevenly spaced along the ridge of the vault; between them are set metal rings (apparently iron), for hanging lamps. The hall is built, in general, of roughly trimmed stones, mostly about 23 cm. long but some as much as 33 cm., set in 28 cm. courses packed with chips. At the corners and around the doors and windows the builders used smooth blocks, which tend to be slightly longer; in spite of this precaution the facing of the corners has broken away from the top downwards. Treasure-hunters have broken up the floor, scattering the paving blocks (which resemble those roughly trimmed in the walls) and revealing an earth fill below a mortar bedding. In the middle portion, this levels the top of the underlying vaulted substructure, but at the east end the earth was heaped over the native rock, and here deep pits have been dug; human bones are said to have been found, as would be explicable had the hall been used temporarily as a chapel. The Armenian archbishop of Aleppo was convinced, in 1937, of the truth of this report, which induced him to conduct a service on the spot. [*The entire vault and much of the walls have now fallen.*]

Windows occur only on the ends of the hall, where the walls are entirely upright. The pointed arch is formed, in each case, by voussoirs that are exposed for much of their height in a rear-arch, which also makes narrow reveals at the sides; the deep embrasure is more steeply arched, with less curvature. The embrasures in the west wall are straight-sided; they frame a central window above and two doorways, in which steps descend from the service court. High in the east wall there is likewise a central window (now broken at the top), but underneath it is a taller, wider window, flanked by two comparable in size to that above; the embrasures splay. The platform outside was apparently a few feet below the floor-level and the sills of the windows stood, perhaps, as high above it.

The south wall contains three doorways. The most westerly, which has a rear arch like those of the west doorways, has been carefully blocked, probably in order that it should not lead into the vault inset behind the facing. [*By 1951 the doorway had been unblocked.*] The end of the vault returns immediately eastward of the doorway. Then follows a second doorway, larger, with only a narrow strip revealed on the inner side. The last doorway is again smaller externally but splayed practically as wide within, where its markedly pointed

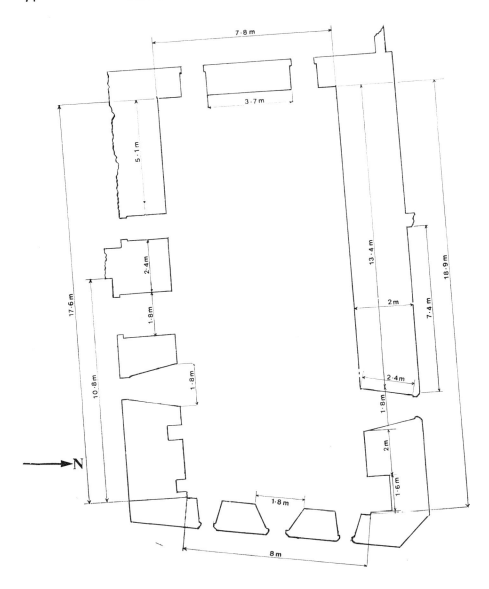

BAGHRAS *The Great Hall*

arch slants sharply upwards and penetrates the side of the vault in a displeasing manner. Smooth blocks, such as are otherwise reserved for coigning, extend all the way between these two doorways, the centre of the stretch being of rather irregular blocks and therefore unsightly, now that most of the plaster coating has fallen. The courses of rough-trim immediately above are out of alignment with those on either side. The splayed doorway might therefore have been inserted or lined later than the other, to replace the doorway blocked by the addition of the vault. The last two doorways open almost side by side, from the same small platform outside the hall. This cannot have been built for the sake of its substructure, the last room of the series which can be entered either through the arch east of the hall, or here from the court, by a doorway in the south wall; a little window in the east wall barely mitigates the gloom within. The roof formed a landing, which must have been the main approach to the hall. Quite a wide ramp or staircase could have ascended eastwards to it from the court. There was certainly need for a landing, such as is commonly found in Europe at the head of the steps leading to a medieval hall, to relieve congestion around the doors. Templars did not go to meals in orderly procession, but entered individually as soon as the bell rang, then waited at their seats for the chaplain before they began to eat; distinct tables were always reserved for the knights and for the lower grades.[47] The two doorways between the hall and its landing, almost side by side, would have made it possible to segregate those entering by rank.

There is only one aperture in the north wall, a doorway opposite that in the south wall with the splayed top and sides, and of similar design. The sill is level with the sills in the east wall and with the terrace outside, but two steps ran from side to side in the splay; there may have been other steps in the centre where a large gap has formed.

Inside the hall there are three niches, all near the east end. Two contribute to the design of the south wall; their heads step up in turn towards the still taller easterly doorway, beyond which the composition is balanced by the lower doorway. The higher-topped niche is actually the smallest, situated just east of the taller doorway. It is covered by a pointed arch 1.20 m. high; the edge was given a rectangular rebate, which seems, however, to have been bevelled off with plaster. There are no signs of hinges; traces of smoke on the haunch are unlikely to be recent. A round-arched niche by the south-east corner contained a washbasin at a comfortable height, 69 cm. lower than the sill of the other niche; the curve towards the round-arched top starts at the

47 H. de Curzon, *La Règle du Temple*, pp. 286–7.

level of the other's intrados. The basin is lost, but the holes for its attachment remain, and the waste-pipe can be seen running back into the wall. It is unusual to find a lavatory placed at even this distance from the door of a hall; from no other spot, however, could a drain discharge straight into the court. A more ornamental recess in the opposite corner of the north wall superficially resembles a pair of sedilia, but is deeper and clearly served as a cupboard. The pointed arches were formerly divided by a pillar; the front was closed by a two-leaved door, the hinges of which have been removed, leaving holes on either side. The recess is framed by a sunken border, 5 cm. wide and deep; the depth within this is 91 cm. and the width 1.50 m. up to the height of 1.44 m. where the sides begin to curve towards the pointed heads, which are 44 cm. above.*

Dating. In many parts of this area a sequence of construction is readily established, but the buildings are so intimately related that they appear to belong to a single, if protracted, campaign of work. The vaults that support the terrace and most of the hall can scarcely have been built for any other purpose. The south walls of the kitchen and hall are continuous, while the stair-arch between the hall and the western twin room is bonded into both, proving that they are contemporary. The south wall of the kitchen was finished before the twin room was applied against it but obviously on a prearranged scheme, and both vaults may well have been built simultaneously, together with that of the other twin room. Only the talus beneath these rooms can be appreciably older. The east curtain must have been backed by the long pentagonal room before the south wall of the hall was built and simultaneously prolonged by the platform arch, into which the courses run without interruption, but all this work, too, seems to have been designed as a unit. Yet the difference in masonry between the east curtain and the tower to the south should imply that the tower is much earlier. Little time need have elapsed between the completion of the hall and the insertion of the vault along the south side.

The main periods of building may be summarised as follows:

Before 1216: east D-shaped tower and adjoining part of east curtain; (?) north talus.

Templar, soon after 1216: substructures, kitchen, hall, stair-arch, twin rooms, terrace, platform, north-east part of east curtain and vault of pentagonal room, landing outside hall.

Templar, later in thirteenth century: vault along south of hall.

* Recent photographs by Miss Ann Epstein show the recess in well-lit detail owing to the collapse of the hall roof; there are prints in the Conway Library of the Courtauld Institute.

5. The south half of the Upper Enceinte

The Entrance. The main gateway of the upper enceinte is near the centre of the east side, immediately to the south of the D-shaped tower, which has already been shown to be older than the curtain adjoining it to the north. The top of the tower has broken away at the centre of the curve, showing the great vault within; perhaps dilapidation of an arrow-slit provoked the collapse, which has been followed by the loss of most of the facing. The base stands on a shelf of rock, which rises high above the ground along which the track from the ramp must have passed, forcing it to keep more or less parallel with the whole length of the east curtain. When the track began to ascend, it probably took a rather more southerly than westerly direction, though the present contours of the ground are somewhat misleading owing to the accumulation of stones fallen from the chapel.

A postern meets the approach, where it formed a ramp-corridor beside the eastern base of the chapel, the facing of which remains intact except towards the north and south ends, where alone there could have been structural attachments. A protrusion at the junction with the D-shaped tower looks as though it had been the spring of cross-vaulting at a height equivalent to 2.85 m. above the extrados of the entrance arch, the northern jamb of which it partially overhangs.* A horizontal row of thin blocks interrupts the facing of the tower at practically the same level and terminates a few metres outwards, immediately under an upright row of similar blocks. [*In 1951 no facing remained on this flank of the tower, but a vertical joint had become exposed in a position more or less corresponding to the upright row, with its foot at the level of the supposed vault-spring; it could have been one side of a blocked doorway. Müller-Wiener's plans, published in 1966, show the whole course of corridor as extant, from a gateway inconsistently marked opposite either the interior of the chapel or (more plausibly) the curve of the south-east tower, up to the flank of the D-shaped tower.*]

The gateway to the upper enceinte is a simple round arch (now choked to the spring), built of large ashlar blocks; the wall immediately above it is faced with smaller ashlar. The gateway leads into an ashlar-lined tunnel, which

---

* In 1951 a low remnant of thin walling had emerged from the rubbish just south of the entrance. It ran south-eastwards from the curtain for 1.50 m., at which point an apparently original gap of 2.40 m. intervened; it resumed its course for only 90 cm. where it met the end of similar walling parallel with the chapel, but too near it to be readily identified with the outer wall of the ramp shown on Müller-Wiener's plans. All this masonry, visible in 1951, seems to have disappeared before his visit. The postern, shown choked on Pl. 9, was open in 1951; cf. plan on p. 59.

runs along the straight flank of the rounded tower; the vault springs from a ledge moulding. There was no door at the exit into the end of an open passage which continues at right angles to the central court; it runs between the back (now fallen) of the tower and the walls, more than man-high, of two sunken rooms, which adjoin the base of the chapel, forming a retaining ledge. A door-way in the end of the passage and another directly opposite the tunnel lead into those rooms and so eventually to a narrow postern underneath the north-east corner of the chapel; its round arch is buried in rubbish except for the voussoirs, which are similar in style to those of the main gateway, though smaller [*but in 1951 the inner face of the wall was exposed, with a bar-hole in each jamb*].

The exterior on south and west. The great height of the sheer walls, and the steepness of the ground outside, would have made flanking superfluous, had it not been necessary to command the roof of the gallery, far below. Apart from that requirement, the plan of the exterior seems dictated by that of the buildings within, rather than *vice versa*.

The chapel stands on substructures, but its south-east corner is rounded off by an apparently solid projection. This continued, above the level of the chapel floor, as a straight-backed tower, which probably contained a small room in each storey in addition to a stair, but the only remaining tall portion adjoins the south curtain, i.e. the south wall of the chapel. A vertical joint in the facing may imply that the tower was completed separately, though in the course of a single programme. A recess, floored level with the chapel, slants through the curtain, narrowing to a slit that overlooks the mouth of the gallery. The masonry is of one build (though divided by a levelling-course from which the vault springs) as far as the west end of the chapel, which is linked with the south-west tower by a short stretch where the upper and lower portions differ in style; the chapel is not bonded into the lower, but the courses run through into the upper. Here, too, a slit is visible but with its top at the level of the chapel floor.

The irregular outline of the south-west tower enabled it to command the roof of the entire gallery. In the lower part of the tower (corresponding to the middle storey internally), the masonry is laid in tall courses which continue those of the lower part of the south curtain around a curved junction. The upper (actually third) storey of the tower is slightly set back; a vertical joint divides it from the south curtain, and the courses correspond only very roughly. It contains, to left and right of the joint, a pair of Gothic windows, so placed that their bases are level with the chapel floor; smooth blocks compose the frames and much of the wall around them. The roof carries a wall, which is about six metres long (although broken at each end) and still almost bisects it diagonally; the axis, from north-east to south-west, was presumably chosen because it passes between the two traps in the crown of the vault. There is no reason to think that any other structure existed on the roof. The single wall, placed at the greatest elevation obtainable in the castle, probably held flag-poles; it would scarcely have been suitable for a windmill.

Inside the lower storey of the tower, a very thick wall emerges from the junction with the south curtain and curves around a half-circumference of at least 4.60 m. to a straight flank on the north-west, ending against the back-wall of the tower. Obviously the wall belonged to an earlier tower, of less projection than its successor, as would be logical if the gallery had not yet been built. An archway through the curve, although large enough for a door, was not fitted with one, as would have been essential for a postern; the lateral splay in the thickness of the wall, and the emphatic upward contraction, would be appropriate to an embrasure, deprived of its front (which faced south-west). The round arch in the facing consists of large voussoirs, with a lop-sided key-stone; the lower part of the facing has been crudely repaired. The remainder of the wall is composed of ill-shaped stones, scarcely trimmed at all, set in very wide mortar-joints; such masonry is found nowhere else except in the tower of similar plan beside the main gateway.

The west curtain continued the alignment of the south-west tower as far as an outward bend in the cliff, above the end of the gallery, but has mostly fallen, probably owing to the collapse of vaults behind. The cliff between the bend and the north side of the hill is virtually perpendicular for its entire height, and certainly required no defensive masonry; any walls built near the verge have slipped to destruction.

The buildings south and west of the Court. At the west side of the central court stands a large vault, which seems to have been separated from the buildings to the north. The sides curve from the present ground level, as do those of the kitchen, and the end-walls have perished. The axis associated it with the south-west tower, being startlingly different from that of the hall and kitchen, and presumably of the vaults which spring off them and which composed the north side of the court; the chapel opposite to those buildings is on an inter-mediate axis. A piece of wall which rises above the south haunch of the large vault probably belonged to the north end of a tall room, the east and south sides of which have completely perished while on the west the few remaining courses of the curtain are twice as thick as elsewhere as though to sustain a vault that had reached to the tower. Fallen blocks, heaped as far back as the tower, must be refuse of the room.

The upper room of the south-west tower is exposed by the loss of the north wall; the rubbish outside stands two metres higher than the floor. A gap in the floor probably began by enlargement of a trap that led to the lower room. A doorway, without coigning, exists in the east wall, facing the chapel. A water-pipe is exposed, 46 cm. from the south jamb, coming down into the face of the vault spring and terminating abruptly. In the roof there are two openings, a square trap towards the north end and a circular lunette in the centre. Two windows with pointed arches (already described with reference to the exterior) open eastward, but the wall of the tower is so thick that they cannot have given much light. The vaults of the window recesses slant upward from the frame, penetrating the main vault, and the jambs are splayed; the inner edge of each recess thus describes an interesting curve. A bench of small stones and plaster, 60 cm. high, cuts across the rounded end of the room, reaching a width of about a metre at the centre. The room must have been the most habitable in the castle and was probably designed to lodge the Templar commanding officer. The windows are Gothic, and the doorway, which is obviously an integral part of the room, opens on a floor which, to judge from the exterior, was not built up to this level before the construction of the chapel.

There is no sign of a roof over the area between the tower and the chapel. The floor here, even after the raising of the curtain, cannot have stood as high as that of the chapel, as is shown by the arrow-slit which is visible externally, though buried on the inner side under heaps of rubbish.

The chapel stands on vaults throughout; the unusually bad condition may be due to that circumstance. Both ends have almost completely fallen, together with the eastern part of the vault and the edge, while the north wall is cracked practically from top to bottom in several places. In this wall there are four uniform windows, each with a pointed vault at the top and the remains of a pointed arch at approximately half the total height; curved blocks just above the spring still project far into the lights. This lower part of the windows resembled the lancets of the hall in shape, and in material, since the frames consist of smooth blocks, almost square, of about the same size as those of the hall windows. The upper halves of the windows are lined with roughly trimmed stones, from which jagged fragments of thin slabs project into the lights and can only be the relics of plate tracery. Each light is covered externally by a pointed arch with voussoirs of long narrow blocks, fairly regular in shape but laid in joints packed with chips; there is no rear-arch. The whole wall was thickly plastered, inside and out, in a buff tint that matches the ashlar frames of the lancets. Holes in the jambs indicate that the lancets could be closed by shutters – a most desirable amenity, because the Baghras valley funnels the winds caused by every difference in temperature between the Amanus range and the Amuq plain. The width of a well-preserved light is 96 cm. which equalled half the height below the tracery, and possibly a quarter of the total height.

The north and south walls are rebated, so that the course beneath the sills forms a ledge upon which a wooden floor might have rested. Otherwise the structure resembles that of the hall. The walls consist of square or oblong rough-trim stones, the vault, which rises to a slight point, of thinner and usually longer pieces; these continue in the heads of the windows.

A pair of shallow niches at the present east end of the north wall are placed 81 cm. above the presumed floor-ledge. The round-arched heads, both cut into the same ashlar block, slope inwards, so that the centre of each reaches a height of only 46 cm. at the back compared with 58 cm. in front. Perhaps the niches formed a double aumbry. The north wall breaks off immediately beyond, at the spring of an arch which probably covered an embrasure. The south wall, preserved for half its original length, is pierced by an oblique recess with a sloping vault, constructed like those over the windows, but closed at the outward end except for an arrow-slit, under a lintel.

The fall of plaster has exposed a vertical water-pipe inset behind the inner face of the north wall, beside the east edge of the window-recess nearest the west. Rain-water from the flat roof must thereby have been conducted through the floor and down the wall below, into a huge cistern, which is cut deep into the native rock but also enclosed by masonry built up on all four sides. The vault, which stands high above the cistern, underlies most of the western half of the chapel; a guard-room (from which the postern opens) supports the east end, while an intervening substructure is known to exist because of a choked archway under the space between the two most easterly windows, the sills of which stand only three courses over the voussoirs. The archway (which perhaps led to another cistern) was necessarily put at this level so as to be accessible from the joint roof of the two sunken rooms built against the exterior of the chapel; the western of these rooms projects far into the court (and was there lit by a shaft now choked) while the eastern room is restricted between it and the entrance.

The cistern is accessible only from the court, through a cross-vaulted ruin and an archway at the back of it, set through the base of the chapel wall which at this point is over two metres thick.[48] A piece of the cross-vaulting remains within, crudely truncated – proof that the north-east corner of the cistern was quarried through a demolished aisle of the vaulted building. That building can be nothing but an undercroft, designed to carry an altogether exceptional weight; the roof is placed very low (under 2.5 m.), the vaults are squat and crowded, and their round arches stand on massive square piers, composed of enormous ashlar blocks. The masonry in the vault consists of larger blocks than are usually found in that position, and is quite neatly dressed. Holes through the corners of the piers probably contained halters for horses, in accordance with both crusader and oriental custom, one which was also practised, at Megiddo, two thousand years earlier. Another part of the undercroft was evidently shortened to enlarge the court, and then given a new external wall, composed of stones put together so carelessly that the joints do not alternate. [*This wall fell between 1938 and 1951.*] The original limits of the undercroft could have been placed far beyond the extremity of the ruin in every direction except the south. The minimum dimensions, estimated by including the complete span of broken vaulting, must have exceeded 14 m. north to south and 9 m. west to east. The undercroft may, therefore, have been the lowest storey of an oblong or square keep. Whether or not that identification be correct, the undercroft was evidently designed to carry at least one exceptionally heavy upper storey, which would surely not have vanished without leaving some trace; more likely the project was never realised. It might have been abandoned when the Templars left Baghras in 1187.

Dating. Sequences of building are visible in two interrelated areas; the undercroft must be earlier than the chapel, while the south-west tower encloses a previous tower and is itself divided into storeys that were not built simultaneously, the upper alone being demonstrably of the same date as the chapel. The latest of the three programmes here is unquestionably Templar work of the thirteenth century. The chapel resembles the hall in details and balances it in the general lay-out, but would not do so if the floor were at a lesser height. Because the substructures are taller than was necessary, or even advisable, on any practical considerations, we may presume that the hall had already been designed, if not completed. The lower storey of the south-west tower may be ascribed either to the Templars of a slightly earlier date in the same generation, or to predecessors, Armenians or twelfth-century crusaders. The tower enclosed

---

[48] In 1951 it was still impossible to measure the cistern; looking at it from just inside the archway, I thought it extended four or five metres N.–S. by three or four metres W.–E.

within may or may not be contemporary with the undercroft, the style of which assigns it to the twelfth-century crusaders, plausibly identifiable on historical grounds as Templars of 1186–7. The main gateway is likely to be of approximately the same period, whereas the tower alongside may be either contemporary or earlier.

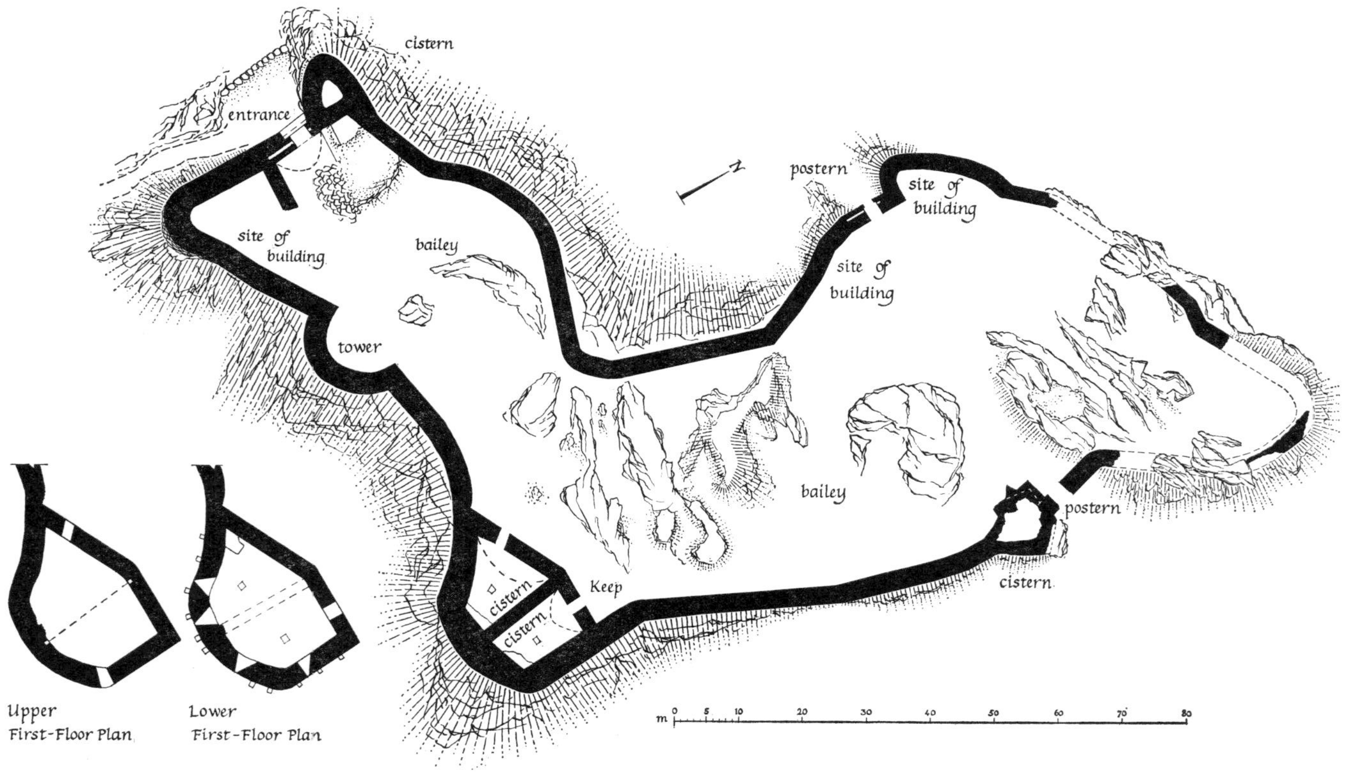

site of building

postern

site of building

postern

cistern

bailey

N

keep

cistern

cistern

bailey

tower

cistern

site of building

entrance

m 0 5 10 20 30 40 50 60 70 80

Upper
First-Floor Plan

Lower
First-Floor Plan

AZGIT   *General Plan*

3

THE CASTLE OF AZGIT

The castle of Azgit has not been certainly identified with any documented Armenian site. The route through the hills from Coxon to Kadirli was one of the most strongly fortified entries to Cilicia. Coxon was on the main route from Caesarea to Marash; Kadirli on a road leading from the Amanus Gates to Sis. Coming south from Coxon, a path branches west to Saimbeyli, Himmetli and Vahka; at Andirin another path leads through to Marash. It is a hilly country, full of small river beds, of which the torrents mostly find their way to the Pyramus. The largest ones are the Andirin river, the Körsulu and the Fornos or Kayagösü, which crosses the main Marash–Coxon route. Three castles are known by name in this area, Gaban, Djandji and Schogagan. Of these Gaban seems to have been the most northerly and was a customs post at the entry into Armenian territory. It is almost certainly the considerable, but not as yet surveyed, castle south-west of Coxon, now known as Kizil Kale. In 1216 when Kai-Kaus I was besieging Gaban, an Armenian relieving force was heavily defeated under the hill of Schoghagan. This would fit well enough with the position of Azgit, but there is another castle, about 20 km. north-east of Andirin on the west bank of the Körsulu river, not far from the small town of Çokak, a name suspiciously similar to Schoghagan. Near by these two castles, to make further complication, is a village called Geben and yet another, Keben, in the neighbourhood, neither with traces of fortifications actually on the site, and neither fitting as well as the northern fortress with what is known of Gaban's history. In the immediate vicinity of Andirin there is another castle, now sometimes called Ak Kale, on the left bank of the Andirin river. Assuming the northernmost castle is Gaban, it is reasonable to place Djandji and Schogagan as two of the other three fortresses. However the names are allotted, this area was the early seat of Rupenid power, and the final retreat in 1375 of the king of Armenia. Remains of a castle have been reported in the Fornös valley, possibly either Gantchi or Pertounk.

G

The castle is situated in the valley of one of the upper tributaries of the Andirinsuyu at a height of about 1,300 m., and some 8 km. north-east of the small town of the same name. The site is a prominent rock outcrop which commands the route leading from Andirin to Coxon by way of the headwaters of the Andirinsuyu and the valley of the Körsulu Dere, a major tributary of the Ceyhan. The castle comprises an approximately L-shaped bailey, which measures about 180 m. from N. to S. by 37 m. over all and incorporates an irregular-shaped keep within its SE. corner. The wall of the bailey follows the outer edge of the summit of the rock outcrop, the total area enclosed being about one and a half acres. Some portions of the fabric show traces of minor alterations and additions, but in general the castle appears to be the product of a single building period. All the buildings are now ruinous to a greater or lesser extent and the fabric shows signs of fairly rapid deterioration.

MATERIALS

The castle is constructed for the most part of roughly dressed blocks of limestone rubble brought to courses and bonded in good lime mortar with numerous small pinnings. Some of the limestone blocks are of considerable size, measuring up to 95 cm. and 53 cm. over all; a number of them appear to bear the marks of the broad-toothed chisel. In general the masonry is not of the highest quality, but carefully dressed limestone blocks with bossed centres and drafted margins have been utilised in the construction of the doorway and window openings. A more porous brownish limestone was used in the construction of some of the vaults and arches. In those sectors where the facing stones of the walls have collapsed the core is seen to be composed of courses of small blocks set vertically or obliquely on edge, somewhat in the manner of 'herringbone' masonry. There is no evidence of the incorporation of horizontal wooden tie-beams in the masonry.

THE ENTRANCE GATEWAY

A narrow path leads up the W. side of the rock outcrop to the main gatehouse, which stands near the SW. corner of the bailey. The path gives access to a small platform bounded on its W. side by a retaining wall, of which the lowest courses alone remain. From the platform the approach leads eastwards into the gatehouse which, although ruinous, still stands to a maximum height of 8 m. 20 cm. The opening evidently comprised a pointed outer arch, behind which there was a machicolation slot accessible from a chamber at first-floor level. Immediately behind the machicolation was the entrance doorway itself; this measured about 1 m. 30 cm. in width and 1 m. 90 cm. in height, and was apparently surmounted by a massive stone lintel, of which a mere fragment now remains. The door was strengthened by a wooden draw-bar. Very little now remains of the interior of the gatehouse, but the entrance appears to have opened into a barrel-vaulted chamber from which direct access was obtained to the bailey. The method of access to the upper floor or floors of the gatehouse cannot now be determined.

THE BAILEY

As already noted the curtain wall follows the outer edge of the rock outcrop; there are few sharp angles, the wall invariably changing alignment by means of gentle curves or rounded angles. The main entrance and the two postern doorways, however, are situated at points where the wall returns fairly sharply, the approaches thus being protected by flanking fire. Apart from the keep itself and a single rounded tower in the S. sector of the curtain no use is made of projecting towers, and the defence was presumably conducted almost entirely from the wall-head of the curtain. This probably incorporated a parapet walk approached by mural stairways, but no traces of such structures are visible today. The original height of the curtain cannot now be determined, but the masonry at present rises to a maximum height of 2 m. 60 cm., 9 m. 30 cm., 9 m. 10 cm., and 6 m. 40 cm., on the N., E., S. and W. sides respectively; the width varies from 2 m. 30 cm. to 4 m. Except in one or two areas on the N. and E. sides of the castle the base of the curtain wall can be reached fairly easily by scrambling up the rock slopes. The uppermost surviving courses of the curtain are constructed, for much of their length, of a rather darker stone than the lower courses, and this suggests that the upper part of the wall may at some time have been rebuilt.

Immediately to the N. of the entrance gateway the curtain wall returns north-westwards to form a small projection before running in an easterly direction for a distance of about 26 m. This projection houses a vaulted water-cistern, now ruinous.

At the main W. re-entrant angle of the bailey the curtain turns northwards towards the W. postern, now the best preserved of the three entrances of the castle. The doorway measures 90 cm. in width and 1 m. 75 cm. in height. The jambs are wrought with a sharp arris, and the centre of the lintel is carved with

PLATE 35   AZGIT

General view from the west, showing entrance gateway and west postern

a Greek cross set within a sunk circular frame; the arms of the cross expand slightly towards forked ends. A second cross, of similar size and shape to the first, is incised at the N. end of the lintel, and a third upon the lowermost rybat but one of the N. jamb of the doorway; both these carvings are much weathered. Behind the door, which was evidently two-leaved, there is provision for a draw-bar. Beneath the door-sill there appears to have been an opening, perhaps a waste chute; this is now blocked.

Immediately beyond the postern the curtain returns sharply westwards before curving north-eastwards to enclose the N. end of the bailey. On each side of the postern a series of joist holes may be seen in the inner face of the curtain wall; these presumably indicate the former existence of a range of buildings running parallel to the curtain. There now appear to be no other traces of this range, which is likely to have been of timber construction with a lean-to roof. Very little now remains of the curtain on the N. side of the bailey, but the line taken by the wall is seldom in doubt.

From the NE. corner of the bailey the curtain runs southwards towards the E. postern, which is placed at a point where the wall bridges a cleft between two rock spurs. The opening is now very ruinous, but appears originally to have had an external width of about 1 m. 10 cm. The door was evidently two-leaved, but no provision for a sliding bar is now visible. The doorway was probably surmounted by a lintel set within a semicircular-headed arch, of which a part remains. A small projection of the curtain immediately to the S. of the postern appears to have housed an irregular-shaped chamber, perhaps a water-cistern, but little of this structure survives.

From the E. postern the curtain runs southwards to the NE. angle of the keep, but no particular features of interest remain in this sector. The remaining section of the curtain links the NW. angle of the keep with the entrance gate-way. This sector incorporates a projecting D-shaped tower, open at the rear, and between the tower and the SW. angle of the bailey a range of timber buildings appears to have abutted on the curtain wall.

THE KEEP

The keep is of irregular plan; it comprises two storeys, and the walls now rise to a maximum height of about 11 m. The structure appears to be integral with the curtain, except at the NW. angle, where a straight joint in the masonry indicates that the upper courses of the curtain were renewed after the erection of the keep. Another straight joint in the N. face of the keep, 5 m. 30 cm. W.

of its junction with the E. sector of the curtain, suggests that the building was originally intended to be much smaller, but was extended to its present dimensions during the course of erection.

The most interesting feature of the keep today is the arrangement for the defence of the exposed portions of its perimeter by means of a projecting timber bretasche. This bretasche encircled the SE., SW., and part of the NW. sides of the keep and was borne on horizontal timbers slotted into the walls and supported by rough stone corbels of two members. Most of the corbels remain, and portions of some of the timbers can be seen embedded in the walls. Access to the bretasche was obtained by two doorways placed respectively in the SE. and NW. sides of the keep, and probably reached from the interior of the first-floor apartment by means of ladders or wooden stairs. The bretasche may have communicated with the parapet walk of the curtain wall of the bailey.

The ground floor of the keep is occupied by two barrel-vaulted apartments, each of which has its own entrance doorway opening from the bailey. Both chambers appear to have been water-cisterns and both communicate with the first floor of the keep by means of hatches. Part of an earthenware inlet-pipe, 13 cm. in diameter, which communicates with the E. cistern, has been exposed by the collapse of masonry in the chamber above, while two similar inlet-pipes communicating with the W. cistern may be seen within the NW. face of the keep. All these pipes were presumably fed by catchment points on the roof of the keep.

The first-floor apartment was entered through a doorway in the N. wall close to the junction of the keep with the E. sector of the curtain. This doorway, of which all the facework has been removed, was presumably reached either from the parapet walk of the E. curtain or by means of a ladder. In the single large apartment that occupies the whole of the first floor four deeply splayed slit-windows pierce the SW. and SE. walls. The rear lintels of the embrasures are shouldered, being carried on rough stone corbels. The roof was probably flat-pitched; it appears to have been carried upon a substantial transverse beam which spanned the centre of the apartment from N. to S. and was supported by wall struts.

THE CHURCH

Although no remains of a chapel can now be identified within the castle, the ruins of a small church stand on the hillside immediately below the castle, some 50 m. S. of the keep.

The church is very ruinous, the walls being reduced for the most part to their lowermost courses; the interior is filled with debris. The building is constructed of coursed limestone blocks bonded with lime mortar. On plan the church is rectangular externally and apsidal within, and measures 9 m. 90 cm. from E. to W. by 6 m. 70 cm. transversely over walls some 90 cm. in thickness. A gap towards the centre of the W. wall evidently indicates the position of the entrance doorway, while another gap in the middle of the apse wall may indicate the site of an E. window. There is also evidence of two small mural recesses, one at each side of the ingoing of the apse.

CONCLUSION

In the absence both of inscriptions and of closely datable architectural features it is difficult to ascribe the castle to any particular period of Armenian history. Indeed, it has been argued that the structure is Byzantine,[1] but this seems unlikely in view of certain similarities of construction between Azgit and the nearby castles of Ak-Kale and Tavutlu, near Çokak, all three being situated in an area having an exceptionally long history of Armenian occupation. Azgit alone of these possesses a keep, however, being one of the few recorded Cilician castles to do so.

[1] Fedden and Thomson, *Crusader Castles*, pp. 46–7.

4

THE TEMPLARS AND THE TEUTONIC
KNIGHTS IN CILICIAN ARMENIA

The massif of the Amanus, an outcrop of the Anti-Taurus mountains, marks the frontier between Asia Minor and Syria. In the twelfth century a march was created to control the two best roads through the range from the north to the city of Antioch only a few miles away. On the shore at the point where the mountains reached the sea there lay the small town of Port Bonnel (Arsuz) with its lands around. Eighteen miles to the east the Syrian Gates (Belen Pass), through which wound the easiest route from Cilicia into Syria, were closed by the important fortress of Gaston (Baghras). Some twelve miles further north ran the pass of Hajar Shughlan, a longer way to Antioch than that provided by the Syrian Gates but a more direct route to Aleppo and having the advantage for the tactician that it could be entered from the west even when the Portella (Saqaltutan), a strip of land between the Amanus and the sea, was held by an enemy. Half-way down this pass a crossroads, from which paths ran in all directions up through the mountain valleys, was overlooked by the castle of Roche Roussel (Sultan or Chilvan Kale), while its western entry was controlled by the fortress of Darbsak (Trapesac). Somewhere in this area there must have stood the castle of Roche Guillaume, although its site has never been identified.[1]

This important march was in Templar hands when Gaston, Darbsak and

[1] C. Cahen, *La Syrie du Nord à l'époque des Croisades et la principauté franque d'Antioche* (Paris, 1940), pp. 140–5. For the Templar possession of Sultan Kale, see also, under Hajar Shughlân, G. Le Strange, *Palestine under the Moslems* (London 1890), p. 447. It is not clear whether the Minat al-Franj, a few miles south of Arsuz, was in Templar hands. There has been no detailed study of the Templars in Lesser Armenia, but see Cahen, op. cit., pp. 511–12. K. Forstreuter (*Der Deutsche Orden am Mittelmeer*, Bonn, 1967, pp. 59–67) has written a chapter on the estates of the Teutonic Knights in Cilicia.

Roche Guillaume were besieged by Saladin in 1188,[2] and it is clear that the brothers were also holding Port Bonnel and Roche Roussel as well.[3] One of these castles, perhaps Roche Roussel, seems to have been already in Templar possession in 1154 when its garrison helped Stephen, the brother of Thoros of Armenia, to ambush and defeat a Selchukid army near the Portella.[4] Other Templar castles in the area were seized by the Greeks early in 1138 at the time of the campaign of the Emperor John Comnenus towards Antioch:[5] in 1156 Reginald of Antioch forced Thoros of Armenia, who had in the meantime taken these strongholds, to return them to the Order.[6] It seems reasonable to assume that the whole area had been acquired by the Templars before John Comnenus' expedition and this gives us a tentative *terminus ante quem* of 1137 for the establishment of the march. It is more difficult to give a *terminus a quo*, but it cannot be placed much before 1131–2 when the Franks lost control of southern Cilicia and the Amanus became the effective boundary of the Princi-

[2] Innocent III, 'Opera omnia', Migne, *PL.* CCXIV, col. 819: '*L'Estoire de Eracles empereur et la conqueste de la Terre d'Outre-mer*', *RHC.Oc.* II, pp. 72–4, 122–3, 125; *Chronique d'Ernoul et de Bernard le Trésorier*, ed. L. de Mas Latrie (Paris, 1871), pp. 255–6; Michael the Syrian, *Chronique*, ed. and tr. J.-B. Chabot (Paris, 1899–1924), III, p. 405; Michael the Syrian, '*Chronique*' (in Armenian translation), *RHC.Arm.* I, p. 401; Gregory Dgha, *Élégie sur la prise de Jérusalem*, *RHC.Arm.* I, p. 303; 'Imād al-Dīn in Abū-Shāma, 'Kitāb al-rauḍatain fī akhbār al-daulatain', *RHC.Or.* IV, pp. 375–9; Ibn al-Athīr, 'Kāmil al-tawārīkh', *RHC.Or.* I, pp. 730–2. See '*Historia de expeditione Friderici imperatoris*', ed. A. Chroust, MGH. NS. V, p. 4; Sichard of Cremona, *Chronicon*, Rerum Italicarum scriptores VII, p. 606; Baha' al-Dīn, *Kitāb al-nawādir al-sulṭānīya wa'l maḥāsin al-Yūsufīya* (Life of Saladin), trs. C. W. Wilson (London, 1897), pp. 135–7.

[3] See Innocent III, CCXV, col. 504, CCXVI, col. 430. From a reference in Gregory Dgha (loc. cit.) it is possible that Roche Roussel also fell to Saladin.

[4] Gregory the Priest, *Chronique*, *RHC.Arm.* I, pp. 171–2. Of the Templar castles, Roche Roussel had the most direct control over the Portella. Most commentators have believed that the fortress involved was Gaston and it is true that the Selchukid army had already passed through the Portella before the engagement. But Gaston may not have been in Templar hands; it had probably been taken by the Greeks in 1138 and seems to have been in Byzantine possession in 1142. William of Tyre, *Historia rerum in partibus transmarinis gestarum*, *RHC.Occ.* I, p. 689. See also below, note 5.

[5] John Cinnamus, p. 19; Michael the Syrian, (Arm. trans.), *RHC.Arm.* I, p. 349: Michael the Syrian, III, p. 314.

[6] Michael the Syrian, III, p. 314; *RHC.Arm.* I, p. 349 (in which there was a rather more favourable account of Thoros' actions). According to the Armenian translation of the Chronicle of Michael the Syrian (p. 354), the prince of Antioch later gave Gaston to Gerard of Sidon. Although this seems to be linked to a story about a Frankish brigand at Gaston in the original redaction (III, p. 318), it must be in error.

pality of Antioch. Before that date, moreover, the newly established Templars, who had faced difficult early years and were only beginning to expand,[7] would have been in no position to take on so important a commitment.

Within the years 1131–7 there seem to be two possible dates at which the Order could have been given the castles. In 1131 King Fulk of Jerusalem, who in 1136 was to give the Hospitallers their first fortress at Bethgibelin (Bait Jibrin),[8] came north to Antioch in order to establish his regency in the face of the opposition of the dowager Princess Alice and the Count of Tripoli, and he put the city 'and its adjacent districts' in order.[9] He returned to Antioch in 1133, but then was concerned with the frontier to the south-east of the city, while his visit in August 1135 seems to have been hardly the occasion on which to make so important a grant, for authority was slipping out of his hands as a result of an alliance between Princess Alice and the new patriarch, Ralph of Domfront. Fulk decided to send to the West for Raymond of Poitiers, whom he wished to become the husband of Constance, the young heiress to the Principality. Raymond travelled out in disguise, reaching Antioch in April 1136. His first campaign as prince was launched against the Armenians in Cilicia, and desultory warfare lasted until 1137.[10] It is possible that it was at this time that the Templars were given their strongholds; in 1140 Templar brothers witnessed two of Raymond's charters.[11] Raymond had been in Europe in the years when the military orders had caught the imagination of the western nobility and he was to make grants to the Hospitallers, giving them freedom from customs duties and a general confirmation of their rights.[12]

[7] See *Un Document sur les débuts des Templiers*, ed. J. Leclercq, *Revue d'histoire ecclésiastique*, LII (1957), p. 83.

[8] *Cartulaire général de l'ordre des Hospitaliers de St-Jean de Jérusalem (1100–1310)*, ed. J. Delaville Le Roulx (Paris, 1894–1906), no. 116; William of Tyre, p. 639.

[9] William of Tyre, *RHC.Occ.* I, p. 613. It might be thought that a grant of this kind was too important to be made by a regent. But *cf.* the gift made in 1170 by king Amalric to the Hospitallers when he was regent of Tripoli, although it was never confirmed. *Cart. gén. Hosp.*, no. 411. In 1133, while Fulk was on his second visit to Antioch, the fortress of Castellum Arnaldi near Jerusalem was built. Although this was later to be in Templar hands, it seems to have been garrisoned at this time by the Patriarch of Jerusalem. William of Tyre, *RHC.Occ.* I, p. 617.

[10] Cahen, op. cit., pp. 350–8; S. Runciman, *A History of the Crusades* (Cambridge, 1951–4), II, pp. 193–202.

[11] *Regesta regni Hierosolymitani*, ed. R. Röhricht (Innsbruck, 1893–1904), nos. 194–5.

[12] *Cart. gén. Hosp.*, nos. 129, 170, 183. A grant to the Templars could perhaps be connected with the recommendation sent in 1135–9 by St Bernard to Ralph of Domfront, patriarch of Antioch. *Cartulaire général de l'ordre du Temple* ?1119–50, ed. Marquis d'Albon (Paris, 1913), I, no. 106. The Templars certainly owned lands in the

The two most likely dates for the establishment of the Templars in the Amanus seem to be 1131 or 1136–7; and it must be seen in the context of the struggle for Cilicia between Latins from Antioch, Armenians and Greeks. If this dating is correct, the acquisition of the castles in the Amanus was probably the consequence of the first really important gift in the Latin East to the Order. The date at which Chastel Blanc (Ṣāfīthā) was acquired is not known – it was before 1152[13] – but Gaza was not garrisoned by the brothers until 1149, nor was Tortosa until 1152. Although there is no evidence for privileges enjoyed by the Templars in the Amanus, it is possible that the grant of this march is the first example of what was to be a standard kind of gift from the rulers of the northern Christian states to the Military Orders. This may have been the prototype for the grants to the Hospitallers of the territories around Krak des Chevaliers (Ḥiṣn al-Akrād) in 1144, 1180 and 1186 and on the south-east and southern frontiers of the Principality of Antioch in 1168 and 1186; and for the creation of a domain for the Templars at Tortosa, Chastel Blanc and Arima in the years around 1152. In the various charters to the Hospitallers and possibly also in those to the Templars concerning the lands round Tortosa and Chastel Blanc there were clauses giving favourable conditions for the sharing of spoil gained on expeditions in which the ruler also took part and a free hand for the Order in the decisions it would make on its relations with neighbouring Muslim princes. The ruler would surrender all his rights over the inhabitants of the territory granted.[14]

The march in the Amanus was considered by contemporaries to be an important section of the frontier defences of the principality.[15] As late as 1305 the Templar master, James of Molay, was to argue in a memoir to Pope Clement V that no future crusade should be sent to Armenia, because the expedition would find it difficult to break into Syria from Cilicia.[16] In spite of the brothers'

Principality by 1149. See the letter from Andrew Montbard, *Recueil des historiens des Gaules et de la France* XV, p. 540.

[13] See 'The Templars and the castle of Tortosa in Syria: an unknown document concerning the acquisition of the fortress', ed. J. S. C. Riley-Smith, *English Historical Review* LXXXIV (1969), pp. 279–80.

[14] J. S. C. Riley-Smith, *The Knights of St. John in Jerusalem and Cyprus c. 1050–1310* (London, 1967), pp. 55–7, 66–9, 131–2, 463–5. The Orders were usually encouraged to reconquer lands beyond the frontiers but there is nothing to suggest that such was the case with the grant of the Amanus.

[15] See ʿImād al-Dīn in Abū-Shāma, *RHC.Or.* IV, p. 379.

[16] *Vitae paparum Avenionensium, hoc est historia pontificum Romanorum qui in Gallia sederunt ab anno Christi MCCCV usque ad annum MCCCXCIV*, ed. S. Baluzius and G. Mollat (Paris, 1916–22), III, p. 147.

claims that before 1188 Gaston had been held by them without challenge,[17] it is clear that their territory stood in the way of possible Rupenid advance to the south-west, although they seem to have had fairly good relations with the Armenian lords for most of the twelfth century: Gregory the Priest took a favourable view of them,[18] while Mleh, who became prince of Cilicia in 1168, had in the past been a *confrater* of the Order.[19] We have seen, however, that Thoros temporarily occupied the castles in the middle of the twelfth century, and Mleh himself made an attempt to extend the lands under his rule at the Templars' expense. In 1172, allied to Nūr ad-Dīn and the Selchukids, he took 'whatever the brothers of the Knighthood of the Temple had in the area of Cilicia', according to the Latin chronicler, William of Tyre.[20] From the arguments in Rome of an embassy of Leon of Armenia in the 1190's it is certain that he occupied Gaston.[21] The Latin reaction was swift. A punitive expedition launched by Bohemond of Antioch and joined by Amalric of Jerusalem advanced onto the Cilician plain, although an attack by Nūr ad-Dīn on Kerak in Moab caused it soon to withdraw.[22] The Templars, however, seem to have reoccupied the Amanus.

In the late summer of 1188 Saladin's march of conquest reached the Principality of Antioch. He seems to have spent the first half of September besieging Darbsak.[23] The Templars sent to Prince Bohemond III of Antioch for aid, but when none arrived they surrendered on condition that they could depart freely, although they had to pay Saladin 5,000 *dinars* and leave behind all their goods.[24]

---

[17] Innocent III, *PL.* CCXIV, col. 819.

[18] Gregory the Priest, *RHC.Ar* I, pp. 171–2, 188–9. The last of these references concerns mediation by the Templars between the Greeks and the Armenians. See also Michael the Syrian, (Arm. trans.), *RHC.Arm.* I, pp. 331–3 (*cf.* Michael the Syrian, III, pp. 201–3). [19] William of Tyre, *RHC.Or.* I, p. 991.

[20] William of Tyre, loc. cit. [21] Innocent III, *PL.* CCXIV, col. 819.

[22] See S. der Nersessian, 'The Kingdom of Cilician Armenia', *A History of the Crusades*, ed.-in-chief K. M. Setton (Philadelphia, 1955 ff.), II, p. 643. The Latin invasion was also occasioned by Mleh's attack upon Count Stephen of Sancerre. In 1169 Gaston was damaged by an earthquake. Bar Hebraeus, *The Chronography*, tr. Budge (Oxford, 1932), p. 296.

[23] According to Ibn al-Athīr (*RHC.Or.* I, pp. 730–1) the siege of Darbsak lasted from 2 to 13 September. Bahā' al-Dīn (trs. Wilson, pp. 135–6) and 'Imād al-Dīn (in Abu-Shama, *RHC.Or.* IV, p. 376), the only writer present, reported that the castle was taken on the 16th, although this can be reconciled with the report in Ibn al-Athīr that the garrison surrendered three days before Darbsak was occupied.

[24] 'Imād al-Dīn in Abu-Shama, *RHC.Or.* IV, pp. 376–7; Bahā' al-Dīn, p. 136, Ibn al-Athīr, *RHC.Or.* I, pp. 730–1. See also the sources above, note 23.

Saladin moved on with part of his army to Gaston, where the garrison was understrength, and which surrendered on 26/7 September on the same conditions as those at Darbsak, after a siege that had not been easy for a Muslim force that was itself too weak.[25] It is possible that Saladin then went on with some troops to reduce Roche Guillaume, but it is certain that his attention was diverted before the castle fell,[26] and the Templars appear to have remained in possession of it as well as of Roche Roussel.[27] Before his departure the sultan created an *iqtā*', comprising Gaston, Darbsak and possibly Port Bonnel, for 'Alam ad-Dīn Sulaimān bin Jandar, the lord of 'Azāz. 'Alam ad-Dīn was believed by contemporaries to have had only a financial interest in the castles, for he sold the goods he found in them at a profit in Antioch and then, on the approach of the German crusaders in 1190, slighted and evacuated Gaston,[28] although he seems to have retained possession of Darbsak until it passed to the ruler of Aleppo, perhaps on the partition of the Aiyūbid empire on Saladin's death in 1193. The empty Port Bonnel and Gaston were seized, probably in 1191, by a force sent by Leon of Armenia.[29] He immediately set about establishing a permanent occupation, carefully rebuilding and garrisoning Gaston before granting it in fief to Adam, his seneschal, who held it at least from 1198 to March 1215.[30]

[25] Bahā' al-Dīn, p. 136. See also 'Imād al-Dīn in Abū-Shāma, *RHC.Or.* IV, p. 378; Ibn al-Athir, *RHC.Or.* I, pp. 731–2.

[26] See the curious story of Saladin's vendetta against the knight John Gale who was in the castle. *Eracles, RHC.Occ.* II, pp. 72–4, 122–3, 125; *Ernoul*, pp. 255–6.

[27] See Innocent III, *PL.* CCXV, col. 504.

[28] 'Imād al-Dīn in Abū-Shāma, *RHC.Or.* IV, pp. 378–9; Bahā' al-Dīn, p. 136; Ibn al-Athīr, *RHC.Or.* I, p. 732 (who reported that Saladin ordered Gaston to be demolished); Innocent III, *PL.* CCXIV, col. 819; *Eracles, RHC.Occ.* II, p. 136. 'Alam al-Dīn, however, was still known as lord of Gaston in the spring of 1191. 'Imād al-Dīn in Abū-Shāma, *RHC.Or.* V, p. 6.

[29] Bar Hebraeus (pp. 336–7) in what seems to have been otherwise an apocryphal account, gave the date of 1191. 'Imād al-Dīn (in Abū-Shāma, *RHC.Or.* IV, p. 379) gave the years 1191–2. See also Innocent III, *PL.* CCXIV, col. 819; Vahram of Edessa, 'Chronique rimée des rois de la Petite Arménie', *RHC.Arm.* I, p. 512; Ibn al-Athīr, *RHC.Or.* I, p. 732; *Eracles, RHC.Oc.* II, p. 136.

[30] Sempad the Constable, *Chronique du royaume de la Petite Arménie, RHC.Arm.* I, p. 636; Röhricht, *Reg. Hier.*, nos. 820, 843, 869, 870, 875. The last of these is dated 15 March. In two further documents of 31 March (nos. 877–8), Adam witnessed without reference to Gaston. The writer of *Eracles* (*RHC.Occ.* II, p. 136) reported that Gaston was occupied for Leon by his cousin Fulk de Bouillon, but added, clearly in error, that he held it in lordship for twenty years. For the care with which the castle was rebuilt, see Ibn al-Athīr, *RHC.Or.* I, p. 732.

In Armenian hands Gaston threatened not only the city of Antioch but also Muslim Aleppo,[31] which may have been why Bohemond drew Saladin's attention to Leon's action. In fact Leon's ambitions soon became clear. In 1193 or 1194 he invited Bohemond to meet him at the Fons Gastonis[32] and then in the fortress itself, perhaps holding out the prospect of its return. There he held Bohemond prisoner with most of his escort until the prince had promised to surrender Antioch to him. But the people of the city were not prepared to accept this. There was revolution, a commune was proclaimed and Armenian occupation was resisted. Henry of Champagne, the ruler of the Kingdom of Jerusalem, negotiated Bohemond's release, but while no ransom was paid for the prince, he may have had to do homage to Leon, he certainly surrendered Gaston and Port Bonnel, and agreed to a marriage between his eldest son Raymond and Alice, Leon's niece and heiress.[33] The couple were wedded at the beginning of 1195, but two years later Raymond died, leaving a small son, Raymond Rupen, who in 1198 was recognised as Bohemond's heir by a full court of the Antiochene barons, and who was of course supported by his great-uncle Leon. The population of the city of Antioch was no more tolerant now than it had been in 1194 of Armenian domination. The commune rose in revolt, deposed Bohemond III and called in to govern it his younger son, Count Bohemond of Tripoli. The rebellion was short-lived, but on Bohemond's death in 1201 the count of Tripoli regained Antioch and was to hold it until 1216 and again from 1219 until his death, in spite of invasions from Cilicia, a strong party of opposition within the Principality and the almost frantic efforts of Pope Innocent III, his legates and the leaders in Latin Syria to bring about peace.

Armenian ambitions and the struggle for power in Antioch not only divided the Christians in the North but also divided the Military Orders. At first the Hospitallers favoured Bohemond of Tripoli, but in 1204 they swung over to the support of Leon and Raymond Rupen.[34] The Teutonic Knights, we will see, were also drawn onto Leon's side. The Templars remained firmly behind Bohemond; the strength of the Armenian position was partly based on the threat

---

[31] Ibn al-Athīr, *RHC.Or.* I, p. 732. See Cahen, op. cit., p. 582.

[32] This place had belonged to the Abbey of St Paul at Antioch before being seized by Leon. *Annales ecclesiastici*, ed. C. Baronius, O. Raynaldus, A. Pagi and A. Theiner (Bar-le-Duc/Paris, 1864–82) XX, p. 203.

[33] Cahen, op. cit., pp. 583–6. See Sempad the Constable, *Royal Chronicle*, part trans. S. der Nersessian, *The Armenian Chronicle of the Constable Sempad or of the 'Royal Historian'*, *D.O.P.* XIII (1959), p. 155. Leon seems to have been acting partly in revenge for the imprisonment of his brother Rupen by the Antiochenes in 1185–6.

[34] Riley-Smith, *Knights of St. John*, pp. 152–60.

PLATE 37

AZGIT

West curtain wall and west postern

The curtain wall follows a markedly sinuous course, changing direction in accordance with the configuration of the summit.

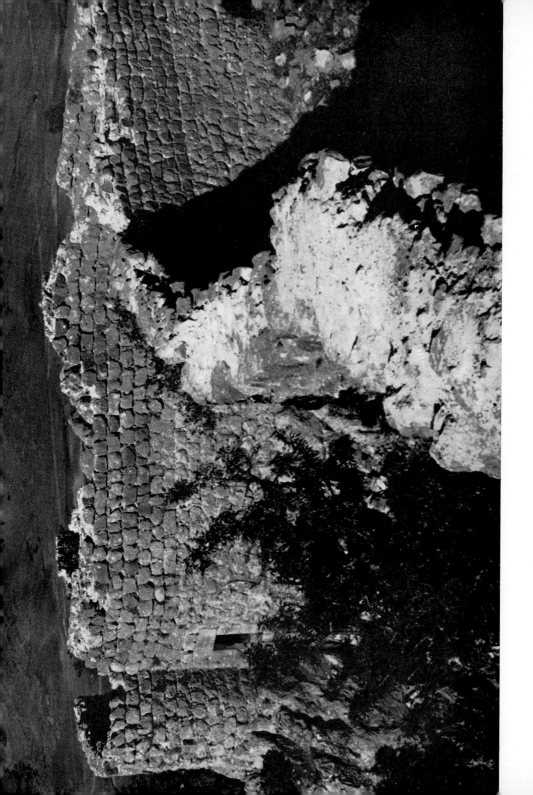

to Antioch posed by Leon's occupation of Gaston and his seizure of the castle remained, as the pope wrote in 1209, the 'principal cause' of their opposition to him.[35] For over twenty years Leon played quite admirably a game of promising and protracting negotiations over the return of the fortress, while sending to Rome for papal decisions that he would then ignore. The attitude of the Templars was not softened by a change in his tactics that can be seen in 1201. His seizure of Gaston seems to have resulted from the desire, shared with his predecessors, of freeing his path into northern Syria. But, hard pressed by the papacy, he began to use the castle as a bait to detach the Templars from Bohemond's side, holding out to them the prospect of its return on condition that they supported the claims of Raymond Rupen. This move merely made the Templars more intransigent.

In 1198 the seizure of Antioch by Bohemond of Tripoli was supported by the Hospitallers and Templars under their masters and it seems that plans were then made to campaign into Cilicia itself. Both Orders, however, soon made peace with Leon,[36] perhaps because of a promise made by him to enter into negotiations for Gaston's return. He assured a deputation which represented all the parties in Antioch that he would act on whatever was advised by the patriarch and the prince, perhaps still in exile in Armenia, thus presumably trying to strengthen Bohemond III's position. Almost at once, however, he changed ground, informing the Templars that he would seek judgment on the case from Rome, where his representative based his claims to the castle on two arguments: that it was his by inheritance because it had once been held by Mleh – a reference to that prince's occupation of Templar possessions in 1172 – and that anyway it was his by right of conquest.[37] Innocent III's reply, written late in 1199, was unequivocal. He told Leon to hand Gaston back to the Templars, then afterwards to bring before the curia or the papal legates soon to come to the East any complaint he had against the Order.[38]

It is possible that the Templars recognised the Armenian occupation of the Amanus to the extent of paying homage to Leon for their other properties, although it looks as if they held the lands from him in free-alms, no service being expected for them.[39] This cannot be dated, but the act of homage may

[35] Innocent III, *PL* CCXVI, col. 55.
[36] Innocent III, *PL* CCXIV, cols. 811–13. See also col. 816.
[37] He was to repeat this second argument in 1216. See below, p. 107.
[38] Innocent III, *PL* CCXIV, cols. 819–20.
[39] Misimus pro Templariis morantibus in regno nostro, de possessionibus valentibus viginti millia bysantiorum, ut venirent in *auxilium nostrum ad honorem Dei et defensionem Christianitatis.*

H

have been performed at the time of Leon's coronation as king of Armenia in 1198, perhaps in the hope that a conciliatory gesture of this kind would restore Gaston to the Templars. When Bohemond of Tripoli took possession of Antioch in 1201 he appealed for support to al-Ẓāhir of Aleppo and Rukn ad-Dīn Sulaimān of Rūm who invaded Cilicia in July. Leon called on the Templars for service proportionate to the size of the fief they held of him, although he was careful to ask for it only 'for the honour of God and the defence of Christianity'. The master of the Templars replied by sending a letter from the pope which demanded that the king should return Gaston to the Order. Leon, as Innocent had suggested, offered to open negotiations, but when he met the master he put six proposals to him. Embassies should be sent by both parties and by the patriarch of Antioch to Rome, and the pope himself would hand the fortress over to the Templars. Leon agreed to this on condition that the brothers took charge of the young Raymond Rupen, whom they would find residing in Gaston, and supported him in his pretensions to Antioch. They must ensure that no harm came to Cilicia through their possession of the fortress. The king asked that he and Raymond Rupen might become *confratres* of the Order and he committed himself to giving the Templars the rents from Gaston's domain until the embassies had returned from Rome. He also offered to help them recover Darbsak. It is not surprising that the Templars refused terms whose acceptance would have implied that their claims on Gaston were doubtful enough in law to be submitted to the papal curia and which bound them to helping Raymond Rupen. They also refused to lend Leon aid against the Selchukid Turks.[40]

In November 1203 a contingent of Armenian troops penetrated the city of Antioch and was only driven out with Templar assistance.[41] Bohemond called in his Muslim allies, and the forces of Antioch, together with those of Aleppo and the Templars, who unfurled their battle-flag,[42] plundered villages in the vicinity of Gaston.[43] Leon claimed that by these actions the Order had broken its feudal contract with him, because it had made no formal diffidation,[44] and

[40] Innocent III, *PL*. CCXIV, cols. 1005–6.

[41] Innocent III, *PL*. CCXV, col. 689; *Les Gestes des Chiprois*, ed. G. Raynaud (Société de l'Orient latin: série historique, 5. Geneva, 1887), p. 16; 'Annales de Terre Sainte', ed. R. Röhricht and G. Raynaud, *Archives de l'Orient latin* II (1884), p. 435. See Cahen, op. cit., p. 604.

[42] 'Vexillum *Balzanum* contra nos paraverunt.' For the importance of this, see *La Règle du Temple*, ed. H. de Curzon (Paris, 1886), pp. 126–7, 229–30.

[43] Innocent III, *PL*. CCXV, cols., 689–90; *Annales ecclesiastici*, XX, p. 201.

[44] 'Sine *diffiducia* facta contra nos dentes.'

he took forcible possession of the rest of the march in the Amanus, including Roche Roussel and Roche Guillaume.[45]

Two papal legates, the cardinals Soffred of Pisa and Peter Capuano, were now in the East with the unhappy task of trying to unravel the Antiochene business. Peter did not behave tactfully on his arrival in Cilicia and Leon, suspecting that he favoured Bohemond, was not ready to listen to demands to restore Templar possessions. He would do so, he said, if the brothers promised to remain neutral as a religious order should, and to stop helping Bohemond. The Order defiantly refused and Peter, obviously at the end of his tether, excommunicated Leon and hurled an interdict on his lands. In spite of the belief of the Armenian catholicos that this sentence had no validity, being issued at a council to which he had not been invited, Leon was prepared to continue negotiations. He promised to abide by the legates' decision concerning Antioch and, when called to a meeting with them in Acre, he sent his cousin Constantine of Camardias with powers to reach agreement. Bohemond of Tripoli, however, remained intransigent and the legates found themselves helpless. Peter's excommunication of Leon and interdict upon Cilicia seem to have been lifted, probably because Leon was prepared to return Roche Roussel, Roche Guillaume and perhaps Port Bonnel,[46] although he was still intent on increasing his control over the Amanus. In the winter of 1205–6 he unsuccessfully tried to take Darbsak from Aleppo.[47] In the short time that they had held Roche Roussel and Roche Guillaume the Armenians had done a good deal of damage and in January 1205 Innocent III informed Leon that he had ordered the bishops of Gibelet (Jubail) and Valenia (Bāniyās) to decide on the terms of compensation to be awarded to the Templars.[48]

Towards the end of 1207 a group in the principality who favoured the Armenians nearly succeeded in taking possession of Antioch. The patriarch Peter of Angoulême, who had been party to the attempt, was thrown into prison, where he died in the most cruel circumstances. In his disappointment Leon devastated parts of Syria in 1208 and 1209. Bohemond appealed for aid to Kai-Khusrau of Rūm who invaded Cilicia in the spring of 1209 and forced

[45] Innocent III, *PL*. CCXV, cols., 504, 689–90.

[46] Innocent III, *PL*. CCXIV, col. clviii, CCXV, cols. 689–91. See also CCXV, cols. 557, 692–4.

[47] Cahen, op. cit., p. 610.

[48] Innocent III, *PL*. CCXV, col. 504. The pope was anxious that the military orders should remain neutral (cols. 557, 558), but he seems to have been nearing desperation over the whole business (col. 698).

PLATE 38   A Z G I T

South curtain wall and keep, showing corbels of former timber bretasche

The uppermost courses of the curtain wall, consisting of dark-coloured stone,
appear to be of secondary construction.

Leon to agree to a treaty by which he promised to restore Gaston to the Templars, and Raymond Rupen renounced his claims to Antioch. The treaty was unenforceable and its terms were not kept.[49] Early in 1208 Pope Innocent had written to the patriarch of Jerusalem, asking him to intervene in the disputes over Antioch and Gaston and to obtain the release of Peter of Angoulême. Now, horrified at what had happened to Peter, the pope again tried to find some solution and in March 1209 ordered the patriarch of Jerusalem to try to bring about agreement between Leon, Bohemond and the Templars. Clearly Innocent did not have much hope of success. He told the patriarch that if it should prove impossible to bring about a reconciliation, he must anyway try to persuade Leon to return Templar property and to refrain from confiscating any more of it. Further, the patriarch was to enforce what seems to have been a new excommunication imposed on the Armenian king for his obduracy towards the Order.[50] In June Innocent wrote to Leon suggesting a compromise over Antioch, in which the Hospitallers and Templars would have custody of the city fortress under the direction of the new patriarch, Peter of Locedio, who was not yet open to charges of partiality. Leon had again complained to Rome of the Templars' support for Bohemond, but the pope defended the Order vigorously. Its master he wished 'to persist in his purity of religion rather than to make war upon you', but he considered that the Templars were only defending themselves, and that it was not surprising that they maintained Antioch against Leon, for Gaston was still in his hands. The pope believed that the Templars would stop attacking Leon when the Armenian king himself ceased to offend them.[51]

Up to this point Innocent seems to have tried to be patient, but now his attitude hardened. In 1210 he sent once more to Syria Sicard of Cremona, who had assisted the papal legates in 1203–4, and this time gave him sterner powers. If Sicard could not bring the parties together he was to decide the case of Antioch himself, together with two prudent men acceptable to both parties, or, if this could not be achieved, with the two patriarchs, and he could call upon physical force to make the claimants submit to his decision.[52] Sicard, however, was no more successful than his predecessors, and when the patriarch of Jerusalem tried to carry out a mandate from Innocent making him a judge delegate in the dispute over Gaston, Leon not only refused to answer the Templars'

[49] Cahen, op. cit., p. 614.
[50] Innocent III, *PL.* CCXV, cols. 132–3, CCXVI, cols. 18–19.
[51] Innocent III, *PL.* CCXVI, cols. 54–6.
[52] Innocent III, *PL.* CCXVI, cols. 310–11.

pleas before him, but also once more confiscated their lands at Port Bonnel and 'in other places in Armenia', presumably nearby, because there is no evidence that at this time they had estates in Cilicia proper. The patriarch ordered Leon to remove the officers he had appointed to administer the Templar lands or to come to answer the case within a set term. Leon remained obdurate and the patriarch published a new excommunication, forbidding all those in the east to lend aid to the king in further damaging the Order. An already tense situation was made worse by the Templars, who now sent a force north to Antioch, ostensibly to revictual their castles, but clearly to bring pressure to bear on the Armenians. Leon's reaction was typical. He confiscated all their remaining properties in Armenia except for two castles, presumably Roche Roussel and Roche Guillaume, which he could not take; he devastated the villages in the Amanus that had come into his hands; and when a convoy under the master William of Chartres marched to the relief of one of the two remaining castles, it was ambushed by the Armenians who killed one Templar and wounded several mercenaries and brothers, including William of Chartres himself. Innocent's response was equally typical. In July 1211 he wrote to the two patriarchs, to the archbishop of Tyre and the bishops of Sidon, Tripoli, Tortosa, Limassol and Famagusta, commanding them to publish a solemn sentence of excommunication against Leon; and he wrote to the faithful in Latin Syria and to King John of Jerusalem giving him the captaincy of a punitive expedition to be launched to recover the Order's rights.[53]

John of Jerusalem did not campaign himself, but he provided 50 knights for a force assembled by the Templars that included troops from Antioch and which ravaged parts of Cilicia, perhaps laying siege to Gaston.[54] The expedition, however, seems to have ended inconclusively with a truce, in which Leon promised to return Gaston at some future but unspecified date.[55] At the time the Templars cannot have been very confident of ever reoccupying the castle, for Leon continued to defy the papacy, even introducing Greek clergy into the Church of Tarsus.[56] But late in 1212 he suddenly decided to come to terms.

[53] Innocent III, *PL*. CCXVI, cols. 430–2. The patriarch of Jerusalem was to act as adviser to the king of Jerusalem in the matter.

[54] *Eracles, RHC.Occ.* II, pp. 137, 317–18.

[55] See *Eracles, RHC.Occ.* II, p. 137, in which account Leon agreed to return Gaston when Raymond Rupen was received in Antioch. According to the writer of *Eracles* (*RHC.Occ.* II, p. 318), Leon was forced to return Gaston after the Templar campaign. This is obviously in error.

[56] Cahen, op. cit., p. 619.

He wrote to the patriarch of Jerusalem, asking for absolution, offering reconciliation with the Order and seeking his judgment over Antioch. In the spring of 1213 the pope agreed to the lifting of the excommunication.[57] Almost certainly one result of this was the return to the Templars of Port Bonnel, if the place had not already been occupied by them on their campaign of 1211;[58] but for Gaston they had to wait until Leon and Raymond occupied Antioch on 14 February 1216. With Antioch in his great-nephew's hands Leon could afford to relax. He restored properties in the Amanus to the Abbey of St Paul in Antioch and to other monastic houses and he returned Gaston to the Templars. although he emphasised again that the castle had come to him by right of conquest.[59]

After 1216 the Templars were again in possession of nearly all their march in the Amanus, although Darbsak was to remain in the hands of the rulers of Aleppo. While there is no evidence that the brothers ever held estates on the main Cilician plain, they were perhaps to gain another important property on the shores of the Gulf of Alexandretta with the acquisition of Calamella (Ḥiṣn al-Tīnāt), a small port some fifteen miles north of the Portella and divided from their march by the fief of Nigrinum.[60] It is not known when they took possession of this place. Calamella was certainly not in their hands in 1190, as it was then held by Leon himself;[61] and in 1214 he gave the Hospitallers the enjoyment of its revenues for two years, although the reference in his charter is to the port[62] and it is possible though unlikely that the castle already belonged to their rivals. Muslim sources, however, reported that it was in Templar hands at the time of its capture by the Mamluke Sultan Baybars in 1266.[63]

[57] Innocent III, *PL*. CCXVI, cols. 792–3.

[58] It is worth noting that the Cistercian monastery of St George of Jubin was affiliated in 1214. It was established in the Amanus, so it may have been in possession of its lands.

[59] *Annales ecclesiastici*, XX, p. 203. For its date, see Cahen, op. cit., pp. 622–3.

[60] For the identification of Calamella, see Cahen, op. cit., p. 150. For Nigrinum, see E. Dulaurier, Introduction to *RHC.Arm*. I, p. lxxxvii. It was given to the Hospitallers for two years at the same time as Calamella. *Cart. gen. Hosp.*, no. 1427.

[61] Abū-Shāma, *RHC.Or*. IV, p. 460.

[62] *Cart. gen. Hosp.*, no. 1427.

[63] U. and M. C. Lyons, *Ayyubids, Mamlukes and Crusaders: Selections from Tārīkh al-Duwal wa'l Mulūk of Ibn al Furāt* (Introduction and notes by J. S. C. Riley-Smith), 2 vols. (Cambridge, 1971), II, p. 99. See al-Maqrīzī, *Kitāb al-sulūk li-ma'rifat duwal al-mulūk*, extr. trs. E. M. Quatremère (Paris, 1837–45), I B, p. 34. Arab chroniclers, however, often confused Templars and Hospitallers and it may be that Calamella was still in Hospitaller possession.

The territory in the Amanus and its foothills seems to have provided the Order with important revenues. Innocent III believed that the returns from these lands played a large part in sustaining 'the brothers made responsible for aiding the Holy Land'.[64] In 1201 Leon estimated that Roche Roussel, Roche Guillaume and perhaps Port Bonnel were worth 20,000 *besants* and this must have been in annual revenue, for in 1205 the Templars were claiming to have lost in damage to movable goods 50,000 *besants* at the time of the Armenian occupation of the villages around Roche Roussel and Roche Guillaume the year before; this estimate may have included the returns from a harvest.[65] From the port of Calamella were exported pine trees that grew on the slopes of the Amanus and wood may have provided the brothers with some wealth.[66] On the other hand while the Templars in Darbsak could pay Saladin 5,000 *dinars* and 'Imād ad-Dīn, who himself drew up the inventories of goods in Gaston and Darbsak after their capture by the Muslims in 1188, reported that there were 12,000 sacks of corn in Gaston and implied that the store-houses of both fortresses were full,[67] Muslim accountants estimated the annual revenues of Gaston at only 8,000 *dinars*, which did not compare favourably with the c. 24,000 provided at about the same time by Turbessel (Tell Beṣir).[68] Gaston, of course, may not have been so rich a domain as the Templar castles just to the north of it, while its estates may have been partially destroyed in the Muslim invasion.

In the twelfth century the group of castles in the Amanus had marked the north-west frontier of the Principality of Antioch. But we have seen that the Templars probably paid homage to Leon of Armenia for Roche Roussel and Roche Guillaume; and by 1211 Pope Innocent seems to have believed that Port Bonnel lay within Leon's kingdom.[69] Willbrand of Oldenburg who visited Cilicia at that time reported that the frontier between the Kingdom of Armenia and the Principality of Antioch ran north of the Syrian Gates, and to writers in the middle of the thirteenth century, Port Bonnel was on the Armenian border.[70]

---

[64] Innocent III, *PL.* CCXVI, col. 430. *Cf.* for the Hospitallers, *Cart. gén. Hosp.*, no. 3308 (vol. iv).

[65] Innocent III, *PL.* CCXIV, col. 1005, CCXV, col. 504.

[66] Le Strange, *Palestine*, p. 455. See also *Cart. gén. Hosp.*, no. 1427. 'portus de Calamella . . . et tablagium, et omnes dricturas . . . tam lignorum quam aliarum rerum venalium.'   [67] 'Imād al-Dīn in Abū-Shāma, *RHC.Or.* IV, pp. 376-9.

[68] Cahen, op. cit., p. 467.   [69] Innocent III, *PL.* CCXVI, col. 430.

[70] Willbrand of Oldenburg, 'Itinerarium Terrae Sanctae', ed. J. C. M. Laurent, *Peregrinatores medii aevi quatuor* (Leipzig, 1864), p. 174 (who reported that Gaston was in Leon's hands); *Gestes des Chiprois*, p. 191; *Eracles*, II, p. 437.

While it is possible that Leon's return of Gaston in 1216 was conditional on a recognition of his authority,[71] at the very least the march in the Amanus was divided by the frontier, and one would expect to find the Templars with responsibilities for the defence both of Cilicia and Antioch. The later history of the relations between the Order and the kings of Armenia is, however, marked by a mutual and almost traditional antipathy. When in 1225 Bohemond of Antioch marched into Cilicia to avenge the death of his son Philip at the hands of the Armenians, the Templars did nothing to prevent his passage through the Amanus, although they would not serve with his army; and it is noteworthy that al-'Azīz of Aleppo answered Constantine of Babaron's[72] call for assistance by besieging Gaston in 1226.[73] Seven years later the Order and King Hetoum I were quarrelling violently, because it was believed in Cilicia that the brothers were planning treason; some of them were arrested and hanged. The Templars under their master, Armand of Périgord, marched into Cilicia together with the new prince of Antioch, Bohemond V, who had not forgiven the Armenians for the murder of his brother. Constantine of Babaron intervened on behalf of his son and reached an agreement with Armand of Périgord who withdrew his forces, much to Bohemond's annoyance.[74] It is noteworthy, however, that when, after the Mongol invasion of Syria, the Khan Hulagu gave Hetoum Darbsak in 1261, the king does not seem to have considered returning it to the Order.[75]

In the 1220's and 1230's the Templars were trying to extend their control eastward of the Amanus across the 'Amouq depression. In this they behaved like their brothers at Tortosa and the Hospitallers at Krak des Chevaliers and Margat; in their great semi-independent marches in the north the Military

[71] Although there is no mention of this in Leon's letter to the Pope on the matter. *Annales ecclesiastici*, XX, p. 203. It is possible that with Raymond Rupen as Prince he would have been content to have it returned to the Principality.

[72] For this man, see W. H. Rüdt-Collenberg, *The Rupenides, Hethumides and Lusignans. The Structure of the Armeno-Cilician Dynasties* (Paris, 1963), p. 58 and Tables II (H.1), III (H.2).

[73] Ibn al-Athīr, *RHC.Or.* II, pp. 168–70; Sempad, *RHC.Arm.* I, p. 648. Bar Hebraeus (p. 370) wrote that in 1217 Raymond Rupen was plotting against Leon, but the conspiracy was revealed to the king by the *frères*. These were almost certainly the Hospitallers and not the Templars.

[74] *Eracles, RHC.Oc.* II, pp. 405–6. It may have been on this occasion that the Templars were given Calamella. It seems that by 1237 trouble was about to break out again between Antioch and Armenia, and pope Gregory IX was writing to the Military Orders, to Bohemond and to king Henry of Cyprus, ordering them to protect Constantine of Lampron. Gregory IX, *Régistre*, ed. L. Auvray (Paris, 1896–1955), nos. 3448–54. See nos. 3597, 4732.   [75] Cahen, op. cit., p. 705.

Orders seem to have adopted a very aggressive approach towards their Muslim neighbours.[76] In 1227 the Templars avenged the murder of one of themselves by raiding the Turkoman tribes in the 'Amouq and it was only threats from Aleppo and the execution of two of their brothers that persuaded them to disgorge most of the loot they had gained.[77] In 1237 they took advantage of a minority in Aleppo to attack once more the Turkoman encampments. A Muslim force under al-Mu'aẓẓam Tūrān-Shāh, the great-uncle of the child-ruler of Aleppo, countered by investing Gaston and devastating the lands around. The castle had almost fallen when it was saved by Bohemond V, who interceded for the Order with Aleppo. But the truce that resulted was soon broken, for in June William of Montferrand, the Templar commander of Antioch, assembled a very strong force of brothers and lay knights at Roche Roussel and marched down the pass of Hajar Shughlan to surprise Darbsak. The Muslim garrison learnt of its coming and held out until the arrival of an Aleppan relieving force that annihilated the tired Christian army. It was reported that more than 100 brothers were killed, including William himself and the Order's standard-bearer.[78]

It seems that, far from being the frontier either of Antioch or of Armenia, the Amanus was a semi-independent territory in which the Templars went their own way, with little reference to their nominal lords in Cilicia. Significantly, the Order does not seem to have appointed a special officer with responsibilities for Armenia until after the fall of Antioch in 1268. Until that date the castles in the Amanus appear to have remained, as presumably they had done in the twelfth century, under the supervision of the commander of Antioch.[79]

*   *   *

[76] See Riley-Smith, *Knights of St. John*, pp. 136–41.

[77] Ibn al-Athīr, *RHC.Or.* II, p. 170.

[78] Kamāl al-Dīn, 'Bughyat al-ṭalab fī tārīkh Halab', extr. trs. E. Blochet, *Revue de l'Orient latin*, V (1897), pp. 95–6; Abu'l-Fidā', 'Mukhtaṣar fī ākhbār al-bashar', *RHC.Or.* I, p. 112; *Annales de Terre Sainte*, p. 439; Matthew Paris, *Chronica maiora*, ed. H. R. Luard (Rolls Series, 57. London, 1872–83), III, p. 404; Philip Mousket, *Historia rerum Francorum*, RGHF, XXII, p. 62; *Annales Colonienses Maximi*, MGH. XVII, p. 846. See Albéric of Trois Fontaines, *Chronica*, MGH. XXIII, p. 942; Gregory IX, *Reg.*, nos. 3991–4000, 4143–4; L. de Mas Latrie, *Histoire de l'île de Chypre* (Paris, 1852–61), II, p. 61

[79] *Règle du Temple*, p. 105. See also the actions of William of Montferrand, the Templar commander of Antioch, above. A Templar commander of Armenia is found only in 1285. al-Maqrīzī, II A, pp. 166, 201, 212. For the Hospitaller commanders, see J. Delaville Le Roulx, *Les Hospitaliers en Terre Sainte et à Chypre (1100–1310)* (Paris, 1904), p. 431. For the Teutonic Knights, see below.

The endowment of the Teutonic Knights in Cilicia early in the thirteenth century was a consequence of the predicament in which Leon found himself, for in his struggle with Bohemond of Tripoli and the Templars he was looking for allies. He discovered them in the Hospitallers and the Teutonic Knights,[80] but the two Orders cannot be compared. The Hospitallers of St John of Jerusalem were as richly endowed and as powerful as the Templars; the Hospitallers of St Mary of the Germans were brothers of a newly founded and as yet poor Order and cannot themselves have been expected to provide significant support. But when their hospice was reconstituted in Acre as an independent Order in March 1198,[81] it was very much the creation of the German crusade which had been present in the Holy Land, and there can be little doubt that the initiative had come from the imperial chancellor Conrad of Querfurt, bishop of Hildesheim, a friend and confidant of the Emperor Henry VI. The later history of the Order shows it to have been closely allied to the policies of the western emperors. Like Aimery of Cyprus, Leon had turned to the West in his search for a crown, and before his early death Henry had agreed to the establishment of Cyprus and Armenia as vassal kingdoms of the empire. In January 1198 Conrad of Querfurt and the papal legate Conrad of Wittelsbach, archbishop of Mainz, were present at Leon's coronation in Tarsus. While there is little evidence that imperial suzerainty was ever an effective force in Cilicia, Leon may have hoped that favour shown to a German Order would bring him the favour of the emperor himself and it may be significant that his first contacts with the Teutonic Knights date from the period after the death of Philip of Swabia when Otto of Brunswick's power in Germany was for a short time in the ascendant. Leon seems to have emphasised his love for the Order to Wilbrand of Oldenburg, the chief of an embassy sent to Cilicia in 1211 by Otto with a new crown for the Armenian king.[82] And it is not surprising that the first of Leon's surviving charters to the Order should have been issued 'out of love for God and the Roman Empire, under the grace of whose power I have been made king'.[83]

<hr />

[80] For the Hospitallers, see Riley-Smith, *Knights of St. John*, pp. 154–9.

[81] See R. Röhricht, *Geschichte des Königreichs Jerusalem (1100–1291)* (Innsbruck, 1898), pp. 677–8. There are problems concerning the relationship between the German hospice in Jerusalem before 1187 and the later Military Order, many of them discussed in Forstreuter, *Deutsche Orden*, pp. 12–34.

[82] Wilbrand of Oldenburg, p. 179. For the relations between Otto IV and Leon, see Cahen, op. cit., p. 618.

[83] *Tabulae ordinis Theutonici*, ed. E. Strehlke (Berlin, 1869), no. 46.

Plate 39

AZGIT

West postern

Masonry of superior quality, comprising close-jointed blocks with drafted margins, are very sparingly used.

In June 1209 a Teutonic Knight was acting as Leon's emissary to the pope over the question of Antioch;[84] and almost at the same time Innocent issued a general confirmation of the Order's properties in which there was reference to two Cilician villages, Cumbethfort and Ayun.[85] Neither has been identified, but Cumbethfort lay on the road from Mamistra to Tarsus and seems to have contained a conventual cell by 1211, in which year the Order was already holding the small fortress of Adamodana (al-'Amūdain/Hematye Kale).[86] Adamodana was for a long time its most important property in Cilicia, lying on the road from the passes through the Amanus to Anazarbus and Sis and one of a group of castles controlling the upper reaches of the Ceyhan river.[87] The Order's possession of Adamodana with an adjacent *casal*, and of Cumbethfort, Ayun and two other villages was formally confirmed in 1212. This charter was issued following a visit to Cilicia of Hermann of Salza, the master of the Teutonic Knights,[88] and it contained, as we have seen, a specific reference to Otto IV's suzerainty. It was an eleemosinary grant, for which no service would be owed. Leon acknowledged himself to be a *confrater* of the Order and he granted the brothers throughout his kingdom freedom from the sales and purchase taxes levied on victuals, necessities and horses bought by them for their own use.[89] This was an important and far-reaching exemption, although the Teutonic Knights could not rival in possessions the march of the Templars in the Amanus or the great tract of territory on the western frontier of Cilicia acquired by the Hospitallers in 1210.[90]

The close relations between the Teutonic Knights and the Armenians continued after Leon's death. In 1225 the Order was supporting Constantine of Babaron at the time of the assassination of Philip of Antioch and the resulting march of Bohemond IV into Cilicia; indeed Bohemond was told that Philip was being held prisoner at Adamodana and that it was there that he was murdered.[91] In the 1230's Hetoum seems to have supported the Emperor Frederick II in

---

[84] Innocent III, *PL*. CCXVI, col. 54.

[85] *Tab. ord. Theut.*, no. 298.

[86] Wilbrand of Oldenburg, pp. 176, 179.

[87] Cahen, op. cit., p. 148; P. Deschamps, 'Le Château de Servantikar en Cilicie', *Syria*, XVIII (1937), p. 381.

[88] Wilbrand of Oldenburg, p. 178.

[89] *Tab. ord. Theut.*, nos. 46–7. See Wilbrand of Oldenburg, p. 179. J. Gottwald, *Burgen und Kirchen im mittleren Kilikien*, *BZ*. XLI (1941), pp. 90–1 believed that the estates of the Order stretched as far as the great Cilician castle of Yilan Kalesi.

[90] See Riley-Smith, *Knights of St. John*, p. 132.

[91] Bar Hebraeus, p. 381. See Cahen, op. cit., p. 635.

his struggle to dominate the baronage of the Kingdom of Jerusalem,[92] and it is not surprising that he should have shown favour to the emperor's most ardent supporters.[93] At this time he was facing pressure on the western frontier of the kingdom from the Selchukids and seems to have been concerned to ensure that the eastern border remained secure.[94] In January 1236 he established the nucleus of a march on his frontiers when he gave the Teutonic Knights at their request the important fief of Harunia (Haruniye) which, together with the neighbouring lordship of Sarvantikar, dominated the roads to Marash and Melitene through the northern Amanus, the main ways into Cilicia from the east.[95] The Teutonic Knights were given the same rights over Harunia as had been enjoyed by its previous lord,[96] but the wording of the charter suggests that the grant was made specifically for Cilicia's defensive needs.[97] Hetoum not only himself became a *confrater*, but appears to have put his whole kingdom into a special relationship with the Order.[98] In Harunia the Teutonic Knights enjoyed the same right to exact tolls as any lord, a right which led to a dispute with Constantine, lord of Sarvantikar, that was only settled after a visit to Armenia of the master Anno of Sangerhausen in 1271. The brothers had built a toll station at some point on the borders between Harunia and Sarvantikar without seeking Constantine's permission. He regarded this as an infringement of his rights, but a compromise was reached that enabled the brothers to continue to levy tolls at a place called the Black Tower.[99]

[92] See *Gestes des Chiprois, RHC.Arm.* II, p. 105.

[93] It has been suggested recently that behind the acceptance of the grant of 1236 by the Teutonic Knights was a desire to strengthen the position of the Hohenstaufen in the East. Forstreuter, *Deutsche Orden*, p. 63.

[94] In 1261 Hetoum was to marry his daughter Rita to the Lord of Sarvantikar, perhaps also a surety for the eastern frontier.

[95] Cahen, op. cit., pp. 145–6; Deschamps, *Servantikar*, passim.

[96] This lord was called in the charter Gaufridus, and may be the same Geoffrey as the father of Constantine of Sarvantikar referred to below. There were at Harunia some 'free' peasants, who answered to royal authority and also some who were owned by other Cilician lords. If the brothers wished, the revenues taken from these peasants would be shared. Otherwise the peasants would be removed from the lands.

[97] *Tab. ord. Theut.*, no. 83, corrected in some important particulars – including the extract quoted in n. 98 b   w – in a partial edition by Forstreuter (*Deutsche Orden*, pp. 235–6).

[98] 'Receperunt nostrum regnum in veram fraternitatem et sororitatem.'

[99] Ed. and trans. L. Alishan, *RHC.Arm.* II, p. 840 note. It was apparently witnessed by three brothers of the Order. Forstreuter (*Deutsche Orden*, pp. 62–3) has argued that the commitments of the Order elsewhere in Latin Christendom made it impossible for there to be further development of this march in eastern Cilicia.

The Teutonic Knights appointed an officer to supervise their properties in the Kingdom of Armenia sometime in the first half of the thirteenth century. The commander of Armenia was a capitular bailiff, appointed by the master with the consent of the General Chapter and therefore in the highest ranks of the provincial administrators.[100] The establishment of this officer presumably followed the acquisition of Harunia, for in 1213 Pope Innocent III had confirmed for the Order in Acre the acquisition of Adamodana and it seems that as late as 1236 the brothers in Cilicia were still answerable to the general authority of the Grand Commander in Palestine.[101]

*   *   *

In 1258 the three great Military Orders made an important agreement covering the procedure to be followed in the settlement of land disputes between them in the East, including Armenia.[102] But the end for them was drawing near. In 1266 Calamella, Adamodana and perhaps Port Bonnel fell to Baybars.[103] Adamodana was burnt down and does not seem to have been reoccupied; there was no garrison there to resist the Egyptians in 1298.[104] After Baybars had taken the city of Antioch on 18 May 1268 the Templars abandoned much of the Amanus. At Gaston they claimed to have taken away everything they could carry and to have burnt the rest, but on 27 May the Muslims found it well provisioned, although inhabited by one old woman only.[105] They also evacuated Port Bonnel and Roche Roussel,[106] but retained control of Roche Guillaume. We have seen that the Teutonic Knights were still holding Harunia in 1271. Sarvantikar nearby fell to the Mamluks in 1299, but was not finally lost by the Armenians until 1337.[107] By this time the attention of the Order had for long been drawn to lands far away on the north-eastern frontiers of Latin Europe

[100] *Die Statuten des Deutschen Ordens*, ed. M. Perlbach (Halle, 1890), pp. 59, 91, 97. The charter of 1271 may contain a reference to the commanders. *RHC.Arm.* II, p. 840 note.

[101] *Tab. ord. Theut.*, nos. 47, 83. The charter of 1236 was issued to the master and to Lutold, the grand commander in Acre.

[102] *Cart. gén. Hosp.*, no. 2902. Confirmation, no. 3565.

[103] Ibn al-Furāt, p. 99; al-Maqrīzī, I B, p. 34; Sempad, *Royal Chronicle*, p. 164, n. 75.

[104] See al-Maqrīzī, II B, pp. 60-5, esp. p. 61, note 18.

[105] *Cart. gén. Hosp.*, no. 3308 (vol. IV); *Eracles, RHC.Occ.* II, p. 457; *Gestes des Chiprois*, p. 191; Ibn al-Furāt, p. 127; al-Maqrīzī, I B, p. 56.

[106] *Eracles, RHC.Occ.* II, p. 457; *Gestes des Chiprois*, p. 191.

[107] Deschamps, *Servantikar*, pp. 387-8.

PLATE 40

SARVANTIKAR

Curtain wall

The castle controlled one of the routes from Marash into Cilicia and was of considerable strategic importance. Hence its constant change of occupiers between Armenia and Antioch. In a thickly wooded area, the ruins are much overgrown by trees but the outer walls still show the small blocks and rounded towers typical of Armenian fortification.

and in the fourteenth century[108] commanders of Armenia were no longer being appointed. It is not possible to be more precise about the date of departure of the Templars. In 1285 their commander of Armenia negotiated with the Mamluk sultan Kalavun on behalf of Leon III[109] and after the loss in 1291 of their castles in Palestine and Syria the brothers, with their headquarters now in Cyprus, lent aid to Cilicia.[110] Roche Guillaume remained in their hands until 1299 when it was taken by a Mamluk army.[111] It must be presumed that with the falling of that fortress they lost the last of their Armenian possessions.

[108] *Die Statuten*, p. 59 (variant of statutes in French).

[109] al-Maqrizi, II A, pp. 166, 201, 212.

[110] Pope Nicholas IV, *Régistre*, ed. E. Langlois (Paris, 1905), nos. 6854–5. See *Annales ecclesiastici* XXIII, p. 237. They may have been interfering in the internal politics of Cilicia. See the statement of James of Molay in 1306–7 that the Armenians were suspicious of Frankish designs. *Vitae pap. Aven.*, III, p. 147.

[111] *Gestes des Chiprois*, p. 292. In 1310 a Templar called Peter of Tripoli told the Papal Commission enquiring into the brothers in Cyprus that he had been received into the Order twenty-two years before in Roche Guillaume. *Processus Cypricus*, ed. K. Schottmüller, *Der Untergang des Templer-Ordens* (Berlin, 1887), II, p. 206.

I

5

THE HOSPITALLERS' INTERVENTIONS IN CILICIAN ARMENIA: 1291–1375

Western attitudes towards the Armenians varied during the period after the last of the Christian possessions in Syria fell to the Mamluks in 1291. The Latins had a general obligation to defend their fellow Christians, and after the loss of their Syrian ports Western traders were increasingly drawn to Ayas, or Laiazzo as it was then known, an important harbour and market in the Gulf of Iskenderum where they could secure the profitable luxury goods of Asia. On the other hand, the Latins mistrusted the Armenians, whose Church was in a state of schism with Rome and whose ruling dynasty seemed perpetually unstable. At a time of troubles and preoccupations in the West, the papacy and the Latin powers showed only mild enthusiasm for a new crusade. Mongol and Armenian envoys visited the West in search of alliances and aid against the Mamluks in Egypt and Syria, but the Latins made no effective response and did little to secure the conversion of the Mongols to Christianity. Western rulers were prepared to undertake limited amphibious operations in which they could exploit their sea-power to temporary advantage, but they were reluctant to involve themselves in major continental warfare which offered little prospect of success against a great land-power such as the Mamluks.[1] James II of Aragon, for example, was typical in that he maintained diplomatic relations with the Armenians and spoke of a crusade, but was in reality concerned above all to secure favourable conditions for his subjects to trade in Cilicia.[2]

[1] There is no satisfactory recent study of Latin interests in Cilicia. For a survey to 1307, with useful bibliography, S. der Nersessian, 'The Kingdom of Cilician Armenia', in *A History of the Crusades*, ed. K. Setton, II (2nd ed. Madison, Wisc., 1969); see also G. Hill, *A History of Cyprus* II (Cambridge, 1948). For recent publications, H. Mayer, 'Literaturbericht über die Geschichte der Kreuzzüge: Veröffentlichungen 1958–1967', *Historische Zeitschrift* CCVII (1969).

[2] F. Giunta, *Aragonesi e Catalani nel Mediterraneo* II (Palermo, 1959), pp. 137–9.

The position of the Hospital of St John of Jerusalem was rather different, for its very existence depended on its being able to maintain a semblance of warfare against Islam. After 1291 the Hospital established its new headquarters in Cyprus, where the brethren of the Order sought to employ the resources which they drew from their European estates in the continuation of crusading activity. The Hospital did take part in various ineffectual campaigns against the Mamluks in Egypt and Syria. It was only after 1306, when they began their conquest of Rhodes, that the Hospitallers shifted the focus of their activities away from Cyprus and the Southern Levant towards *Romania* and those Aegean lands disputed between Byzantines and Turks.[3]

Before 1306 there had however been an alternative to intervention in *Romania*, that of assisting the Armenians of Cilicia in the defence of what was almost the last major Christian foothold on the mainland of Asia. The Hospitallers had long been established in the western part of Cilicia, where the Armenian crown intended that they should defend the country against the Selchukid Turks. Early in the thirteenth century the Hospitallers increased their Cilician holdings through their intervention in succession disputes; they secured considerable estates at important points, such as Silifke, but they soon lost control of many of these possessions, being compelled to retreat, like the Armenians themselves, under continual pressure from Turks, Mongols and Mamluks. In 1252 the Hospitallers helped to arrange the marriage of an Armenian princess, and in 1281 the prior of England and other brethren fought with the Armenian king alongside the Mongols at Homs in the battle against the Mamluks. The Hospital's Cilician possessions were organised as the preceptory of Armenia, and towards the end of the thirteenth century the preceptor of Armenia had his own seal and was assisted by a treasurer. In fact the brethren in Syria valued their Cilician estates, depending to a considerable extent on their resources.[4] But their estates continued to dwindle; the Mamluks took

[3] The standard works are J. Riley-Smith, *The Knights of St. John in Jerusalem and Cyprus: c. 1050–1310* (London, 1967), and J. Delaville le Roulx, *Les Hospitaliers à Rhodes jusqu'à la mort de Philibert de Naillac: 1310–1421* (Paris, 1913); the latter is somewhat outdated. For a general assessment of Hospitaller policy, A. Luttrell, 'The Crusade in the Fourteenth Century', *Europe in the Late Middle Ages*, ed. J. Hale *et al.* (London, 1965); on the Templars' involvement, M. Barber, 'James of Molay, the last Grand Master of the Order of the Temple,' *Studia Monastica*, XIV (1972).

[4] Riley-Smith, pp. 132, 152–63, 432, 442, 495–505 *et passim*; C. Cahen, *La Syrie du Nord à l'époque des croisades et la principauté franque d'Antioche* (Paris, 1940), pp. 510–526 *et passim*. These authors use the documents in J. Delaville le Roulx, *Cartulaire général de l'Ordre des Hospitaliers de S. Jean de Jérusalem: 1100–1310*, 4 vols. (Paris,

PLATE 41

CORYCUS

The land castle from the east

The castle was built among the ruins of a Roman and early Christian city; hence it consists almost entirely of re-used material, which accounts for the unusual prevalence of smooth-dressed blocks. The mediaeval walls are tied at short intervals by column-drums laid horizontally, and incorporate ornamented marble blocks where exceptional coherence was advisable. The intact Roman doorway, through which one tower is still entered, could have been robbed from a tomb, but the seaward gateway as a whole can scarcely be later than Byzantine; it led to a causeway in the sea, popularly supposed to have reached the fortified island (Pl. 42) though in fact a mere jetty. The 'very strong fortress' of which these are relics became an abandoned ruin, says Anna Comnena, but the repairs her father undertook at the beginning of the twelfth century may have left much of the older work still in place. Alterations in the following 300 or more years were probably made not only by the Armenians but also by their European allies and successors.

The castle is surrounded by a ditch, which on the east side is cut in hard rock to sea-level; except where a drawbridge crossed, the outward edge was heightened by masonry of which remnants are visible in the foreground of the photograph. One line of wall rises from the inward edge, and another of greater height stands behind so narrow an intervening strip of ground as to produce the effect of a second ditch.

A. W. L.

Arsuf from the Hospitallers in 1265, and Safad and *Arassous* from the Templars in 1266. These places were described by an Armenian chronicler as the fortresses of the brethren 'who wear the garments marked with the cross'.[5] Yet as late as 1282 the Hospital sent a hundred armed horsemen, 50 Hospitallers and 50 turcopoles, to aid the Armenians at their king's request.[6]

After the loss of Syria the Hospital continued to hold certain estates in Armenia and to maintain an interest in that country. During the years that they were based in Cyprus the Hospitallers, having lost their original mission of the defence of Jerusalem and Syria, needed to justify their continued possession of vast estates in the West by some show of crusading activity in the East. On 23 January 1292 Pope Nicholas IV was already instructing the Hospital and the Temple to use their galleys in defence of the Armenians.[7] Certainly there were still Hospitallers with a knowledge of the country such as Boniface de Calamandracen, grand preceptor of the Hospital and one of the most important brethren of his time.[8] He was probably at Ayas in March 1279[9] and he possessed a translation of Albertus Magnus' *Libellus de Alchimia* given to him by one of the Armenian kings.[10] In 1294 the masters of the Hospital and Temple were present at the coronation, probably at Sis, of King Hetoum of Armenia.[11] Hetoum's reign was a troubled one, but his pro-Latin leanings resulted in closer contacts with Cyprus; he was a convert to the Roman Church who became a Franciscan, and he married his sister to Aimery of Lusignan, lord of

1894–1906), but it is difficult to decide which properties were granted to the Hospital, where they were, and for how long the Hospital held them; a detailed analysis of these questions was made in J. Riley-Smith, *The Knights Hospitallers in Latin Syria* (unpublished Ph.D thesis: Cambridge, 1964). Little or nothing can be said on the basis of surviving buildings or inscriptions. On the Latin military orders in Armenia, see also V. Langlois, *Le Trésor des chartes d'Arménie: ou Cartulaire de la Chancellerie royale des Roupéniens* (Paris, 1863), pp. 72–82, and now Riley-Smith, *supra*. For Silifke, see J. Langendorf and G. Zimmermann, in *Genava* n.s. XII (1964), pp. 155–65.

[5] S. der Nersessian, 'The Armenian Chronicle of the Constable Sempad or of the "Royal Historian" ', *DOP.* XIII (1959), p. 164 and n. 1; *Arassous* remains unidentified.

[6] Text in *Cartulaire* III, no. 3782.

[7] Text in *Cartulaire* III, no. 4183.

[8] Cf. Riley-Smith, pp. 205–6, 370–1; Boniface was dead by 1298.

[9] Text in C. Desimoni, 'Actes passés en 1271, 1274 et 1279 à l'Aïas (Petite Arménie) et à Beyrouth par devant des notaires génois', *AOL.* I (1881), pp. 511–12. In 1288 the king of Aragon complained that because Fr. Boniface was his kinsman he had been sent to die of the bad climate in Armenia: *Cartulaire* III, no. 4007.

[10] J. Morelli, *I codici manoscritti volgari della Libreria Naniana* (Venice, 1776), p. 48.

[11] Hetoum of Gorighos, *Flos Historiarum Terre Orientis*, in *RHC.Arm.* II, p. 330.

Tyre, the brother of King Henry II of Cyprus. From Cyprus the Hospitallers kept in contact with Armenia, and when in 1299 Hetoum overthrew his brothers Sempad and Constantine, who had seized power a few years earlier, the Hospitallers in particular apparently gave him a measure of assistance.[12]

In 1299 Ghazan, the Mongol Il-Khan of Persia, invaded Syria, accompanied by Armenian forces which assisted in the rout of the Mamluks near Homs in December. Ghazan twice invited Henry II of Cyprus and the masters of the Temple, the Hospital and the Teutonic Order to join in his campaign. In November the king of Cyprus, the master of the Temple and the grand preceptor of the Hospital conferred together, but inconclusively; the traditional rivalries between the orders probably came into play.[13] The Hospitallers were involved in an acute constitutional crisis during 1299 and 1300, and their master reached Cyprus from the West only late in 1300,[14] while at the same time the Templars were openly quarrelling with King Henry.[15] The Templar castle of *Rocca Guillelmi*, where there was a *domus* and a preceptor of Armenia in about 1288,[16] was taken by the Muslims in 1299,[17] and it is possible that certain brethren of the Hospital and Temple who were stationed in Cilicia may have fought with the Armenian king alongside the Mongols. There were even rumours in the West that Ghazan had temporarily restored to the two orders their former Syrian estates;[18] in fact, Ghazan did offer to return to the Latins their possessions in Syria, but the envoys who took back a reply to Ghazan arrived from Cyprus only after the battle at Homs.[19] In 1300 however the Latins

[12] *Infra*, pp. 123, 129 and 130.

[13] Amadi wrote: *Et fatto conseglio el re con li maestri del Tempio, et commandator del Hospital, che teniva el loco del maestro, non se accordavano troppo tra loro*: in *Chroniques de Chypre d'Amadi et de Strambaldi*, ed. R. de Mas-Latrie, I (Paris, 1891), pp. 234–5. Bustron wrote that the envoy *parlò con li maestri dell'Hospital e del Tempio, quali non furono d'accordo tra loro*: in *Chronique de l'île de Chypre*, ed. *idem* (Paris, 1886), pp. 129–30.   [14] Riley-Smith, pp. 207–8.

[15] Hill, II, pp. 198–9, 202–3; Barber, pp. 97–8.

[16] Text in K. Schottmüller, *Der Untergang des Templer-Ordens* II (Berlin, 1887), p. 206. The Templar Preceptor of Armenia was entrusted in 1285 with the negotiation of a peace between the Armenian and Egyptian rulers (*RHC.Arm.* I, p. lxxxii).

[17] *Les Gestes des Chiprois*, ed. G. Raynaud (Geneva, 1887), p. 292, which does not, however, state whether the Temple still held the castle in 1299.

[18] References in R. Röhricht, 'Les Batailles de Hims (1281 et 1299)', *AOL*. I (1881), p. 649, n. 76.

[19] See Hetoum, II, pp. 319–20, and three letters of 1300: texts in L. Muratori, *Rerum Italicarum Scriptores* XII, part 1 (revised ed.: Bologna, 1938), pp. 396–8; H. Finke, *Acta Aragonensia*, 3 vols. (Berlin-Leipzig, 1908–22), III, pp. 90–1.

responded to Ghazan's invitations, and in July Cypriot, Templar and Hospitaller forces sailed to attack the Egyptian and Syrian coasts; they had some success at Tortosa, but the Hospitallers' troops were routed in a small engagement at Maraclea. Subsequently the Templars and the Hospitallers, who were now led by their master Fr William of Villaret, briefly occupied the island of Ruad off Tortosa.[20]

Statutes of the Hospital passed in 1300[21] and 1301[22] showed that brethren still went fairly regularly to Cilicia, while between 1300 and 1305 the master Fr William of Villaret led two considerable expeditions to Armenia and stayed there some time.[23] But if there was a moment when the Hospitallers considered some more serious involvement in Cilicia, it passed. The country continued to suffer from Mamluk attacks, while Hetoum abdicated in 1305 and was killed in 1307. The Hospitallers were in an unsatisfactory position on an island from which it was difficult to prosecute an effective semblance of crusading activity and where they were at the mercy of the Crown. The political situation in Cyprus deteriorated in 1306, and in that year the Hospitallers initiated the conquest of Rhodes, which provided them with an independent base from which they could oppose the Turks.[24]

A few crusading propagandists still advocated intervention in Armenia. One theorist, possibly Otto of Grandson, had argued at the end of the thirteenth century for a landing at Ayas, where the Armenian king would give assistance and a junction could be made with the Mongols.[25] Others, such as Fidenzio of Padua and the Armenian historian Prince Hetoum, also favoured an overland attack on Syria using Cilicia as a base; they emphasised the advantages of good harbours in Christian hands, of deflecting trade through Ayas, and of the

[20] Hill, II, pp. 212–16; Riley-Smith, pp. 198–9.

[21] *illis exceptis qui ibunt ad ultramarinas partes seu Erminie, aut de hinc ad Suriam* (*Cartulaire* III, no. 4515, para. 16).

[22] The statutes spoke of brethren *qui sera par le mareschal en Ermenie*, and *quant freres partent dou covent pour aner en Ermenie* (*Cartulaire* IV, no. 4549, paras. 8–9).

[23] . . . *eundo bis in Armeniam cum magna comitiva equitum et peditum et ibidem morando aliquo tempore*: text in Finke, III, p. 146.

[24] A. Luttrell, 'The Hospitallers in Cyprus after 1291', *First International Congress of Cypriot Studies* II (Nicosia, 1972), pp. 163–5; contrary to the accepted view, it is clear that the initiative for the conquest actually came from the Hospital.

[25] C. Kohler, 'Deux Projets de croisade en Terre-Sainte composés à la fin du XIIIe siècle et au début du XIVe', *ROL*. X (1903–4). One text (pre-April 1289) suggested that the Hospitallers and Templars should assist the crusade when it reached Armenia; the other (probably post-1312) mentioned only the Hospitallers (ibid., pp. 413, 430, 453).

availability in Armenia of horses and supplies. The majority considered the overland route too difficult and expensive, and judged that victuals would be in short supply. Most of the Latins never overcame their suspicions of the Armenians, especially over the religious issue. James of Molay, master of the Temple, reported to the pope in 1305 that the Armenians were suspicious of Latin intentions and would refuse to co-operate or would flee to the mountains, and that the country and climate were so unhealthy that within a year a force of 4,000 Latin knights would be reduced to 500. A more balanced judgment was that of the Venetian Marino Sanudo who knew Cilicia well; he opposed the use of Armenia as a base for an attack on Syria, but saw the economic advantages of maintaining Christian rule there, and he repeatedly called for an expedition to assist the Armenian Christians against the infidel.[26] In 1309 a crusading *passagium* did sail to the East under Fr Fulk of Villaret, master of the Hospital, but it went to Rhodes and there was no hint in the various crusade projects drawn up by Fr Fulk, nephew of Fr William of Villaret, that he had any particular intention of fighting in Armenia.[27]

Their implication in Cypriot politics created difficulties for the Hospitallers in Armenia. In 1306 Henry II of Cyprus was forced into retirement by his brother Aimery, whose wife Isabella was a sister of King Oshin of Armenia; in the ensuing struggle Aimery was encouraged by the Templars, while the Hospitallers at first remained neutral and then supported Henry. When Aimery was assassinated on 5 June 1310 his Armenian supporters accused the Hospitallers, who were active in the subsequent restoration of Henry. Aimery had previously moved Henry into custody in Armenia, where the grand preceptor of the Hospital, Fr Guy of Séverac, was sent by the master to see him; Oshin prevented the grand preceptor from seeing the king, but Séverac was able to return to Cyprus with a sealed letter by which Henry appointed the master of the Hospital, Fr Fulk of Villaret, to rule for him in Cyprus. Séverac reached Famagusta with this letter on the very day of Aimery's death; he at once returned

[26] Survey in A. S. Atiya, *The Crusade in the Later Middle Ages* (London, 1938), pp. 41–3, 55–6, 59, 62–4, 79–80, 105–6, 122–6, *et passim*.

[27] Text by a Master of the Hospital in *Cartulaire* IV, no. 4681, where it is assigned to Fulk of Villaret and probably to 1305; text of Villaret's letter of 1309, ibid., IV, no. 4841; text in Paris, Bibliothèque Nationale, MS. Lat. 7470, ff. 172–8, which was probably composed after 1306 but during Villaret's Mastership, possibly *c.* 1309. J. Delaville le Roulx, *La France en Orient au XIVe siècle* I (Paris, 1886), pp. 79–81, summarised this last document, dating it to 1323/28; the present author plans to publish this text, which deserves further study.

to Cilicia in an unsuccessful attempt to secure Henry's release, but was compelled to sail back to Famagusta, having narrowly escaped capture.[28] The Hospitallers were clearly in conflict with Oshin; Armenian exiles were finding refuge at Rhodes, and it was rumoured that the master planned to remove Henry from Armenia to Rhodes.[29] It was probably at this time that Oshin sequestrated the Hospital's Armenian estates, and effective participation by the Hospital in the defence of Armenia was scarcely possible, though it was still discussed. In March 1309 James II of Aragon reported to the pope that his advisers considered that the Hospital's coming expedition could deter the Mamluks from attacking Cyprus or Cilicia, but the Aragonese king correctly foresaw that the Hospitallers would concentrate on the conquest of Rhodes and he discounted their empty boast that in five years they would be in Jerusalem.[30]

Once the subjugation of Rhodes was complete the Hospitallers were occupied with the fortification, colonisation and defence of their new territories, which included certain conquests on the mainland,[31] but they retained at least some of their Armenian possessions. The fate of the Cilician estates of the Templars after their dissolution in 1312 is obscure; it is unlikely that any of their lands passed to the Hospital, as they should have done according to the pope's instructions. The possessions of the Teutonic Order were united with those in Sicily and administered by a *magnus preceptor* of Sicily and Armenia.[32] The Hospitallers' Armenian estates still constituted a preceptory which in 1319 was granted for life to Fr Maurice of Pagnac, who became *generalis preceptor Hospitalis . . . in regno Armenie*.[33] Pagnac was an influential Hospitaller; he had been elected master of Rhodes in 1317 on the deposition of Fr Fulk of Villaret, but the pope quashed the election two years later. At this time the Hospital's lands were in fact in the hands of the Armenian king who had confiscated them.

[28] Hill, II, pp. 216–62; Riley-Smith, pp. 210–15; Luttrell, 'Hospitallers in Cyprus', pp. 165–7. These accounts are based mainly on the chronicles of Amadi and Bustron.

[29] Text in C. Perrat, 'Un Diplomate gascon au XIVᵉ siècle: Raymond de Piis, nonce de Clément V en Orient', *Mélanges d'archéologie et d'histoire* XLIV (1927), pp. 70–1.

[30] Text in Finke, III, pp. 198–9.

[31] A. Luttrell, 'Feudal Tenure and Latin Colonization at Rhodes: 1306–1415', *English Historical Review* LXXXV (1970), pp. 755–7.

[32] Text of 1336 in C. Trasselli, 'Sugli Europei in Armenia', *Archivio storico italiano* CXXII (1964), p. 490, n. 25; cf. K. Forstreuter, *Der Deutsche Orden am Mittelmeer* (Bonn, 1967), pp. 59–67, 200, n. 21, 234–7.

[33] Text in J. Richard, *Chypre sous les Lusignans* (Paris, 1962), pp. 115–17. There seems to be no reference in the documents from which any of the Hospital's Cilician properties held during the period after 1291 can be identified.

The Hospitallers were still closely involved in Cypriot affairs, and they arranged the marriage of the king of Cyprus' daughter to James II of Aragon which took place in 1315.[34] The Hospitallers' support of the regime in Cyprus may have increased King Oshin's antagonism towards them. Pope John XXII in a bull of 5 May 1318 commended to the Hospitallers his legates to Armenia, who were to request the cessation of persecutions against the Hospital there.[35] On 13 August 1319 John XXII instructed Pagnac and the papal collector in the East to exhort King Henry of Cyprus and King Oshin of Armenia to observe the truce they had made,[36] and the two papal agents did succeed in securing a new truce.[37] Over a year later, on 22 September 1320, the pope wrote to Leon, the new king of Armenia, requesting the return of the Hospital's properties and promising that Pagnac would reside on these estates and defend them. This bull rehearsed the story of how, following the fall of Acre, the Hospitallers had failed to defend their Armenian lands so that the Crown had justifiably confiscated them, and of how for a space of time they had served once again so that Oshin, who became king in 1308, had returned their properties, only to take them away again when the Hospitallers once more failed to provide the service due.[38] A similar bull of the same date instructed that Pagnac or a substitute should take up residence in Armenia and assist in its defence.[39]

The situation in Armenia became desperate when the Mongols, Turks and Mamluks all attacked in 1321. Discussions about a projected Armenian expedition had been dragging on for years at the papal and French courts;[40] and in response to the new crisis Pope John XXII arranged for money to be sent to the Armenians. In fact a total of only 37,722 florins was paid to the bankers, who were to send it to the Armenians, during the whole of John XXII's long pontificate; some of this money was used to rebuild the fortifications at Ayas and elsewhere, while ships were constructed in Cyprus and supplies sent to Cilicia.[41] Fr Maurice of Pagnac, the preceptor of Armenia, apparently did serve

[34] A. Luttrell, 'The Aragonese Crown and the Knights Hospitallers of Rhodes: 1291–1350', *English Historical Review* LXXVI (1961), pp. 5–6.

[35] Archivio Vaticano, Reg. Vat. 109, ff. 207v–208; text in S. Pauli, *Codice diplomatico del Sacro Militare Ordine Gerosolimitano* II (Lucca, 1737), p. 67.

[36] Archivio Vaticano, Reg. Aven. 12, ff. 83v–84.

[37] Reg. Aven. 14, ff. 124–24v.

[38] Reg. Aven. 14, f. 426v (text *infra*, pp. 135 and 137).

[39] Reg. Aven. 14, f. 123–23v.

[40] G. Tabacco, *La casa di Francia nell'azione politica di Papa Giovanni XXII* (Rome, 1953), pp. 218–34.

[41] Texts and references in Richard, pp. 36–49.

with a force of horse and foot in defence of the kingdom; on 25 October 1324 the pope exempted him from the payment of papal tenths in Cyprus on the grounds that he had maintained *plures equites et armigeri* for the defence of Armenia at his own expense, and that the destruction inflicted on Armenia by the Muslims had reduced his Armenian incomes to little or nothing.[42] At this time there was possibly some sort of rapprochement between the Hospital and the powerful baron Oshin of Gorighos, the leading member of the regency council which sent John and Bohemond, sons of Aimery of Lusignan, lord of Tyre, into exile at Rhodes; they were courteously received by the Hospitallers and stayed in Rhodes for three years. Subsequently Bohemond became count of Gorighos while John, who was constable of Armenia, ruled the country for a brief spell in 1341.[43] Pagnac himself was one of three agents instructed by the pope on 9 April 1323 to work for a peace between King Leon of Armenia and King Henry of Cyprus.[44]

Meanwhile plans for more active assistance remained under discussion in Avignon until news arrived that the Armenians had made a truce with the Mamluks, that they had agreed to pay tribute, and that they were themselves opposed to the idea of an armed expedition.[45] None of the many crusading schemes presented to John XXII in 1323 envisaged any Hospitaller participation in such a crusade,[46] but the *Ramenbranze* which Marino Sanudo wrote when presenting his crusade treatise to the king of France in 1323 did call for a force which would defend Armenia and to which Cyprus and Rhodes were to provide galleys; Sanudo added: *Les Isles de Cypre et de Rodes pourront bien aider Armenie continuellement de cccl. hommes a cheual.* A Latin variation of this preface, written at about the same time, claimed that the Hospital, which was by then spending less on the defence of Rhodes, could afford 150 armed horsemen from its Cypriot and Armenian incomes: *Hospitale tum propter diminutionem custodiae Rodi Insulae, tum de redditibus quos in Cypro et Armenia percipit posset large dicto regno Armeniae de cl. armatis equitibus subuenire.*[47] On 1 September 1326 James II of Aragon had heard that the master of the Hospital and Louis of Clermont, who had been nominated as the commander of an eventual French

---

[42] Reg. Aven. 22, ff. 338–338v.

[43] According, at least, to Jean Dardel, *Chronique d'Arménie*, in *RHC.Arm.* II, p. 19; cf. ibid., II, p. 21 notes.

[44] Reg. Vat. 62, ff. 12v–13.

[45] Tabacco, pp. 234–7.

[46] Texts in *Lettres secrètes et curiales du pape Jean XXII (1316–1334) relatives à la France*, ed. A. Coulon (Paris, 1906), nos. 1682–1711.

[47] Texts in G. Bongars, *Gesta Dei per Francos* II (Hanover, 1611), pp. 5–7.

expedition, were proposing to lead a force of nobles to Armenia.[48] Meanwhile Pagnac died in Armenia and was buried in Cyprus.[49] Following his death, and acting upon the master's request, John XXII wrote once again on 25 September 1328 demanding that the Hospitallers' Cilician estates be returned to them.[50] In effect the preceptory of Armenia was gradually disappearing; from about 1330 it was not expected to pay *responsiones*, though it still existed on paper.[51] There was a preceptor of Armenia, Fr Nienaut of Pomiers, in 1340,[52] and there were *gubernatores* in the preceptory as late as 1347.[53]

By 1332 the Armenian king was in such trouble that he begged John XXII to persuade the Hospitallers to accept the offer, as a gift in perpetuity, of two castles which the Armenians could not defend and would otherwise have to sell to the Turks or raze to the ground; the Hospitallers were to undertake the defence of the castles, and the pope wrote on 2 August 1332 exhorting them to do so. The papal bull referred to *duo Castra situata in marchia paganorum Turchorum, quorum unum Siquinum prope mare ad miliare, et aliud Anthioceta in Rupe supra mare posita . . .*[54] Both these places were on the coast and accessible to the Hospital's vessels. The former was apparently Sechin, on the Cilician coast between Anamur and Silifke; the latter was Anthiochia Parva or *ad Cragum* just west of Anamur.[55] In April and May 1336 the new pope, Benedict XII, unable to arrange immediate military aid, responded to desperate pleas from Armenia by sending grain and according indulgences to any inhabitants of Sicily, Cyprus, Rhodes and other eastern islands who would serve against the infidels in Cilicia.[56] Ayas was lost to the Mamluks in the following year.[57] The

[48] Barcelona, Archivo de la Corona de Aragón, Reg. 249, ff. 218–218v. (Señorita Mercedes Costa kindly traced this document, misleadingly cited in Finke II, p. 742).

[49] According to one version of a brief chronicle of the Masters of the Hospital: Toulouse, Archives départementales de la Haute-Garonne, H Malte 12, f. 56.

[50] Reg. Vat. 115, f. 92 (*olim* 64).

[51] Text in C. Tipton, 'The 1330 Chapter General of the Knights Hospitallers at Montpellier', *Traditio* XXIV (1968), pp. 302–3, 308.

[52] Valetta, Royal Malta Library, Archives of the Order of St. John, cod. 280, f. 46.

[53] Reg. Vat. 140, f. 280 (text *infra*, p. 141).

[54] Reg. Vat. 102, ff. 104v–105: text in Pauli, II, pp. 81–2 (inaccurately), and Raynaldus, 1332, xxiv. *RHC.Arm.* I, p. xxxiv, wrongly gives 22 August. O. Raynaldus, *Annales ecclesiastici*, 15 vols. (Lucca, 1747–56), is the edition used here, with references *ad annum* and by paragraph.

[55] Cf. L. Alishan, *Sissouan ou l'Arméno-Cilicie* (Venice, 1899), pp. 352–4, 377, 383.

[56] C. Daumet, 'Benoît XII et la Croisade', in his *Benoît XII 1334–1342: lettres closes, patentes et curiales se rapportant à la France* (Paris, 1920), p. liv; texts ibid., nos. 109, 151–2, 155, 175–6.   [57] *Infra*, pp. 137ff.

PLATE 42   CORYCUS

The Sea Castle seen from the moat of the Land Castle

The land castle on the beach and the island castle, a short way from the shore, form one of the most romantic groups of medieval buildings. The island castle, now only an outer circle of walls and towers, has Armenian inscriptions of 1206 and 1251. Its wanton diversity of tower-shapes is unparalleled in any specifically Armenian fortification and may be due to the retention of earlier features.   A. W. L.

Hospitallers had done nothing; in fact, they were at last solvent and preparing for some sort of expedition in 1336 when Benedict himself cancelled any further crusading activity, partly perhaps because the Hospital's considerable credits were deposited with the pope's own hard-pressed bankers. Thereafter the Latins were increasingly preoccupied in the Aegean rather than in Cilicia, and this concern resulted in the Latin crusade which captured Smyrna from the Turks in 1344.[58] In any case, while the Latin and ecclesiastically Roman elements in Armenia looked to the West for support, the 'national' party was suspicious of papal aid since it was accompanied by strong pressure on the Armenian Church. An Armenian appeal for aid, made in 1343, produced no effective response from the West,[59] though on 8 September 1344 Clement VI did instruct the papal legate at Smyrna to send vessels to assist the king of Armenia.[60]

During 1346, in the face of renewed Mamluk attacks, King Constantine of Armenia sent his *secretarius* Constantius to seek help in the West.[61] Clement VI in turn ordered the bishops of Gaeta and Coron to inspect the orthodoxy of the Armenian Church, and on 3 September 1346 he recommended them to the master of the Hospital, who was to secure their passage from Rhodes to Cyprus;[62] they reached Cilicia in March 1347.[63] Following their report, Clement took action. On 26 September 1347 the pope sent Constantius back to the Armenian king to urge him to settle the doctrinal differences between the Roman and Armenian Churches, hinting that this would be the prerequisite for Latin assistance.[64] Clement also instructed the archbishop of Crete, who was his legate in the East and captain of the Latin fleet in the Aegean, to send vessels to provide help if the Armenian king requested it, but only in so far as this would not prejudice the Latin position at Smyrna: . . . *auxilijs et fauoribus oportunis quantum poteritis sine preiudicio negociorum fidei, ad que estis specialiter*

---

[58] Luttrell, 'The Crusade', pp. 133–5, with references.

[59] J. Gay, *Le Pape Clément VI et les affaires d'Orient: 1342–1352* (Paris, 1904), pp. 133–46.

[60] Text in C. Kohler, 'Lettres pontificales concernant l'histoire de la Petite Arménie au XIVe siècle', *Florilegium . . . Melchior de Vogüé* (Paris, 1909), p. 320.

[61] Reg. Vat. 140, ff, 210v–11.

[62] Reg. Vat. 140, ff. 111–12.

[63] Reg. Vat. 141, ff. 88–88v: text in G. Golubovich, *Biblioteca biobibliografica della Terra Santa e dell'Oriente francescano* IV (Quaracchi, 1923), p. 374. *Clément VI (1342–1352): Lettres closes, patentes et curiales intéressant les pays autres que la France*, ed. E. Déprez–G. Mollat (Paris, 1960), no. 1488, wrongly gives May.

[64] Reg. Vat. 141, f. 90: text in Raynaldus, 1347, xxix, and Déprez–Mollat, no. 1493.

deputati, efficaciter assistere studeatis.[65] On the same day, 26 September, the pope wrote to the master of Rhodes, Fr Dieudonné of Gozon, and to Hugh of Lusignan, king of Cyprus, encouraging them to continue to provide assistance or *auxilia* for the defence of the Cilician coast; these bulls stated that the Hospitallers and Cypriots had already made some contribution to the defence of Cilicia: *oportunis favoribus potenter assistere studuisti.*[66] The Hospitallers were involved and may have recovered some of their Armenian possessions, for on 29 April 1347 Clement had recommended Fr Dalmacius de Baucio to the *Gubernatores Prioratus Armenie hospitalis Sancti Johannis Jerosolomitani, eodem Prioratu uacante*, whom the bull did not actually name.[67] In addition, on 25 September, Clement wrote requesting the doge of Venice to use his influence with the Mamluk sultan in Cairo to obtain the restitution of Ayas, Constantine having sent envoys who were to ask the Venetians for help in the recovery of the town.[68]

Following various negotiations conducted by the Armenian envoy Constantine of Portella, who had been three years in Avignon, Clement sent him on 24 September 1351 to the kings of Armenia and Cyprus and to the master of the Hospital; on the same day he ordered the master of the Hospital, the king of Cyprus and the captain of Smyrna to send aid to Cilicia. As in so many papal exhortations of the period, no specific action was suggested in these bulls, which simply referred to assistance in the most general terms.[69] Clement also sent Fr Raymond Berenguer, preceptor of Castelsarrasin, with a message to the master but his letter of credence, dated 12 September 1351, gives no hint as to the nature of the message.[70] These appeals produced no action. At this time the Hospitallers in particular and the Latins in general were concerned with the retention of Smyrna, and they were also planning to aid Byzantium against the

[65] Reg. Vat. 141, f. 89v.

[66] Reg. Vat. 141, f. 89v: both texts in Kohler, *Lettres*, p. 323. Gay, p. 148, wrote of 'quelques vaisseaux . . . peut-être aussi quelques troupes de terre'; presumably he followed Bosio, who wrote of 'ships' and 'soldiers', which are not explicitly mentioned in the bull (*infra*, p. 140).

[67] Reg. Vat. 140, f. 280: text *infra*, p. 141.

[68] Reg. Vat. 141, ff. 89–89v: text in Raynaldus, 1347, xxviii; partially, in Déprez–Mollat, no. 1489; and *infra*, pp. 146, 147. Reg. Vat. 62, ff. 86–7, also contains the bulls of September 1347.

[69] Reg. Vat. 145, ff. 83–4: texts in Déprez-Mollat, nos. 2502–4: cf. nos. 2306, 2306 bis, 2498, 2501, 2505.

[70] Reg. Vat. 145, ff. 63v–64: text in *Clément VI (1342–1352): Lettres se rapportant à la France*, ed. E. Déprez–G. Mollat III (Paris, 1959), no. 5057.

Ottomans, who established themselves across the Dardanelles in 1354. Only for a brief period did effective Latin assistance reach Armenian Cilicia; this came after the papal legate Peter Thomas had abandoned the Greeks in 1360 and 1361 and, in alliance with Peter of Lusignan king of Cyprus, had transferred the centre of crusading activity to the Southern Levant. The Hospitallers provided four galleys and a number of brethren for the campaign in which King Peter captured Adalia in Cilicia in August 1361, their experienced troops playing a distinguished part at a difficult moment in the battle. The Hospital participated fully in Peter's great crusade of 1365 which set out from Rhodes and might well have attacked the Muslims in Armenia, though in fact it sailed to capture Alexandria in Egypt. In 1367 the Hospitallers again sent four galleys and a good number of other vessels to assist Peter, whose action included the restoration of order among the Latins at Adalia, a period of refitting at Rhodes, and the temporary recapture of one of the castles at Ayas.[71]

After the assassination of Peter of Lusignan in January 1369 no further Latin help reached Armenia. However on 7 April 1369 Pope Urban V, realising that both Adalia and Smyrna were in danger as a result of King Peter's death, wrote to the master and convent of the Hospital to send help to both cities if need be; he also appealed to the other petty Latin powers in the Aegean to give assistance, presumably to Smyrna rather than to Adalia.[72] Early in 1372, on 22 January, having received news from Armenia that much of the country had fallen to the infidels, the next pope, Gregory XI, sent an appeal to Venice, Genoa and the Eastern Latin powers, including the Hospital, to give assistance in Armenia.[73] The Latins, however, were divided among themselves; in fact, the master of the Hospital, Fr Raymond Berenguer, died in Cyprus in February 1374 whilst attempting to settle the quarrels between the Genoese and King Peter II,[74] and nothing was done to prevent Leon VI, the last king of Armenia, being captured by the Mamluks at Sis in April 1375. In that year Pope Gregory XI was organising a *passagium* of Hospitallers, destined to intervene against the Turks in 1377. The bull of 8 December 1375 by which Gregory convened

---

[71] Delaville, *Rhodes*, pp. 140–2, 158–60. On 8 February 1366 the Hospitallers granted favourable terms for certain Armenians from Mytilene to settle on Kos, an island north of Rhodes. Delaville, p. 155 and n. 1, gives details of this and assumes that the Armenians came from Cilicia, but the document (Malta, cod. 319, f. 270v) shows that their envoy was a *Vanes de Cafa Armenus*, and presumably they were from the Black Sea, as were other Armenians who in 1363 received similar concessions to settle in Crete: cf. F. Thiriet, *Régestes des délibérations du sénat de Venise concernant la Romanie* I (Paris–The Hague, 1958), pp. 105, 107.   [72] Reg. Vat. 244M, ff. 44–5.
[73] Texts in Kohler, *Lettres*, pp. 324–7.   [74] Hill, II, pp. 402–3.

this expedition did refer to Armenia, along with Serbia, Bulgaria and Constantinople, among the places suffering from the Turks,[75] but other similar
documents concerning the scheme made no mention of Armenia at all.[76] In the
event everything to do with the organisation of the *passagium* made it clear
that the plan was to intervene in the Aegean; in fact, the expedition eventually
sailed to Epirus.[77]

King Leon was taken in chains to Cairo, and on 20 March 1382 King
Peter of Aragon wrote to Fr Juan Fernández de Heredia, the master at Rhodes,
asking him to assist an Aragonese messenger being sent in an attempt to secure
the liberation of Leon and his family.[78] On 21 October of the same year Leon
reached Rhodes, where he found his kinswoman Isabella of Lusignan. While
he was at Rhodes news arrived of the death of Peter II of Cyprus, and the
master agreed to lend Leon a ship to take letters of condolence to Cyprus.
Leon thought of trying to assert his rights to the throne of Cyprus but the
Hospitallers, afraid of the Genoese who had their own interests in the island,
prevented him from going there himself; so Leon left Rhodes on 21 November
to seek aid in the West, accompanied by the Hospitaller Fr Domenico de
Alamania and by the Rhodian landholder Giovanni Corsini, who in 1383
became Leon's Chancellor.[79] In May 1385 the Avignonese pope, Clement VII,
sent Giovanni Corsini back to Rhodes and Cyprus on certain affairs connected
with Leon, with a recommendation addressed to the master of the Hospital,
who was then at Avignon, or to the lieutenant master and convent at Rhodes;
he was to return within a fixed period of time.[80] Giovanni Corsini was well
established at Rhodes,[81] and King Leon must still have hoped to secure or

[75] Text in Pauli, II, pp. 97–8.

[76] Eg. text in F. Cerasoli, 'Gregorio XI e Giovanna I regina di Napoli: documenti
inediti dell'Archivio Vaticano', *Archivio storico per le provincie napoletane* XXV (1900),
pp. 6–8.

[77] Details and references in Delaville, *Rhodes*, pp. 184–91, 199–204; O. Halecki,
*Un Empereur de Byzance à Rome: vingt ans de travail pour l'union des Églises et pour la
défense de l'empire d'Orient: 1355–1375* (Warsaw, 1930), pp. 248–329. *RHC.Arm.* I,
721, is clearly wrong in stating that the expedition was intended for Armenia.

[78] Text in M. Sáez Pomés, 'La ayuda de Valencia a León V de Armenia, I de
Madrid', *Estudios de Edad Media de la Corona de Aragón* III (1947–8), p. 413.

[79] Dardel, in *RHC.Arm.* II, pp. 103–5.

[80] Reg. Vat. 296, ff. 1v–2v, in which Corsini is *Senescallus Regni Armenie*; cf. N.
Valois, *La France et le Grand Schisme d'Occident* II (Paris, 1896), p. 221 n. 3.

[81] Cf. A. Luttrell, 'Interessi fiorentini nell'economia e nella politica dei Cavalieri
Ospedalieri di Rodi nel Trecento', *Annali della Scuola Normale Superiore di Pisa:
lettere, storia e filosofia*, 2nd ser., XXVIII (1959), p. 325.

recover some sort of advantage in Cyprus or Armenia. Such initiatives were however in vain and the Hospitallers were unlikely to give aid. At some point after 1377 the master, Fr Juan Fernández de Heredia, had the crusading tract composed by Prince Hetoum of Gorighos, who had included in it a wealth of information about Armenia, translated into Aragonese along with many other chronicles and treatises,[82] but Cilician Armenia was in Muslim hands and the Hospital's interests there were extinct.

The Christian Kingdom of Armenia, which ceased to exist in 1375, had been in a state of siege, turmoil and internal strife for the best part of a century. Ayas in particular had an economic importance for the Latins, and the kings of Cyprus had dynastic and strategic interests in the country. The papacy recognised a general duty to assist the Armenians, but this did not go beyond diplomatic and financial support. When the popes were looking for a military force capable of serving in Cilician Armenia they often turned to the Hospital, but Cilicia can seldom have represented an attractive objective for the Hospitallers. The Hospital had been quite securely established in the Armenian kingdom during the thirteenth century; then in the difficult period after 1291, when the Hospitallers were seeking an alternative to their base in Cyprus, they sent forces there on several occasions and may even have considered some more permanent form of involvement. However, the conquest of Rhodes, completed by 1310, provided the Hospital with a permanent base, and thereafter their interests were in the Aegean, in Smyrna or the Morea, rather than further south. Crusading was the principal *raison d'être* of the Hospitallers and from time to time, when encouraged by the pope or dragged in the wake of the king of Cyprus, they did participate in expeditions to Armenia, yet on the whole, once they were established at Rhodes and had lost any effective control of their Armenian properties, their interest in Cilicia was very marginal. After about 1345 the Hospitallers were largely responsible for the defence of Smyrna. Furthermore the Hospital lacked a fleet, so that for military activity it was dependent on the maritime powers. The great plague came in 1347, and war between Venice and Genoa began in 1351; effective action was scarcely possible. Only after 1358, in the time of Peter I of Cyprus, were the Hospitallers again galvanised into active, but temporary, intervention in Armenia.

*   *   *

This preliminary sketch of the Hospitallers' involvement in Cilician Armenia

[82] W. Long, *Flor de las ystorias de Orient, by Hayton, Prince of Gorigos* (Chicago, 1934).

K

in the period after 1291, a topic never before treated, is not based on any exhaustive examination of original documents and chronicles or even of all the sources in print; the Armenian sources in particular may have more to reveal. Nor has any detailed description of the obscure and chaotic course of political and religious events in the decadent Armenian kingdom been attempted. One question of general importance which does, however, merit more detailed treatment concerns the myth of a Christian recapture of Ayas with Hospitaller assistance in 1347. This myth, together with certain other errors examined below, derives from the works of Giacomo Bosio and of other sixteenth-century historians of the Hospital, notably Fr Joan Antoni de Foxa, whose writings require examination. Bosio and his predecessors as official historiographers of the Hospital worked in the Vatican and other archives, but they made or repeated a number of careless errors. Subsequent historians, many of whom still use the first edition rather than the far superior second edition of Bosio's work, have treated him as a reliable authority. Certain mistakes he made are reproduced in such standard publications as the continuations of Cardinal Baronius' *Annales Ecclesiastici*; the relevant sections of the first edition of this were published in 1618 by Abraham Bzovius, who cited Bosio, though the key documents of 1347 appeared only in the later edition by Raynaldus of 1652. From the *Annales*, these errors passed into another standard work, the two *Documents arméniens* volumes of the *Recueil des historiens des Croisades*, which appeared in 1869 and 1906. What follows shows, once again, that it is essential to check the documents before following Bosio.[83]

According to Bosio, Hetoum of Armenia sought aid in Cyprus during 1295 against his brothers who had ousted him. The king and the Military Orders favoured Hetoum but lacked the strength to assist him; subsequently they did provide a small force (*poche genti*) in 1298 or 1299 when Hetoum recovered his throne. When Fr William of Villaret reached Cyprus – Bosio wrongly gives the date of his arrival as 1298 rather than 1300 – Hetoum's envoys arrived to congratulate him on his election as master; to give thanks to the Hospital and Temple, with whose assistance their king had reduced his kingdom to obedience and had forced his brother Constantine into exile; and to ask Villaret to exhort the king of Cyprus and the master of the Temple to participate with the Tartar and Armenian forces in an attack on the Mamluks in Syria. The gist of all this

---

[83] G. Bosio, *Dell'Istoria della Sacre Religione . . . di San Giovanni Gierosolimitano* II (1st ed. Rome, 1594; 2nd ed. Rome, 1630). On Bosio, Foxa and their predecessors, and their sources and inaccuracies, see A. Luttrell, 'The Hospitallers' Historical Activities: 1530–1630', *Annales de l'Ordre Souverain Militaire de Malte* XXVI (1968).

was to be found in Foxa's manuscript history of the Hospital, from which Bosio presumably took it.[84] The sources for it are unknown though the general inaccuracy over dates suggests that it was derived from chronicles rather than documents. The story that the Hospitallers and Templars assisted Hetoum in deposing his brothers Sempad and Constantine is given, again without any source, in the *Recueil*,[85] which presumably derived it from Bosio; there may be some truth in it. There seems to be no evidence of any significant Latin cooperation with the Mongols or Armenians, except in amphibious attacks on the coasts, yet in Bosio's long and confused account of the Mongol campaigns of 1299 and 1300 he states that the Hospitallers and Templars sent the largest possible force to Ruad, and that they were still there when the Mongols won their great victory near Homs in December 1299; in fact, it seems that the Orders sent forces to Ruad only in 1300. Bosio was again following Foxa in much of this, though he does differ from him and adds a considerable amount of detail not found in Foxa; Foxa's chronology was also confused. Bosio wrote that after Homs, the Hospitallers and Templars collaborated in attacks on the retreating Mamluk forces and were left to garrison Jerusalem until the Tartars withdrew; the Hospitallers and Templars then lacked the force to defend Jerusalem on their own and were compelled to withdraw to Cyprus. Bosio also describes an expedition of the two Orders to Ruad in 1300, which did in fact take place, and their supposed participation, together with the Armenian king, in another Tartar campaign in Syria which failed to take Damascus in 1303. The only source for all this which Foxa and Bosio actually mentioned was a crusading treatise, the *Flos Historiarum* of the Armenian Hetoum of Gorighos.[86]

Bosio, like Foxa before him, had some idea of the papal bulls of 5 May 1318 and 20 September 1320 which showed that King Oshin had confiscated the Hospital's Armenian lands.[87] The latter bull, addressed to Leon of Armenia, read:

> Carissimo in Christo filio Leoni Regi Armenie Illustri Salutem. Dudum pro parte clare memorie Ossinj Regis Armenie genitoris tui dum adhuc uiueret fuit expositum coram nobis quod olim quidam [de] pro genitoribus tuis Regibus Armenie opera pietatis que magister et fratres

---

[84] Bosio, II (1594), pp. 4, 6; (1630), pp. 11–12, 17; Foxa, in Madrid, Biblioteca Nacional, MS. 3027, ff. 159–163v.

[85] *RHC.Arm.* I, p. 545, presumably followed, e.g., by H. F. Tournebize, *Histoire politique et religieuse de l'Arménie* I (Paris, 1900), p. 224, who also gives no source.

[86] Foxa, ff. 159–163v; Bosio, II (1594), pp. 6–11; (1630), pp. 17–18, 20–3, 26–7; cf. Hetoum, II, pp. 197–9 and *supra*, pp. 121–3.

[87] Bosio, II (1630), pp. 50–1; Foxa, ff. 173v–174.

PLATE 43

ANAMUR

East face of curtain wall

The Armenian occupation of Anamur was for a short period at the end of the twelfth century and beginning of the thirteenth. The splendid castle as it stands today is almost entirely Islamic work, dating from Ala'ud-din Kau-Qobad's capture of Anamur in 1221, still commemorated by an inscription on the walls. The upper stages of its towers and machicolations have certainly had later restoration and it is a remarkable instance of a castle that over a long period has been kept in working order. Its double lines of defences are planned with a mastery that few Armenian fortifications can equal.

Two unsightly towers on the inland side are rounded and taper upwards like those of the Byzantine period in Cyprus (at St Hilarion). There is nothing patently Armenian. The Turkish structures, perhaps owing to Italian influence, present a startling contrast to ordinary Armenian work. They are built of scraps of stone laid in thick mortar, whereas the Armenians put little mortar around squared blocks of a size a man could carry with effort, and usually dressed them to fit at the edges, leaving the rest of the face bulging. Nearly all their towers are D-shaped, a few rectangular, and all were walled at the back; at Anamur most are semicircular and often open at the back (open-gorged), many square and one triangular, while the largest (in the foreground of the photograph) is a polygon of fourteen facets with a turret in the centre.

A. W. L.

hospitalis sancti Johannis Jerosolimitani [tunc] in illis partibus
exercebant diligentius attendentes et considerantes attentius, quod
fratres ipsi hostibus catholice [fidei] continue se [uir]iliter exponentes,
contra eos strenue dimitabant, quasdam terras infra Regnum suum
Armenie sitas, eidem hospitali sub certis conditionibus concesserunt.
Cunque postmodum eiusdem hospitalis [fratres], Terris Tiri, et Ciuitate
Acconensis, ab eisdem hostibus occupatis, a dictis cessarent operibus,
[et] circa defensionem dicti Regni Armenie quamuis super hoc fuissent
cum instantia requisiti intendere non curarent, idem Rex, undique
dictorum hostium circumseptus insultibus, et grauatus inportabilibus
oneribus expensarum, ad se terras huiusmodi reuocauit, nonnullos
stipendiarios ad Regni defensionem eiusdem necessitate cogente, de
ipsarum terrarum redditibus conducendo. Et licet demum magister et
fratres hospitalis prefati, eidem Regi circa Regni defensionem eiusdem,
per aliquod temporis spatium fideliter astitissent, tamen quia postmodum,
jidem magister et fratres ab huius assistencia destiterunt, Rex prefatus
terras ipsas quas eisdem magistro et fratribus restituerat, ad se iterum
reuocauit. Cum autem dilectus filius Morisius de Ponacho frater
hospitalis eiusdem, terras ut accepimus repetat supradictas nos
intendentes, ut idem Morisius pro terrarum ipsarum tuitione resideat in
eisdem, damus, ei, per nostras litteras in mandatis ut in eisdem terris
pro ipsarum tuitione resideat, uel alium loco suo faciat residere, tot de
redditibus dictarum terrarum ad tuitionem ipsarum, fratres hospitalis
eiusdem, uel alios ydoneos, usque ad apostolice sedis beneplacitum
retinendo, quot redditus ipsi comode poterunt sustinere. Alioquin tibi
memoratas terras, usque ad beneplacitum dicte sedis, ut de ipsarum
redditibus circa custodiam et defensionem ipsarum ualeas prouidere in
pace dimittat. Volumus autem quod idem Morisius si eum in dictis
terris residere, uel alium ad residendum deputauerit, ut prefertur,
nemini teneatur interim de prefatis redditibus respondere, quodque
tibi, uel hospitali predicto seu nature uel conditioni concessionis eiusdem
nullum propter hoc jmposterum preiudicium generetur. datum
Auinione .x. kalendas Octobris Anno Quinto.[88]

It is certain that the Mamluks took Ayas in 1337 and they still held it in and
after 1347, yet the secondary works repeat a strong, though evidently erroneous,

[88] Reg. Aven. 14, f. 426v, damaged but completed from the similar bull of the
same date addressed to Pagnac in Reg. Aven. 14, ff. 123–123v=Reg. Vat. 71, ff. 133–133v.

tradition according to which the Mamluks took Ayas only in 1347, or alternatively that the Christians retook Ayas and lost it again in that year. As late as 1966 the *Cambridge Medieval History* spoke of the Armenians defeating the Mamluk invaders with the aid of the king of Cyprus and the Hospitallers in 1356, the date presumably being a printing error for 1346,[89] while the revised *Encyclopédie de l'Islam* stated in 1960 that Ayas finally fell into Muslim hands in 1347.[90] In a book which appeared in 1930 Niculai Iorga wrote that Ayas was retaken in 1347 with the aid of the Hospitallers, citing a work published in 1899 by L. Alishan.[91] The latter gave no source for the same affirmation but reproduced a picture painted by Henri Delaborde for Louis-Philippe in 1844, which showed the Mamluks surrendering Ayas after their supposed defeat by the Hospitallers.[92] Jules Gay wrote in 1904 of the Mamluks taking Ayas in 1347, a misinterpretation of the bull of 25 September 1347, which he cited.[93] Iorga had already, in a work published in 1896, stated that 'Lajazzo et Alexandrette furent prises par les Égyptiens', and that the Hospitallers and the Armenians recaptured 'Alexandrette'; his source was Giacomo Bosio.[94] Iorga even cited the description given by the pilgrim 'Jacob von Bern' or 'Jacques de Berne' of the refugees reaching Famagusta from Ayas after its fall in '1346';[95] Iorga was citing a German translation of this text, wrongly dated to 1346 because the editors found in the standard works that Ayas fell in 1346 or 1347,[96] whereas this account was actually written in Latin by Jacopo da Verona and described his experiences in 1335.[97] Iorga also used De Mas Latrie who wrote of Ayas being taken by 'les Arabes d'Égypte' in 1320, being reconquered by the Armenians in 1347, and being lost again soon after; De Mas Latrie took this information from A. Saint-Martin, who in turn cited the work of M. Tchamt-

[89] *Cambridge Medieval History* IV, part 1 (revised ed. Cambridge, 1966), p. 636.

[90] *Encyclopédie de l'Islam* I (revised ed. Leyden–Paris, 1960), p. 802.

[91] N. Iorga, *Brève Histoire de la Petite Arménie: l'Arménie cilicienne* (Paris, 1930), p. 144.

[92] Alishan, pp. 470–1. Tournebize, p. 677, also stated that Ayas was retaken with Hospitaller and Cypriot assistance.

[93] Gay, p. 148; cf. *infra*, pp. 142, 143.

[94] N. Iorga, *Philippe de Mézières (1327–1405) et la Croisade au XIVᵉ siècle* (Paris, 1896), pp. 60, 369.

[95] Ibid., p. 3 n. 1.

[96] R. Röhricht–H. Meisner, *Deutsche Pilgerreisen nach dem Heiligen Lande* (Berlin, 1880), pp. 46, 51.

[97] *Liber Peregrinationis di Jacopo da Verona*, ed. U. Monneret de Villard (Rome, 1950), pp. 17–18. Ayas finally fell in 1337 but the first attack did come in 1335, according to the chronicle of the Constable Sempad (*RHC.Arm.* I, pp. 671–672).

chian published in 1786.[98] Tchamtchian used Nerses Balientz' chronicle and made it clear that Ayas remained in Armenian hands in 1321 and 1322; but he also wrote of the king of Cyprus and the master of Rhodes assisting the Armenians in 1347, and he stated that 'the infidels took Ayas' at that time, giving his source as Raynaldus.[99]

Nerses Balientz, who inserted passages concerning Cilician events into his Armenian version of Martin of Poland's Chronicle of the Popes and Emperors which he translated between 1347 and 1362, stated that Ayas was attacked by the Mongols, who withdrew in the spring of 1321; that it was then temporarily captured by the Mamluks who destroyed the fortresses, an event which he wrongly dates to 1321 rather than 1322; and that subsequently the Armenians rebuilt the castles with the help of 30,000 gold florins sent by the pope. Some sixteen years later, that is in 1337, the Muslims forced the Armenians to give up Ayas, 'and they took it and the same Muslims hold it to this day'.[100] This last remark is quite explicit, and nothing is known which contradicts it. A note in an Armenian short chronicle confirms this: 'In the year 1337 the lawless nation of Ismail took Ayas.'[101] In a colophon added in 1337 to a manuscript dated 1297, the writer Vasil relates how the sultan took Ayas in that year,[102] as does a detailed letter written by the sultan himself.[103] The anonymous continuator of the chronicle of the Constable Sempad confirms that Ayas was destroyed by the Mamluks in 1322, and gives no hint that they retained the town,[104] while it is known that in 1323 the sultan undertook to rebuild the *castrum* he had destroyed there.[105] John XXII's letters also spoke of Ayas being

[98] L. de Mas Latrie, *L'île de Chypre* (Paris, 1879), p. 234; A. Saint-Martin, *Mémoires historiques et géographiques sur l'Arménie* I (Paris, 1818), p. 198.

[99] M. Tchamtchian, *History of Armenia* [in Armenian], III (Venice, 1786), pp. 320, 350.

[100] Text in V. Hakopian, *Short Chronicles: XIII–XIV Centuries* [in Armenian], 2 vols. (Erevan, 1951–6), II, pp. 188–9.

[101] Text ibid., I, p. 88.

[102] Text (in English) in A. K. Sanjian, *Colophons of Armenian Manuscripts: 1301–1480* (Cambridge, Mass., 1969), p. 79. The inhabitants of Ayas had killed certain Muslims in 1335 (ibid., p. 75). All the information in the first part of this paragraph was most kindly supplied by Miss Sirapie der Nersessian.

[103] Translation in M. Canard, 'Les Relations entre les Mérinides et les Mamelouks au XIVᵉ siècle', *Annales de l'Institut d'Études orientales: Université d'Alger* V (1939–41), pp. 53–4 and notes; this article provides a number of details concerning Cilician history drawn from Mamluk sources.

[104] *RHC.Arm.* I, p. 667.

[105] Text in Langlois, pp. 232–3.

taken by the Mamluks in 1322, and they made it clear that the castles at Ayas were in Christian hands and awaiting repair.[106] A text of 1325 confirmed that 30,000 florins were put aside to repair the *castra de Alaiacio maris et terre et alia loca regni Armenie*, though the money was not all spent.[107]

Gay, Iorga and De Mas-Latrie were presumably influenced by the *Recueil des historiens des Croisades*, which stated that Hospitaller and Cypriot forces aided the Armenians and which cited the bulls of September 1347, apparently taking them from Raynaldus. The *Recueil* spoke of the Mamluks taking and sacking Ayas in 1347, of Pope Clement VI sending money and a body of Hospitallers in 1348, and of the Armenians and Hospitallers in the year following 22 December 1348 taking 'Alexandrette'; no source was given, but presumably this too was taken, somewhat inaccurately, from Raynaldus.[108] Raynaldus, in describing the bulls of September 1347, made the assumption, which Gay subsequently made, that Ayas was recaptured in that year. In commenting on the bull of 25 September 1347 addressed to the doge of Venice, Raynaldus wrote: *Expugnatum est ab infidelibus Ajacium.* He also wrote of *Isso, . . . olim dictam Alexandretam, . . . a Constantio Rege recuperatam*, giving his source as Giacomo Bosio.[109]

Many of these confusions, therefore, derived from Bosio. In 1347, according to Bosio, the master of Rhodes learnt that the Mamluks had attacked various parts of Armenian Cilicia and had newly taken *Isso*, also known as *Alessandria* or *Alesandretta*; forgetting the damages which earlier Armenian kings had inflicted on the Hospital, the master at once despatched galleys and other ships with Hospitallers and their soldiers to assist the Armenians; together with the king, the Hospitaller forces repulsed the Mamluks and recovered Ayas; and, on hearing this in a letter from the king's ambassador *Costanzo*, the pope wrote to congratulate the master. This story appears in both editions of Bosio. In the second edition Bosio added that at this time the Hospital's grand preceptory of Armenia, called a *prioratus* in the papal registers, became vacant and the master and convent at Rhodes sent several governors or lieutenants instead of

---

[106] Texts in Coulon, nos. 1571–2.

[107] Texts in Richard, pp. 37–49.

[108] *RHC.Arm.* I, pp. 708–9.

[109] Raynaldus, 1347, xxviii–xxix; these phrases appear in the 1652 edition. V. Langlois, 'Documents pour servir à l'histoire des Lusignans de la Petite Arménie: 1342–1375', *RA.* XVI (1859), pp. 146–7, spoke of the Muslims taking Ayas despite the Hospitallers' participation in its defence in 1346/7, and of Hospitaller troops intervening in Armenia in 1349 (!), and he too cited Raynaldus and Bosio.

appointing a new preceptor; Clement VI therefore wrote to them on 5 May 1347 recommending the provision of Fr *Damario* de Baucio to the preceptory; Bosio cited *epistola* no. 1248 in the Vatican register for 1347.[110] This *epistola mccxlviij*, actually dated 29 April 1347, recommended Fr Dalmacius de Baucio to the governors of the *prioratus* of Armenia, the *prioratus* being vacant:

> Dilectis filijs . . Gubernatoribus Prioratus Armenie hospitalis Sancti Johannis Jerosolimitani eodem Prioratu uacante.
> Cum dilectum filium Dalmacium de Baucio hospitalis Sancti Johannis Jerosolimitani audiuerimus fidedignorum testimonijs multis uirtutum meritis adiuuari, Nos ipsum quem obtentu meritorum suorum huiusmodi, ac consideratione quorundam amicorum suorum deuotorum nostrorum et ecclesie Romane fauore dilectionis specialis prosequimur, ut uos, qui meritorum huiusmodi habere potestis noticiam pleniorem, eum super promotionem sua prout ipse petierit, et per vos honeste fieri poterit fauorabiliter prosequamini, uestre beniuolentie propensius propensius [*sic*] commendamus. Datum Auinione iij kalendas maij Anno Quinto.[111]

Bosio had three main sources: copies of documents from the Hospital's archives which had been transferred to Malta after the loss of Rhodes; the papal registers at the Vatican, from which much of the additional material in the second edition was drawn; and the manuscript history of the Hospital written by his predecessor as official historiographer of the Hospital, the Catalan Hospitaller Fr Joan Antoni de Foxa. The Vatican documents, discussed below, provide no evidence that Ayas fell to the Christians in 1347. Nor is there any evidence for this in the records of the Hospital now at Malta, though a fragment of the master's *liber bullarum* for the year 1347 to 1348 does survive. Furthermore it is unlikely that any relevant documents for this period which were then at Malta have been lost since Bosio's time. Bosio, therefore, presumably based his statement about the recovery of Ayas on Foxa, though he added information not given by the latter. Foxa wrote that in 1348 the Hospitallers, in response to a papal appeal, assisted Constantine of Armenia to retake *Issa* and to expel the Mamluks who had taken Ayas: . . . *le havia tomado en Cilicia la uila de issa.* The version of Foxa preserved at Malta, which Bosio may have used, gives a confusing variant: *la villa de Layassa.* Foxa wrote that, with the assistance of the master, *se covro la çiudad de la issa, no e podido hallar como ni otra cosa sobre esto mas de lo que tengo dicho y sea sacado de unas notas de fray antonio*

---

[110] Bosio, II (1594), p. 48; (1630), pp. 75–6. [111] Reg. Vat. 140, f. 280.

Jofre, en que dize aver leydo esto en unos cuadernos viejos de nuestra canzilleria.
Fr Antoine Geoffroi was Foxa's predecessor as historiographer, and in addition
to various papers and old *cuadernos* Geoffroi may have seen at Malta, he had
himself used copies of documents from the Vatican registers. It seems likely,
therefore, that Geoffroi or Foxa either copied or made an error, which may
possibly have arisen through confusing the events of 1347 with those of 1367
when the Hospitallers did participate in the temporary recapture of Ayas. It
seems most probable that this error arose from the misinterpretation of documents in the Vatican registers which were available to Geoffroi, Foxa and
Bosio, and which have subsequently been interpreted wrongly by other historians. The events of 1347 should therefore be reconstructed from the Vatican
bulls.[112]

In his bull of 25 September 1347 Clement wrote of the sultan taking Ayas:
Dilectis filijs Nobili Viro Andree Dandulo Duci et Communi Venetiarum.
Occurrunt frequenter considerationis nostre conspectu deuotionis et
fidei studia quibus insignis Terra uestra, erga deum et Romanam
ecclesiam euidentibus signis et operibus claruit occurrit qualiter uos pro
defensione fidei christiane ac ipsius cultu diffusius dilatando, tan quam
Viri catholici et uere fidei prefate cultores aduersus ipsius persecutores
et hostes labores et solicitudines subijstis hactenus et subitis propter
quod in hijs que christi et ipsius ecclesie beneplacitis conueniunt et
eiusdem fidei fauorem concernere dinoscuntur tanto [fiducialius?]
eadem requirit ecc[lesi]a, quanto sperat in hijs per uos satisfieri
promptius uotis suis. Sane ad notitiam uestram iam dudum credimus
peruenisse qualiter Soldanus Babilonie immanis persecutor nominis
christiani ad eiusdem fidei hanhelans exitium post impugnationes
hostiles post uexationes innumeras post clades depopulationes et spolia
aduersus Christianos orientalium partium per eum ut nostis a longis
retro temporibus crudeliter peccatis exigentibus perpetrata Ciuitatem
Aiacen. insignem utique locum Armenie prodolor occupauit et eam
detinet occupatam Christianos illius ciues et incolas affligens iugo
miserabilis seruitutis de cuius Ciuitatis recuperatione Carissimus in
Christo filius noster Constantius Rex Armenie Illustris anxia cura

---

[112] Foxa, f. 185 (variant in Royal Malta Library, Biblioteca, MS. 314, II, p. 79);
cf. Luttrell, 'Hospitallers' Historical Activities'. In addition to Raynaldus and Gay,
others, such as Golubovich, IV, pp. 371–8, cited and discussed the bulls of 1346–1351,
but further reference below is mostly to originals and published texts.

solicitus, ad uos quorum interuentionibus apud eundem confidit diuina
fauente gratia, super hoc exaudiri ut intelleximus Nuncios suos mittit,
petiturus a uobis ut pro recuperatione huiusmodi, uel aliqua cum eodem
Soldano super hoc habenda conuentione siue concordia ad prefatum
Soldanum speciales Nuntios destinetis. Quocirca Vniuersitatem uestram
attente rogamus, quatenus, diuine remunerationis intuitu ac pro nostra
et apostolice sedis reuerentia eisdem Regi et Regno, consueti fauoris
auxilia impendentes, petitionibus Regis ipsius super hijs et alijs que deo
gratia et ipsi fidei pro futura noueritis liberaliter condescendere
prudentia uestra uelit ut redemptor noster cui prestabitis in hac parte
gratum obsequium mercedis uobis premium tribuat, Nosque deuotionem
uestram dignis gratiarum actionibus prosequamur in domino. Datum
Auinione vij kalendas Octobris Anno Sexto.[113]

It seems clear that Clement was referring to the capture of Ayas, not 'a
few months earlier', as Gay interprets the bull,[114] but several years earlier, that
is in 1337, and that Clement considered that the Mamluks still held the city.
Raynaldus printed the text of the bull of 1347, but glossed it *Expugnatum est
ab infidelibus Ajacium* probably because Bosio, whom he cited on the next page,
had written of the Christian recovery of Ayas in 1347. Presumably Bosio found
Ciuitatem Aiacen. in the bull, but in a misguided display of classical erudition,
and with Foxa's mistake to mislead him, he rendered it in his history as *Isso,
Alessandria* or *Alesandretta*, not realising that Alexandretta, a name not mentioned in any of the documents cited here, is not the same as Ayas, but lies in
the place now known as Iskenderum. Raynaldus glossed his printed text
correctly, but then followed Bosio in writing of *Isso, . . . olim dictam Alexandretam, . . . a Constantio Rege recuperatam.*[115] Medieval Alexandretta was of
very minor importance,[116] yet Iorga, citing Bosio, later wrote of the Mamluks
capturing *Lajazzo et Alexandrette*, and of *Alexandrette* alone being recaptured.
In fact, all this derived from the bull which mentioned only Ayas, and referred
to its loss in 1337. Presumably the errors in Bosio and Foxa originated in a
misinterpretation of the same bull. In any case, the myth that the Mamluks
captured Ayas in 1347 was established.

A similar pattern of errors was repeated with regard to the events of 1351.
Iorga wrote that a Latin league was formed in 1350 and that *Alexandrette*,

[113] Reg. Vat. 141, ff. 89–89v (=Reg. Vat. 62, ff. 86–86v).
[114] Gay, p. 148.
[115] Raynaldus, 1347, xxviii–xxix.   [116] Alishan, pp. 499–501.

which he thought of as a different place from Ayas but which was not mentioned as such in any of the sources discussed here, was retaken with the aid
of the Hospitallers. Iorga cited the *Recueil*, which in fact simply stated that
the Armenians were working to secure the formation of a league in which the
kings of France and England as well as the Hospitallers were to join, and that
the pope called upon the Hospitallers and others to assist the Armenians; in
fact, neither the *Recueil* nor the relevant section in Raynaldus made any mention
of Alexandretta.[117] Bosio provided correct information clearly derived directly
from the papal registers: in response to an appeal from the king, Pope Clement
VI instructed the master of the Hospital to send aid to Cilicia; in a separate
letter of the same date he also recommended to him the Armenian envoy,
Constantine of Portella, who was returning to Armenia after three years at
Avignon; Clement also sent the preceptor of Castelsarrasin, Fr Raymond
Berenguer, with a letter to the master and convent of the Hospital.[118] Foxa
provided similar information apparently derived from the same source.[119]
Once again, the correct version of events can be deduced from the Vatican
bulls discussed above, but in this case the errors embedded in modern scholar-
ship were not the fault of Foxa or Bosio.

[117] Iorga, *Brève Histoire*, p. 144; *RHC.Arm.* I, pp. 710–11; Raynaldus, 1350,
pp. xxxviii–xxxix.
[118] Bosio, II (1630), p. 81; cf. *supra*, p. 130.
[119] Foxa, f. 187.

PLATE 44

BODRUM

The castle seen over the ruins of the classical town

The ruined castle stands on a rock, in which probably in classical times, a passage has been cut, separating it from the town. Some of the columns of the main street of Hierapolis Castabala are still standing with their late Corinthian capitals.

6

GAZETTEER

Modern place-names have been simplified as much as possible. Some of the more obscure are cited in the form used in the source but Turkish official spelling has been followed wherever it could ascertained, only ignoring the distinction between the undotted and dotted *i*; ç represents the English *ch*, ġ a *gh*, ş our *sh*. The word *Kale*, 'castle', is printed without the suffix *-si* which would often be grammatically appropriate. The transliteration of Arabic disregards sounds unknown in English.

The nomenclature of the Cilician and north Syrian area presents endless problems. As early as the thirteenth century a writer could complain that 'perpetual wars have brought great changes to the names of these provinces'.[1] The papacy was constantly at a loss in identifying ancient sees with their present descriptions. Greek, Latin, Byzantine, Arabic, Armenian, Turkish names replace one another bewilderingly and the process continues today with an official policy of standard Turkish place names, which often are at variance with local usage. The various maps available are by no means consistent, even in their physical details. Nineteenth-century travellers, primarily interested in identifying ancient sites, added their hypotheses to the general confusion. In particular, Armenian names have been politically consigned to oblivion. Some of the principal castles and lordships of the Armenian kingdom can still not be accurately placed on the map, while buildings as important and well preserved as Yilan or Tumlo have lost their Armenian names and cannot be assigned to any known Armenian lordship or historical incidents. This gazetteer is therefore tentative in many instances, and can only be regarded as a basis for further work and greater certainties. It represents our present knowledge of the subject, gaps, debatable points and all. Where map references are given they are to the sheets of Turkey 1 : 200,000, Harta Genel Müdürlügu (Ankara: Harita Umum Müdürlügu).

[1] Bergeron, ed. 'Observations du Moine Bacon', p. 5.

The Castles

The key piece of information is a list of Cilician barons compiled in 1198 by Sempad (see *supra* pp. 17 and 27). The list, which has been thought to be a record of those who attended the coronation of Leon II,[1] exists in two versions. The first is in a manuscript of the late thirteenth or early fourteenth century, not published in its entirety until 1956 (*Chronicle of the General Sempad*, in Armenian, ed. S. Akelian); the second is found in two later, but better-known, manuscripts, published and translated in various ways in the nineteenth century (e.g. *Chronique du royaume de la petite Arménie*, ed. and trs. E. Dulaurier, *RHC.Arm.* I). As the later manuscripts are now known to have been derived directly from the earlier one[2] we give only the earlier list, in the form in which it was quoted by L. M. Alishan in *Léon le Magnifique* (translation by G. Bayan, 1888, pp. 174–7). Our explanations of place names are added in square brackets.

Le Seigneur de Baghras, Adan
Le Seigneur de Dgighère, Hoste
Le Seigneur de Hamouss, Arevekouyne
Le Seigneur de Sarvantave, Sempad
Le Seigneur de Haroun, Leon
Le Seigneur de Simana-cla, Sirouhi
Le Seigneur de Ané, Henri
Le Seigneur de Goudafe [Gouda], le Connétable Aboulgharib
Le Seigneur de Engouzoud (Les Noyers), Baudouin
Le Seigneur de Torenga, Etienne
Le Seigneur de Pertouce, Léon et Gregoire
Le Seigneur de Gantchi, Achod
Le Seigneur de Fornauce [Fornos], Aboulgharib
Le Seigneur de Gaban, Tancrède
Le Seigneur de Djandji, Constantin
Le Seigneur de Schoghagan, Geoffroy
Le Seigneur de Mazod-Khatche, Simon
Le Seigneur d'Amouda, Simon
Le Seigneur de Till [Til Hamdoun], Robert
Le Seigneur de Tilsab [Thelbaghd], Thoros
Le Seigneur de Vaner, le Maréchal Vassil
Le Seigneur de Partzer-perte (Haute forteresse), Georges
Le Seigneur de Gobidara, Constantin
Le Seigneur de Molévon, Ajaros
Le Seigneur de Gouglag, Sempad
Le Seigneur de Lambroun, Hethoum

[1] S. der Nersessian in *History of the Crusades* II, p. 648, n. 23.
[2] S. der Nersessian, *DOP* XIII, pp. 143–68.

Le Seigneur de Loulva, Schahenchah
Le Seigneur de Babéron, Pagouran
Le Seigneur de Asgouras [Pertgan], Vassagh
Le Seigneur de Manash, Hethoum
Le Seigneur de Pertig (Petit fort), Michel
Le Seigneur de Bragana, Tigrane
Le Seigneur de Sivile, Ochine
Le Seigneur de Coricos [Corycus], Simon
Le Seigneur de Séleucie et de Bounard, Constance
Le Seigneur de Sinide et de Govasse, Romanos
Le Seigneur de Vède et de Vériski, Nicéphore
Le Seigneur de Lauzade et Timidoupolis, Christophore
Le Seigneur de Manion, de Lamos, de Germanicae [Jamengane] et Anamour, Halgam
Le Seigneur de Nor-perte (Château nouveau) et de Goumardias, le Sébaste Henri
Le Seigneur de Antouchezda et de Gouba, Baudouin
Le Seigneur de Maghva de Sig et de Paleopolis, Kyr Sag (Isaac)
Le Seigneur de Manoughade et Alare, Michel
Le Seigneur de Lagravène, Constance et Nicéphore
Le Seigneur de Calanonoos, Aijoudabe, Sainte-Sophie et Naghlon, Kyr Varte.

Of the forty-five holdings listed, twenty-nine can be identified with known places, though even with some of them exact localities are not known. The list appears to be arranged in a roughly geographical order, beginning with Baghras and working north and then west. There are several omissions. Neither Vahka nor Anavarza is included, at least by any identifiable name. There are no places that appear to fit with Yilan and Tumlu. The main towns Tarsus, Adana, Mamistra, Ayas, Sis are not mentioned. Yilan and Tumlu may not yet have existed, but all the others omitted were presumably on the royal demesne. Round the Amanus Gates we have Hamus, Sarvantikar, Harounia and Til Hamdoun. Between Simana-gla and Pertous there is a group of unplaced names, Ane, Goudafe, Engouzoud and Torenga. Pertous is followed by Gantchi, Fornos, Gaban, Djandji, Schoghagan, the castles of the Coxon–Andirin–Marash area. Then Partzapert, Gobidara and Molevon lead up to Goulag, Lampron, Loulon, Babaron and Asgouras, the defences of the Cilician Gates. Silifke and the western approaches include twenty-four names, many of them identifiable, though unfortunately the MSS. of Sempad's chronicle have here several variants. Norpert and Goumardias (? Camardias) were part of the Hospitaller holding based on Silifke. Antchouzeda and Sinida were other castles of this area.

The list of barons at the Council of Sis in 1307 (Galanus, *Concilationis* I, p. 460; Langlois, *Cartulaire*, pp. 59–60) gives some further names: Mikhailagla, Sempadagla, Cizistra, Djofregla and Gigraschentz. The Council of Adana

1308 (Galanus, p. 504) substitutes Khentzorovid (valley of apples) for Cizistra, and Ghorriculi for Gantchi. A Venetian list under Oshin (1307–20) gives Alticovanci for Gantchi, Mons Livonis (Molevon), Coquelaqus (Gulek) and Roisso. Such divergences show the haphazard nomenclature in use.

Adalia, v. Antalya

Adamodana, v. Amoudain

Adana, Athena: An ancient, possibly Hittite, town. The Roman bridge over the Seyhan was built by Hadrian. Taken by the Arabs in the mid-seventh century, it was retaken by Basil II in 964, and the area was repopulated by Christians, largely Armenian. Between 1064 and 1071 the Selchukids occupied the coastal plain and were still holding it when it surrendered to Tancred in 1097. In 1132 it was occupied by Leon I, but retaken by John Comnenus in 1137. The Armenians regained it c. 1170 and held it till the Mamluk conquest of the Cilician plain and the cession of Tarsus and Adana by Constantine V in 1360. N. Maggiore, *Adana* (Palermo, 1852).

Adana, Plain of, Cilicia Campestris: The great fertile area stretching from the Lamas river to the Amanus mountains. To the north it is bounded by the Taurus mountains, and the longest fertile stretch is that reaching to Sis, about 120 km. from the southern point at Cape Karatas. All travellers comment on the richness of this alluvial area. Wilbrand of Oldenburg in 1211 writes of it: 'In the midst indeed it is flat and very fertile and contains many animals suitable for hunting. In length it is sixteen days' journey, in breadth up to the mountains two. It is inhabited by Franks, Greeks, Syrians, Turks, Armenians and others but it is the Armenians that hold rule' (Laurent, *Peregrinatores*, p. 174). Ainsworth (*Travels* II, p. 81) in 1841 found there gazelles, foxes, hares, jerboas, ground squirrels and large and small bustards. See M. Gough in *AS.* II (1952), pp. 86–7.

Adiyaman, Carbanum, Cholmodana, Hisn Mansur: Between Behesni and Kiahta. Built round the citadel mound; some remains of both castle and town walls, all Arab or Selchukid work. Ainsworth, *Travels* I, p. 267; *Guide Bleu* (1965), p. 655.

Afrin, River: River flowing from the Kurd Dagh into the lake of Antioch. Its valley provided the main route for the early stages of the journey from Antioch to Edessa.

Agner, Aguener: Convent near Partzapert. Alishan, *Sissouan*, pp. 162–6.

Aintab, Hatab, Gaziantep: At the junction of the Marash, Edessa, Aleppo route. Fortified by the Selchukids, it constantly changed hands, and for a period formed a county with Duluk and Raban; *c.* 1125 under a Latin, Mahuis; ceded to the Greeks in 1150. The considerable ruins of the citadel are probably mainly Mamluk work. William of Tyre, *RHC.Occ.* XVII, p. 17; Poujoulat, *Voyage*, p. 2; Cahen, *Syrie*, pp. 115–16; Humann and Puchstein, *Reisen*, with drawing and photograph of citadel, pp. 168–72.

Ak Kale: Placed by Thomson south of Azgit; presumably the castle by Andirin (q.v.) on west bank of Andirin Su. Fedden and Thomson, *Crusader Castles*, pp. 22, 54. (Mut, H–VII; 64, IIc.)

Ak-Kale,? Bonbilico: A small Byzantine site between Ayas and the Lamas river, where a ruinous basilica was repaired and continuously machicolated to make a little castle; it seems to have been called Lamas Kale in Langlois' time. The Bonbilico of mediaeval charts is perhaps the inlet described by Beaufort (*Karamania*, p. 253) as 'a little creek or nook, cut out of the rock, and large enough for the admission of a small galley: it seems to have been intended for the purpose of watering, as a shallow water-course leads into it, which we traced up the slope of the hill to a tank of 100 feet long, by 50 wide, hollowed to the depth of 28 feet, and covered with a groined roof, supported by two rows of piers.' This building, which is actually a Byzantine cistern, stands near the fortress.

Alahan: Monastery in the hills east of the Göksu valley; a remarkable group of buildings including two churches and a baptistery dating from the fifth and sixth centuries. These buildings must have been known to the Armenians, but there is no record of their use of them. Forsyth, *DOP.* XI (1955), pp. 233–36. M. Gough, *AS.* XII (1962), pp. 173–84, *AS.* XIII (1963), pp. 105–15, *AS.* XIV (1964), pp. 185–90. *AS.* XXI (1972), pp. 199–212. (Mut, H–VII; 64, IIc.)

Alanya, Alaya, Calanorus, Coracesium, Candelor Scadelorum, Escandeleur: Under Leon II it was in Armenian hands, and must be the Calanonoos of the Coronation list, when it was held by Kyr Varte. A man of the same name surrendered it to Ala'ud-Din Kai-Qobad in 1221. The town was then renamed Alaiyya and the existing fortifications were built. In 1324–59 Candelor, Anamur, Siki and Satalia paid tribute to Hugh IV of Cyprus. When Peter I took Antalya in 1361 he received tribute from Alanya. In 1403 Marshal Boucicaut raided it from Rhodes (Delaville le Roulx, *La France en Orient* I, pp. 427–30). In 1450 John II of Cyprus

L

made a trading treaty with Alanya. The Red Tower was restored in 1951–3. Lloyd and Rice, *Alanya*; Bean, *Turkey's Southern Shore*, pp. 101–7; Stark, *Alexander's Path*, pp. 48–52.

Alara, ? Karaköy Kale: The Alara river flows through gorges to the Bay of Antalya, between Alanya and Mangavat. In its upper reaches at Karaköy are the ruins of a medieval castle. 'The *kale* itself is now almost inaccessible, since the track from the spring on this saddle, which alone gave access, has been carried away. The three tiers of barracks stepped up to the fort on the actual summit were doubtless barracks for the retainers of a *derebey* or Armenian baron.' (Bean and Mitford, *Journeys 1964–68*, p. 121.) Alara in the 1198 list was held with Manavgat. See also de Tchihatcheff, *Asie Mineure* I, p. 279. (Antalya, H–V; 50, IIç.)

Albistan, Ablastha, Elbistan, Arabissos: Held by the crusaders from 1097 to 1105, when the Armenians called in Moslem help and massacred the crusading garrison. (*RHC.Arm.* I, p. 81.) Besieged unsuccessfully by Leon II in 1205. It was at Albistan that Baybars in 1277 defeated a combined Selchukid–Mongol army. There are considerable ruins of the citadel, which may be largely Aiyubid work. *Guide Bleu* (1965), p. 661.

Alexandretta, Myriandrus, Issa, Iskanderun: This port, probably on account of its malarious marshes, was of little medieval importance. De la Broquière (ed. Schefer, p. 92) describes it as ruined, but with a castle on the sea, surrounded by marshes on the land side. The coast has changed so much here, owing to silt brought down from the mountains, that this could be the fortress of which the octagonal base can still be seen in a garden on the land side of the present town. Jacquot, *Antioche*, pp. 64–77.

Amanus Mountains, Montaine Noir: Divided into two ranges by the Beylan Pass (Pylae Syriae); the southern the Kizil Dağ (Skopelos) with the Gebel Akmar and Gebel Siman (Monastery of St Simeon), and the northern the Nur Dağlari stretching up to Marash.

Amanus Gates, Pylae Amanides, Derbendal Marrim: It lies between the modern towns of Osmaniye and Fevsipaşa. On the south it is approached by a group of shallow valleys, and a southern track runs through them from Osmaniye to Islahiye. To the north another pass, the Bahçe, leads to a route between the Hamus and Pyramus rivers.

Amouda, Amoudain, Amuda, Hemite, Adamodana: First castle taken by Thoros II on his escape from Constantinople in 1145. Acquired by Teutonic knights by 1211. Sacked in 1266. On the Pyramus west of

Bodrum, guarding a ford. Possibly the square keep was added by the knights. Alishan, *Sissouan*, pp. 226–9; Hazan Bekir Ulug, *Tarih Boyanca Çukurova* (Mersin, 1948), p. 144 with photograph; Fedden and Thomson, p. 44; Favre and Mandrot, *Guide*, p. 760. (Kozan, G–IX; 88, Iü.)

Amuq: The marshy plain north of Antioch, stretching in a long but little used corridor up to Marash, between the Amanus mountains and the Kurd Dagh.

Anahṣa-Kale, Eskianahṣa, Rodentos, Butrentrum: Castle commanding the junction of the Çakitsuyu and a tributary on the northern side of the Cilician Gates. Schaffer (*Cilicia*, p. 81) calls the tributary the Aivabesu, and states that the river is only fordable at low water. Ruined Armenian church. Alishan, *Sissouan*, p. 139; R. P. Harper in *AS*. XX, p. 150 (with photograph). (Ulukisla, G–VIII; 77, Iu.)

Anamur, Stalemura, Anemourion, Mamur, Kalesçi, Memoriyeh, Pl. 43: In the list of 1198 Anamur is held by an Armenian, Halgam, a son of Sempad of Babaron and uncle of Leon II. He is also described as Lord of Manioun. When the Hetoumids had occupied Anamur is uncertain, but presumably *c.* 1188, the period when Leon occupied Silifke. It was taken by Ala'ud-Din Kai-Qobad following his occupation of Alanya in 1221, and an inscription records his conquest. The remarkable castle as it exists today is mainly his work, with later adaptations for cannons. It consists of a keep on a small rocky eminence commanding two open courts, which are surrounded by a chain of towers of all shapes – dodecagonal, octagonal, square, triangular, round and semicircular. The extreme dimensions are about 270 by 110 metres; there are three arched gateways, the main one through a square tower on west side, over which is a tablet encompassed by fillets of alternate black and white stone, finishing in a flat pointed arch and containing a long Arabic inscription. The landside ward is defended by a shallow ditch, probably easily flooded. The towers here are closely placed, and the variations in their design suggest that some may have been added to decrease the distances between them. At most periods the threat to Anamur was from the sea, but during the Armenian occupation the land defences must have been the first consideration. The large blocks in the foundations of the sea wall may be re-used classical material, but seem to have been used in places where projection into the sea or uneven rock bases made stability of particular importance. The mosque is an Ottoman building, and its masonry is quite different in style from any other in the castle. Anamur passed under Cypriot control

PLATE 45

TIL HAMDOUN

View of castle from south-east

On a small hill, rising from comparatively flat country, the castle commanded a main cross road. Here the route from Alexandretta met that from Marash and the Amanus Gates, continuing westward to Adana. Its importance led to frequent changes in ownership and also to various stages of rebuilding.

The Byzantines may have been the first to fortify the hill called Til Hamdoun (a name of Syriac or even perhaps Aramaic origin), which appears in history as one of their possessions in 1137; certainly no minor power would have raised an artificial platform on the summit to make a foundation for the court as well as the surrounding buildings. The Armenians captured the fort in 1151 but twice lost it again before it came firmly into their hands in 1194; almost complete rebuilding during or soon after these vicissitudes resulted in the strong castle on which a German traveller remarked in 1212. The towers, or at least their rounded ends, rise from the sloping edge of the platform. Half of the circuit is surrounded by an outer wall, the flat roofs of attached rooms aided defence of the other half, and a fine hall, built on an undercroft, overtops all else; it shows towards the left of the photograph. The external enclosure farther left (cf. Pl. 46) was a late addition, perhaps for temporary occupation by reinforcements or by refugees.   A. W. L.

for the brief period (1361–73) when Cyprus held Antalya and exacted some form of allegiance from the coastline as far as Corycus, ceded to Cyprus by Constantine III. Until very recently the castle was in military occupation.

Beaufort, *Karamania*, pp. 105, 187–8; Schaffer, *Cilicia*, p. 73; Fedden and Thomson, *Castles*, pp. 97–8; Müller-Wiener, *Castles*, p. 81, pl. 117; Stark, *Alexander's Path*, pp. 36–40.

Anavarza, Anazarbus, Ain Zarba: Known as 'La Nouvelle Troie' (*RHC.Arm.* I, p. 30). Possibly the strongest of all the Armenian fortresses; the capital of Thoros I and remained the chief seat of government till *c.* 1162. In 1137 it withstood a Byzantine siege for thirty-seven days, but finally capitulated. John Comnenus took to Constantinople the sacred icon from the church built for it by Thoros I, after he had found it amongst the treasures of Gakik, when he took vengeance on the sons of Mandale at Cybistra. The church was dedicated to the warrior saints, Sargis and his companions, martyred by Sapor II. The castle is built on a limestone outcrop dominating the eastern plain, and rising to a height of 200 m. On its eastern side flows the river Sumbas. It was the seat of an Armenian archbishop. Langlois, *Voyage*, pl. XXVI; Davis, *Asiatic Turkey*, pp. 152–7; *TLN* (26.2.1938), p. 356; Gough, *AS*. II (1952), pp. 85–105. (Kozan, G–IX; 97, Iu.)

Andirin: On the river of the same name, and on the route from Coxon to Kadirli. It is not identified as an Armenian site, but there is a castle (Ak Kale) on the opposite bank of the river. See *supra*, p. 148. (Kozan, G–IX; 90, Ir.)

Andouchedza, Antouchezda: Held in 1198 along with Gouba by Baldwin; in Western Cilicia, but site unidentified, possibly Antiochetta, or at the nearby village of Endişegüney.

Antalya, Attaleia, Adalia, Satalia: Founded by and named after Attalus II of Pergamon *c.* 158 B.C. In Byzantine hands till fourth crusade; it was from here that Louis VII sailed for Antioch, while the troops that attempted the land route were massacred. From 1204 to 1207 it was held by an Italian adventurer, Aldobrandini, and was taken from him by the Selchukids. Under Ala'ud-Din Kai-Qobad it was embellished by many buildings, particularly the great minaret. Captured by Peter I of Cyprus in 1361 (carved inscription in Museum), but surrendered in 1373 to secure Turkish help against the Genoese in Famagusta.

Antalya, Bay of; Mare Pamphylium, Antalya Kürfezi: The coastline from Antalya to Anamur was for Armenia debatable ground first with Byzantium, then with the Selchukids. Between Antalya and Alanya there is a narrow coastal plain; from Alanya to Selinus the hills come steeply down to the sea. On the former, the port of Side, abandoned in the tenth century, at the mouth of the river Melos, was probably replaced in the Middle Ages by a landing stage at the present Manavgat. Beyond Alanya classical fortifications seem to have been at times re-used: Selinus, Antiochia ad Cragum, Charadus, Platanistus. Some of these were certainly occupied by Armenia under Leon II and again in the fourteenth century during the Cypriot possession of Antalya. See Beaufort, *Karamania*, pp. 113–206.

Antiochetta, Antiochia ad Cragum: On a rocky cliff above the sea, 77 km. north-west of Anamur. Remains of fortifications. John XXII (Raynaldus, *Annal. Eccl.* V, p. 538) offered Sechin and Antioch ad Cragum to the Hospitallers on behalf of Leon V. Possibly the Antouchezda of the baronial list. Beaufort, *Karamania*, p. 193.

Arioudz-pert (Castle of the Lion): Occupied by Thoros II (1146) in the Amouda neighbourhood.

Armenia: Originally is the tableland lying north of Lake Van and south of Georgia. The transfer of the name to Cilicia was a gradual process. The twelfth-century rulers there were known as lords or princes of the mountains, and the term Cilicia remained in use. Leon II was however crowned as King of Armenia, and from then on this is the designation of his dominions. They were sometimes known as Armenia Minor, but never in official use. The name Sissouan is used in the rhyming chronicle of Gregory Dgha (Alishan, *Sissouan*, p. 40). For title 'King of Armenia', see Rüdt-Collenberg, *Rupenides*, p. 38.

Arsuz, Rhossus, Rosus, ? Port Bonnel: Jacquot (*Antioche*, p. 41) wrongly identifies it with Roche Roussel. Cahen (*Syrie*, p. 141) identifies it with Port Bonnel (q.v.). (Adana, H–IX; 87, IId.)

Asgouras: Alishan identifies with Asers. Bertrandon de la Broquière (*Voyage*, p. 104) places the castle of Essers between Leve and Heraclea and Schéfer identifies it with Ivris (Ibriz) in the hills to the south of Heraclea. Originally held by the Nathanael family and then passed to the Hetoumids. In 1166 it was held with Lamas by Vassag, brother of Pagouran of Babaron. In 1316 it belonged to Sempad the Marshal, who held it with Binag. Alishan, *Sissouan*, pp. 118–19.

Ayas, Lajasso, Laiazzo, Laicum, Laiacium, Laizo, Yumurtalik: The
port was strongly fortified with a land and sea (island) castle. According
to Bar Hebraeus (p. 465) the island fortress had been recently built in
1282, when the inhabitants took refuge there during a raid. Marco Polo
in 1295 described it 'as the mart for all the riches of the East. All the
spicery, and the cloths of silk and gold, and other valuable wares that
come from the interior are brought to that city . . . Whoever would travel
to the interior takes his way by this city of Layas.' (*La Description du
monde*, trs. L. Hambis (Paris, 1955), p. 20.) After the sack of 1322 only the
land castle was rebuilt. Pope John XXII contributed towards the repairs
of the fortifications in 1331. In 1337, however, another raid resulted in
terms by which all the fortifications were destroyed, and the Mamluks
occupied a defenceless town, that was never to regain its importance. In
1367 it was raided by Peter of Cyprus and the town burned.

The site has never systematically been examined. Beaufort, who gave
such a detailed account of the coastline in 1812, was unfortunately attacked
and severely wounded when he landed there. It was rebuilt by Sulaiman
the Magnificent.

Heyd, *Commerce* II, pp. 74–95; Langlois, *Voyage*, pl. V. For variants
of name see P. Pelliot, *Notes on Marco Polo* (Paris, 1963) II, p. 760.
(Adana, H–IX; 86, IIb.)

Ayas, Elaeusa: Ruins of Roman and Byzantine town between Corycus and
the Lamas river.

Ayun: Unidentified holding of the Teutonic Knights.

Azaz, Hasarth, Hazart: N. of Aleppo. Captured in 1118 by Roger of Antioch
and Leon and annexed to the county of Edessa. The surrender of Azaz
was part of the terms of Baldwin II's ransom in 1124; Baldwin, however,
broke the agreement, and retained it, and when it was besieged by al-
Bursuki and Tughtigin in 1125, the Franks succeeded in raising the siege;
taken by Nur-ad-Din in 1150. It was the cross-roads of the Antioch–
Turbessel and Aleppo–Marash routes. There are some few remains of
the medieval fortifications on the tell. Cahen, *Syrie*, p. 139; *Guide Bleu*
(1965) p. 332.

Azgit: See *supra*, pp. 85–91; Fedden and Thomson, *Castles*, p. 47 (with plan).

Babaron, Barbaron, Paperon, Candirli, Çandir Kale: About 11 km. north-
east of Gösne on the southern side of the Deli Su. It seems to have
blocked a possible route through the Taurus, and this was used by Kai
Khusrau II, guided by Constantine of Lampron, in his raid of 1245 on

Tarsus. It was generally held by the younger branch of the Hetoumids. It was here that Rita, daughter of Sempad of Lampron and sister of Pagouran of Babaron, took refuge with her two sons, Rupen and Leon, and brought them up during the usurpation of Mleh. Pagouran is described by Sempad the Constable as 'a good and generous man, beloved by God and men' (*RHC.Arm.* II, p. 623); he was still lord of Babaron at the time of Leon's coronation in 1198. It was later held by his brother, Vasag, passing to his son, Constantine the Regent, and then to the latter's son, Sempad the Constable. On the death of his grandson, another Sempad, it was held by Oshin of Corycus, on whose assassination in 1329 it passed to the crown. Henry II of Cyprus was imprisoned there in 1309. In 1347/8 it was occupied by the Karamanids.

The ruins of the castle are on a plateau, approximately 500 by 300 m. in extent, approached by a flight of 112 steps, passing at one point through a tunnel. There is also inside the walls a flight of 25 steps leading to sub-terranean rooms under the plateau. The buildings within the walls included a triple-apsed chapel and the remains of the hall, as shown by Gottwald's plans and photographs. On the side wall of the chapel was an Armenian inscription stating that it was built in 1251 by Sempad the Constable in honour of his father, Constantine, but Sir Dennis Wright in 1946 could find no trace of the inscription and the inner buildings were much decayed. There is a description of the castle in E. J. Davis, *Life in Asiatic Turkey* (1879), largely based on a visit made in 1875 by Father Sibilian and a 'Mr. M. Anketell' (possibly the Rev. H. K. Anketell who later, in 1893, was Chaplain to the Embassy in Constantinople). It seems possible that Babaron was also known as Sempadagla (q.v.).

Gottwald, *BZ.* XXXVI (1936), pp. 86–100, pls. II–IV; Alishan, *Sissouan*, pp. 72–7; E. J. Davis, *Life in Asiatic Turkey*, pp. 42–5; A. F. Townshend, *A military consul in Turkey* (London, 1910), photograph. Information from Sir Dennis Wright. (Mersin, H–VIII; 76, Iz.)

Baghras, Bakras, Pagrai, Gaston: See *supra*, pp. 34–83. (Adana, H–IX; 90, IId.)

Bahçe Pass, Pass of Marra: The pass north of the Amanus gates, on a route from the Marash–Antioch road to Osmaniye.

Barsoma, Convent of, Boursum Kale: Residence of Patriarch of Syrian Jacobites near Gargar. Joscelin II of Edessa briefly occupied it as a strong point. *RHC.Arm.* I, p. 342.

Behesni, Behetselin, Besni: On a pass between two valleys, leading down to the Euphrates; remains of citadel or a rocky spur between two ravines. Part of the county of Marash, it was lost in the mid-twelfth century, but regained for a time by Hetoum I. Ainsworth, *Travels* I, p. 265 (with engraving of castle); Cahen, *Syrie*, p. 120.

Beylan, Belen, Pass of: On the route over the Amanus mountains from Alexandretta to Antioch.

Binag: Unidentified site held in 1316 by Sempad the Marshal along with Asgouras, and presumably in that neighbourhood.

Bira, Bir, Birta, Biredyik: On the east bank of the Euphrates between Tur-bessel and Edessa. An important crossing; considerable remains of citadel, with much later restoration. Ainsworth, *Travels* I, p. 304; Des-champs, *Crac des Chevaliers*, p. 41, pl. VIIa; Cahen, *Syrie*, p. 122; Pou-joulat, *Voyage*, pp. 432–4.

Bodrum, Budrum, Hieropolis Castabala (Pl. 44): On the north side of the Pyramus river, at the crossing of a road from the Amanus Gates to Kadirli. The castle is on a rock above the ruins of the classical town. Bell, *Rev. Archéologique* VI, pp. 1–29; Alishan, *Sissouan*, pp. 229–31; Stark, *Alexander's Path*, pp. 8–12, and *RCAJ*. XLIII, p. 9. (Kozan, G–IX; 89, Iü.)

Bounard: Held with Silifke in the 1199 list, possibly Dio-Caesarea (q.v.).

Bragana, Prakana, ? Alâkapi: Almost certainly to the south of the Göksu on the route from the crossing at Köserlerli to Gülnar and Silifke; possibly the site at Alâkilise, where there are some medieval remains. In 1188 it was taken by a Selchukid emir, and the constable Baldwin was killed in an attempt to retake it. Two months afterwards Leon retook it. In 1198 it is listed between Pertgau and Silifke. It was taken by Kai-Khusrau II in 1246. Two years later the Armenians surprised and retook it. Bean and Mitford, *Journeys*, pp. 221, 222. (Silifke ve Mersin, I–VII; 66, 67, IIf.)

Caesarea of Cappadocia, Kayseri: The main stronghold of Byzantium and then of the Selchukids north-west of the Cilician Gates. It was besieged by Leon in 1211, but was never occupied by the Armenians.
Texier, *Description* II, pp. 53–60; *ILN*. (26.2.1938), p. 356.

Çakitsaya: River flowing through the Cilician Gates and ending in the lake on the Seyhan, N. of Adana.

Calamella, Canamella: Port on the coast north of Alexandretta, sometimes identified with Payas, but more probably Hisn at-Tinat. It was in Templar hands when taken by Baybars in 1266. Cahen, *Syrie*, p. 150.

Calendria, Chelindri, Gilindire, Celenderet, Candalar (Pl. 7): On the coast 47 km. east of Anamur; a road leads north to join the main Silifke–Karaman route. Beaufort describes the ruins of a hexagonal tower (*Karamania*, p. 209), Leake (*Journal*, p. 115) 'a square tower on the end of the cape'. For an early nineteenth-century engraving see Carne, *Syria, the Holy Land, Asia Minor* . . . illustrated (London, 1836), I, p. 71. Certainly held by the Armenians, but difficult to identify in any list. (Silifke ve Mersin, I–VII; 56, IIh.)

Camardias, Camardesuim, Camardes: Fedden and Thomson (pp. 37, 103–5) take this to be the castle above the town of Silifke: but it is probably the Goumardias of the coronation list, held with Norpert by the Sebastos Henry. His son, Constantine, held the lordship of Silifke. Camardias may be the ruin at the crossing of the Saleph further north than Silifke. The Charter of 1210 refers to *Civitatem Seleph, castellum novum et Camardesium*: but the French summary from an Inventory of Charters (*Cartulaire*, p. 119) refers to 'the town of Seleck with its castle, Camerdes and Château neuf'. Langlois, *Cartulaire*, pp. 115–16.

Çardak Kale: Ruined fortress on route to Islahiye, near Yarperz. Possibly Hamus (q.v.).

Cassius, Mt, Mt Parlier, Jebel Akra: South of Antioch, above the port of Seleucia-in-Pieria. On it was the monastery of St Barlaam, built on the site of a classical temple (excavations carried out by the University of Utah). *Guide Bleu* (1965), p. 645.

Castrum Nigrinum, Mandjilike Kale, Mancinik: Wilbrand (Laurent, *Peregrinatores*, p. 175) left it on his right going from Portella to Canamella. Cahen (*Syrie*, p. 149) identifies it with the ruined castle of Mandjilike Kale in the hills to the north-east of Payas. Taken and destroyed by the Mamluks in 1336. An Armenian inscription mentions a restoration in 1290 (Sanjian, *Colophons*, p. 22). Heberdey and Wilhelm, *Reisen*, p. 75. (Adana, H–IX; 90, IIa.)

Castrum Puellarum: v. **Sari-Saki**

Cavalieri, Cape, Aphrodisias, Zephyrion: The names of the two capes on the bay formed by the Saleph delta have frequently been transposed, but Cape Sarpedon on the east and Cape Zephyrion on the west are now accepted. Aphrodisias was on Cape Zephyrion and this in the Middle Ages was known as Cape Cavalieri. Beaufort (*Karamania*) and Heyd (*Com-*

merce du Levant, I, p. 303) both attribute the name to the Hospitallers. 'Every accessible spot of this peninsula has been defended by walls' (Beaufort, *Karamania*, p. 213). Schaffer (*Cilicia*, p. 74) describes ruins with a strongly fortified isthmus.

Ceyhan River: v. Pyramus

Charadus, Kaladran Kale, Celandro, Scalandros: Ruins of a Byzantine citadel 58 km. north of Anamur. Leake (*Journal*, p. 124) described a building 1 mile up the valley which seemed to be of Venetian or Genoese construction. Cleave reports only low remains of walls.

Chilvan Kale, Shalan Kale, Sultan Kale, ? Roche Roussel, Hajar Shuglan or Shoglan: On a peak, 1,250 m. in height, above the Hajar Shuglan Pass through the Amanus mountains. A Templar fortress, it was attacked by Leon II in 1204. Cahen (*Syrie*, pp. 142, 143) identifies it convincingly with Roche de Roissol (Roussel). See Jacquot, *Antioche*, p. 119, for full description and plan and photograph. *Guide Bleu* (1965), p. 648.

Cilicia: Traditionally its name came from Cilix, brother of Europa. Occupied by Assyrians, Greeks, Persians and constantly changing hands, it became a Roman province in 102 B.C. Cicero was governor in 50 B.C., and describes the country in his letters. In 23 B.C. Augustus combined it with Syria, but it became a separate province again a century later. In the organisation of the themes under Heraclius, Cilicia was part of the theme of Seleucia, but much of the plain, including Tarsus, was in Arab hands. Including the southern slopes of the Taurus mountains and the coastal plain, it was divided into Cilicia Trachaea, the rugged western half, and Cilicia Campestris, the fertile eastern plain. The length from east to west is about 400 km.; the breadth varies from 48 to 80 km.; the length of the coastline is about 800 km.

Cilician Gates, Pylae Ciliciae: The main entry from Cappadocia to Cilicia through the Taurus mountains. The route from Kayseri via Niǧde (Tyana) joins the routes from Ankara and Konya at Ulukişla (Zeyve). From there the road continues, following the valley of the Çakit Suyu to Tahta Kopru, where it is joined by a more easterly and mountainous route from Niǧde; from there to Pozanti (south of the ancient Podandus) beyond which two valleys branch, that of the Çakitsuyu to the east, followed by a narrow road to Adana, and that to the west, following the course of a tributary stream to the main pass at Gulek Bogazi (1,050 m.), whence the road descends to (54 km.) Tarsus. The junction of the two rivers below Pozanti is commanded by the castle of Anahṣa Kale. On the Tarsus road, 17 km. below the pass, a road leads westward to (38 km.) Namrun (Lampron). The main Armenian castles on the routes to the pass were Lampron, Gouglag (in the pass), Molevon and Loulon.

There are very many discussions of the routes and sites of the pass but they are mainly concerned with classical problems, and the Armenian sites are still hard to place with any exactitude. Bertrandon de la Broquière's account in *Le Voyage d'outremer* (p. 102) is an important medieval description.

See, amongst many others: Ainsworth, *Travels* II, pp. 71–9; Kotschy, *Reisen*, pp. 40–53, 276–88; Ramsay in *Geographical Journal* XXII (1903), pp. 357 ff.; Davis, *Asiatic Turkey*, pp. 198–244; M. H. Ballance in *AS.* XIV (1964), pp. 139 ff.; R. P. Harper in *AS.* XX (1970), pp. 149 ff.

Çinçin Kale: Texier (*Description* II, p. 43) states that overlooking a pass, which forms the only practicable route between Marash and Coxon, there is a great limestone mass, isolated on all sides like a pyramid, with a castle on the top. The castle is impregnable and commands the whole valley. All existing structures are Saracenic; there are two vast halls with ogival vaults, some cisterns, and a fortification follows the edge of the rock all round. He suggests it may be the Azamora which Strabo reports in one of the defiles of Amanus. No recent investigation has been made of this site, and its exact locality is uncertain; possibly Gantchi or Pertounk (q.v.).

Commagene: Bounded on south-east by Euphrates and to the north-west by the mountains; known to the Assyrians as Kummuk, the boundary state between Melitene and Carchemish. Samosata was probably its chief city. For all this area see atlas of Humann and Puchstein, *Reisen in Kleinasien.*

Corycus, Le Courco, Curco, Gorighos (Pls. 41, 42): An important Roman and Byzantine site; refortified by Alexius Comnenus after the first crusade; in Armenian hands under Thoros II, when Benjamin of Tudela describes it as the beginning of the Armenian dominions. The island castle, known as Kiz Kale, has Armenian inscriptions of Leon II (1206) and Hetoum I (1251). The land castle is built of much re-used earlier material, including a gateway which may be in its original position. From 1359 to 1448 Corycus was held by Cyprus, and for much of that period was the main, if not only, Christian port on the southern coast. The ruined church is

PLATE 46   TIL HAMDOUN

The south-west corner

The hill, formerly called Til Hamdoun, as well as much of its neighbourhood,
consists of basalt, and the castle was built almost entirely of that material.
The blackness of the great D-shaped tower is, however, enlivened by a course
of white stone. The tower stands above a sloping revetment, which continues
along the west of the *enceinte* and to the middle of the north side. There
was originally no outer wall behind this half of the fortress, but an extensive
outer enclosure was afterwards added (cf. Pl. 45); its comparatively thin wall
is seen on the right, at the outset of one of its small towers.   A. W. L.

late Byzantine or Armenian work. Close to Corycus are the two great craters known as 'heaven' and 'hell', with at the bottom of the former a Byzantine church. These extraordinary features, the centre of a long cult, must have been known to the Armenians, but there is no identifiable reference to them or traces of Armenian work. Langlois, *Voyage*, pp. 200–16, pl. IX; E. Herzfeld and S. Guyer, *MAMA*. II, pp. 161–94; Müller-Wiener, *Castles*, pp. 79, plan and pls. 111–14; Forsyth, *DOP*. XI, pp. 225–228. (Mersin, H–VIII; 72 IIe.)

Coxon, Cocussus, Gôgison, Göksun: On the route from Caesarea to Marash, at the point where it is joined by the road from Melitene and Albistan. There is no evidence of an Armenian fortress here, but there must still have been Byzantine fortifications, and it was a place of considerable strategic importance. The main body of the first crusade made a halt of some days here, before crossing the Taurus.

Crambusa, Papadula, Babadil, Kizbalesi: Island lying off the coast between Cape Zephyrion and Calendria. Schaffer, *Karamania*, p. 74.

Crasson, Kesoun, Cesson: Occupied by Kogh Vasil at time of Baldwin's advance on Edessa; the citadel rebuilt by Baldwin of Marash, but nothing now remains. A Frankish archbishopric, and in the twelfth century a town of considerable Armenian and Syriac culture. Cahen, *Syrie*, p. 120.

Cumbethfort: Holding of Teutonic Knights, south of Adana, *in territorio Meloni* as was the Hospitaller's castle of Vaner. Wilbrand in Laurent, *Peregrinatores*, p. 176.

Cybistra, Cyzistra, Guizisdara, Guentrosgoi, Guentrosgavis, Dhu'l Kila: The fortress of the Mandalean family and scene of the murder of Gakik in 1079/80, and the vengeance taken by Thoros I. Baladhuri (p. 263) says the name Dhu'l Qila or Kila (possessor of fortresses) was given it because it was made up of three castles. Ibn Khordadbah (trs. Gaye, p. 80) calls it 'a mountain crowned with fortresses', but says its real name was Jusastorun ('approaching the stars' = Armenian Guizisdara). Matthew of Edessa describes it as a very strong castle in the 'plain of Ardzias'. Dulaurier suggests (Matthew of Edessa, p. 420) that this is a plain leading into Mt Argaeus, south-west of Kaiseryi. This would correspond with Cyzistra (Yesilhisar) on the route from Kayseri to Niğde.

Cydnus, Tarsus Çayi: Rises in the Taurus near the Cilician Gates and flows south to the coast; originally navigable as far as Tarsus, it had already silted up in the medieval period.

Dadjig, Danzoud: To escape the Emperor Manuel, Thoros retired in 1159 to this rock, which had never before been inhabited (Mat. of Edessa, ed. Dulaurier, p. 353). Alishan (*Sissouan*, p. 119) thinks that it was a castle in the valley of the Cydnus; possibly Dausid Kalesi (q.v.).

Darbsak, Trapesac, Terbezek: On the eastern slopes of the Amanus between the entry to the Syrian gates and the northern pass of Chilvan Kale, overlooking the route by the Amouq to Marash. Some ruins with bossed stonework. Cahen, *Syrie*, p. 141; Jacquot, *Antioche*, p. 176.

Dausid Kale: Small castle on left bank of Cydnus, 3.2 km. from Beglor or Fekeler Koi; most of wall fallen into river, only a tower and some scraps of aqueduct remained '40 years ago' (Alishan, *Sissouan*, p. 119).

Dio-Caesarea, Uzuncaburç: Roman town with intact Hellenistic residential tower, 29 km. north of Silifke: possibly the Bounard of the 1198 list. *MAMA.* II, pp. 44–79; *Guide Bleu* (1965), p. 624.

Djandji: Probably one of the castles on the Coxon–Andirin–Kadirli route, but there is as yet no certain identification. Alishan (*Sissouan*, pp. 213–14) identifies it with Çinçin Kale (q.v.), but Gantchi or Pertounk seems a more probable candidate for that site.

Djegher, Dgigher, Giguer: The district on the western slopes of the Amanus, north of Alexandretta. It is not certain what castle was the headquarters of this area; ceded by Leon II in 1214 to the Hospitallers as guarantee for a loan. Cahen, *Syrie*, p. 620.

Duluk, Doliche, Telouch, Tulupa: In the valley of the Nahr Kerzin, at the junctions of the roads from Marash and Mamistra to Edessa. Cahen, *Syrie*, p. 115.

Durak, Dorak: North of Tarsus, on the southern slopes coming down from the Cilician Gates. Edib (*Itinerary*, p. 99) refers to a castle of 'Doulek' at approximately this site. Gottwald (*BZ.* XLI, p. 94, pl. III) describes a rectangular tower with continuous machicolations, and calls it Kys-Kale. (Ulukişla, G–VIII; (78/79, Iv.)

Edessa, Roha, Urfa: The name Edessa was given it by the Macedonians. *C.* 132 B.C. it passed under the control of a local Semitic dynasty, the Abgars, and in A.D. 204 Abgar IX (170–212/3) accepted Christianity. In 260 it was conquered by the Sassanides. *c.* 637 it was occupied by the

Arabs. It was taken by the Byzantines in 944 and remained vaguely under their control till occupied by the Selchukids in 1087. In 1095 the Armenian, Thoros, seized it and held it till the arrival of the crusaders in 1098. The fortifications, much damaged and rebuilt, are basically Byzantine. A Greek inscription refers to work carried out under Alexis Comnenus; on a round tower in the east wall an Armenian inscription mentions a restoration in 1122 under Count Joscelin. The citadel, on rising ground, is cut off from the hillside by a rock-cut ditch, with a pillar left for a drawbridge. The Latin cathedral of St John the Baptist was destroyed by fire in 1183, and the famous Byzantine church of Hagia Sophia was demolished under Zengi. Poujoulat, *Voyage*, pp. 413–16; Cahen, *Syrie*, pp. 111–13; T. E. Lawrence, *Oriental Assembly*, pp. 6–9; J. B. Segal, *Edessa*.

Engousoud: Fortified township and bishopric in eastern Cilicia; held by a lord, Baldwin, in 1198; unidentified site.

Ermenek, v. Jamengane

Fornos, Fornauce, Fernus, Fernuz: In Coronation list between Gantchi and Gaban. On the hill above it was the monastery of St Stephen of Oulni. The village of Fornos, on the river of the same name, is in the upper part of a valley leading to Zeytin. Gantchi seems to have been in the same valley, further to the east.

Frenk Kale, Karafrenk Kale: Ruins of castle. Favre and Mandrot, *Voyage*, p. 35; Cahen, *Syrie*, p. 145.

Gaban, Geben, Gheiben: The Armenian name means 'narrow pass' and the castle commanded a defile through the mountains on the route from Kayseri to Marash. It was a customs post, and also a bishopric. It was always a site of some strategic importance. It was here, in 1072, that the Armenian lord of Antioch, Khatchadour, fighting on behalf of Romanus Diogenes, then a refugee at Adana, was defeated by the forces of Michael Doukas, commanded by the Norman, Robert Crespin. Occupied by the Rupenids it was taken by John Comnenus in 1137, and then by the Danishmendids around 1140. It was retaken by Thoros II and was given by Rupen III to his brother Leon. At the time of the latter's coronation it was held by Tancred, presumably a Latin; by 1215 it was in the hands of an Armenian baron, Leon, and in 1216 was besieged by Kai-Kaus I. The relieving force was heavily defeated, but the castle held out. At the end of the thirteenth century it was held by Constantine, brother of Hetoum II. It was the last stronghold to which Leon VI fled in 1375, and it was there that he was forced to surrender after a nine months' siege. After 1375 the widow of Leon's general, Hetoum, of the Lampron branch, rallied the Armenian forces and reoccupied Gaban; her son George is called Lord of Gaban and seems to have maintained a certain independence there in the first half of the fifteenth century.

No certain identification of the site has been made.

Alishan, *Sissouan*, pp. 198, 210; Fedden and Thomson, *Crusading Castles*, p. 37; information from Mr John Dunbar and Dr Richard Cleave.

Gabnupirath, ? Gaban (q.v.): Captured by Malik Mohammad of Melitene in 1139 along with Vahka. Barhebraeus, ed. Budge, p. 266.

Gaënsin, Ghensin, ?Kantze: Near Tahtaçi on headwaters of Cydnus, east of Lampron. Alishan, *Sissouan*, p. 123.

Gantchi, Gaintchi, Gantchoug, Ghorriculi, Cukur Hisar: Probably in Fornos valley, though Rüdt-Collenberg places it north-west of Gaban. Held by brother of Hetoum I, Oshin, who died there in 1265. Guy, brother of Oshin the Regent, held it in 1320. Alishan, *Sissouan*, p. 213.

Gargar, Gerger, Karkar, Roche-Jaune, Tegenkir: Castle on the Euphrates north of Kahta. The Armenian lord, Constantine, was an ally of Baldwin I but Baldwin II later imprisoned him. Gargar was ceded to Belek of Aleppo in 1123, when Baldwin II was captured. In 1124 it was retaken by Constantine's son Michael, by a surprise attack with only fifty men. The Franks seem to have regained possession of it, and to have installed there Basil, brother of the Catholicos, St Nerses Schnorhali, in 1136. Basil was still lord of Gargar when the town was taken in 1149 by Kara Arslan, the Artukid ruler of Hisn Kaifa on the Tigris. Cahen, *Syrie*, pp. 125–6. Ainsworth identifies it with Juliopolis (*Travels*, p. 275, with engraving). Matthew of Edessa, ed. Dulaurier, pp. 330, 464.

Gaston, Gastum, Guastone, v. **Baghras**

Gaston, Fountain of: Spring behind the castle of Baghras. It was here that Leon II and Bohemond III of Antioch met in 1188. (See *supra*, pp. 18, 19.)

Ghuikhath: Monastery burnt in 1275, but not reached in 1279/80. Bar Hebraeus, p. 462.

Giguer, v. **Djegher**

Gobidara, Colidara, Gobidurh: According to Matthew of Edessa in the Taurus mountains in the 'district of Maraba'. In the list of 1198 between Partzapert and Molevon. Rüdt-Collenberg places it to north-east of Sis. Pegolotti (*La Pratica della Mercatura*, ed. A. Evans, Cambridge, Mass. 1936, p. 28) describes it as 'on the boundary of the lands of the king of Armenia'. Dapper (*Asia*) places it on his map in the nills north-west of the 'Syriae Portae' (Amanus Gates). It was the seat of an Armenian bishop. Favre and Mandrot (*Cilicie*, p. 766) mention three castles north of Sis – Turris Kale, Ardal Kale and Kara Sis. One of these must be Vahka; another is probably Gobidara; the third may possibly be Partzapert. The Catholicos Gregory V was imprisoned here in 1194 and fell to his death in trying to escape. Alishan, *Sissouan*, p. 167.

Gökvelioǧlu, Gueval-oǧlu, Kizlar Kale, Mosku (of Circassian settlers): 13 km. south of Mamistra. The castle is built on an outcrop of rock on the southern extremity of the Gebel-i-Nur mountains. It must have had an Armenian name, but it is so far impossible to identify it. Youngs, *AS*. XV (1965), pp. 118–25. Favre and Mandrot, *Voyage*, p. 122. (Adana, H–IX; 84, IIa.)

Gorighos, v. **Corycus**

Gösne, Gösnekoy: In the hills north of Mersin, in the neighbourhood of Babaron. On a hill above it are the ruins of a church. Possibly the convent church of Melidseh, the burial place of the Hetoumids.
Gottwald, *BZ*. XLI (1941), pp. 96–7.

Gouglag, Gülek, Cogueloch, Cublech: Overlooking the Cilician Gates, on a hill 1,600 m. above sea level, 600 m. higher than the gorge. Approached by about sixty steps cut in the rock. The west wall is the best preserved, and the upper part is built of well-shaped blocks. On the south-east it overlooked a high cliff.

Held by Sempad in 1198; at the end of the thirteenth century it was held by Alinak, brother of King Oshin. Bertrandon de la Broquière (p. 102) thought it the highest castle he had ever seen. It was a customs post.

Kotschy, *Reisen*, pp. 40–53, 73–204; Favre and Mandrot, *Voyage*, p. 135; Schaffer, *Cilicia*, p. 55; Alishan, *Sissouan*, p. 132. (Ulukişla, G–VIII; 77, Iv.)

M

Gouvaira, ?Govasse: Held in 1198 with Sinida: in the region of Silifke. Ceded in 1233 by Constantine of Lampron to the Hospitallers. *RHC.Arm.* I, p. lxxiv.

Hajar Shoglan (Shuglan), Pass of: The route through the Amanus mountains from Darbsak to Sari-Saki, passing below the castle of Chilvan Kale (q.v.).

Hamus, Hamouss, ?Bodrum, ?Çardak Kale: Held by Vardan at the time of his revolt against Leon II. It was here that Stephen, brother of Thoros II, was captured by the Greeks and boiled alive. Cahen (*Syrie*, p. 147) suggests identification with Bodrum, but not convincingly, though no castle in the 1198 list is identifiable with Bodrum. Hamus in the list is placed between Djegher and Sarvantikar. The only ruins that seem appropriate are those of Çardak Kale, north-east of Osmaniye.

Hamus, River: Rises in the hills above the Bahce pass and flows south-west joining the Pyramus by the crossing to Bodrum.

Harunia, Haroun, Harouniya: North of Amanus Gates. Said to have been founded by Harun ar-Rashid. Ceded to the Teutonic Knights in 1236. Alishan, *Sissouan*, pp. 236–8; Cahen, *Syrie*, p. 146. (Maras, G–X; 92, Iu.)

Heraclea (of Cappadocia), Eregli: On the route from Iconium to the Cilician Gates. It was taken in 1211 by Leon II, but evacuated almost immediately afterwards.

Hromgla, Ranculat, Kala-Rhomaya, Rum Kale: On the Euphrates, north of Bira. Taken by Baldwin in 1116. The Patriarch moved there in 1147 and bought it from Beatrice of Edessa in 1150. According to Bar Hebraeus (ed. Budge, p. 277) the Catholicus was invited there by an Armenian, Michael, whom he then dispossessed by treachery in 1150: it is more likely that negotiations with Beatrice bypassed the local holder. It was taken by Mamluks in 1292. There are considerable remains of the castle, which is built on a rock tongue *c.* 400 by 200 m. wide, cut off by moat *c.* 30 m. deep. Walls follow the contours at 50 m. higher than the river while the edge of rock in the centre of the moat rises 30 to 40 m. higher. The entrance path rises on an artificial ramp below the west wall to the first gate, passing below an Armenian inscription flanked by a pair of Selchukid lions. This first gate is entirely rock cut. The path then climbs on the native rock more steeply to the second, which is of masonry and has a small room overlooking the Merziman Su, beside the passage.

The path continues under the wall to the third, below which flows the Merziman. Then it turns and passes through a rock gate into a small court, from which a fourth vaulted gateway leads to an outer court, bounded on the east by the rising rock and on the west by the wall. Many caves offer shelter to man and beast. The wall round the citadel has for long stretches a vaulted passage, from which arrow-slits open. On the north-west the passage is two-storeyed. Gateway on east with rock-cut stairs to Euphrates.

A. Nöldeke, *Petermanns Mitteilungen* LXVI, p. 53; F. Frech, *Geog. Zeitschrift* XXII (1916), p. 5, pl. 1; Dussaud, *Topographie*, p. 450; Humann and Puchstein, *Reisen*, pp. 175–80 (with plans and photographs); T. E. Lawrence, *Oriental Assembly*, pp. 28–37, pls. 14–18.

Isauria: Strictly a district on the northern slopes of the Taurus, but as a Byzantine administrative area it included Rough Cilicia, the hill-country west of the Lamas river.

Islahiye: At the point where the road through the Amanus Gates joins the main Antioch–Marash road. No Armenian name can be identified with it; possibly the classical Nicopolis.

Jamengane, Germanicae, ?Germanicopolis, Ermenek: Held with Manion, Lamos, Anamur and Halgam in 1198 list. Germanicopolis on the route from Laranda to Anamur seems a likely site; in the two versions of 1198 list, one gives Jamengane, the other Germanicae. In the face of the cliff above the town identified as Germanicopolis are medieval fortifications (information from Dr Terence Mitford).

Jofre-Cla, Château de Geoffroi: Held by Thoros, the Proximos, in 1316 (Galanus, *Conciliatio* I, p. 504). It is not so far possible to identify either the castle, or the Geoffrey who gave his name to it, but v. **Schoghagan.**

Jonah's Pillar, Portella (q.v.), **Bab Iskanderun:** A Roman gateway, now reduced to a single pier; here the crusaders kept a customs post on the coast road from Alexandretta to the Armenian Kingdom. See Sari-Saki. The site was traditionally the spot where Jonah was belched out by the whale.

Kadirli, Kars, Flaviopolis: At the junction of the routes from Mamistra to Sis and to Coxon via Andirin. This site must have been occupied by the Armenians, and may be that of Simona-gla or Arioudzepert. *Guide Bleu* (1965), p. 629; Bent, *JHS.* XI (1890), p. 233.

PLATE 47 YILAN KALE

View of castle from river

Overlooking the Pyramus river, and controlling the route along its western bank from Adana to Sis, this castle has as splendid a setting as any in Cilicia. Undoubtedly built by the Armenians, it has strangely never been securely identified with any of their known castles. Neither of the names that have been applied to it since, at least, the sixteenth century bears the slightest resemblance to any recorded in the mediaeval chronicles or lists of baronial holdings. Indeed both Yilan, which is Turkish for 'Snakes', and the Kurdish alternative Shah Meran, meaning 'King of Snakes', probably arose from ignorant interpretation of a carving over the main gateway – a figure, seated in the manner of an oriental potentate, holding upright in each hand a sceptre-like object which could easily be mistaken for a snake. The block on which this had already been carved forms the keystone of an arch, and on the next block a rampant lion faces it. But for the fact that neither the potentate nor the lion wears a crown he could be identified with Leon II, who used a crowned lion for his symbol; perhaps the representation is of this Leon between 1186 and his coronation in 1198, when Cilicia officially became a kingdom. But the style of the castle may be too advanced for that period and seems more appropriate to Leon III as Crown Prince, before his capture by the Arabs in 1266; cf. Pl. 48.   A. W. L.

Kahta, Kiahta: On a hill overlooking the Kahta river (Nymphaios) and con·trolling the route from Edessa to Melitene. The river is here crossed by a Roman bridge, with inscriptions of Vespasian and Severus. The Byzantine castle was rebuilt by the Aiyubids, and is well preserved, 'one of the most imposing ruins of the Turkish territory' (Cahen, *Syrie*, p. 124). Occupied by Armenians and crusaders during the periods in which they held Gargar, but there is surprisingly little reference to it in the chroniclers. The medieval occupants were probably unaware of the great Commagene Mausoleum of Nemroud Dagh in the hills above the castle. Humann and Puchstein, *Reisen*, pp. 232–353; Ainsworth, *Travels* I, p. 270; Percy, *Highlands of Asiatic Turkey*, pp. 101–4.

Karaköy Kale, v. Alara

Karaman, Laranda: Captured from Byzantium in the early twelfth century by the Danishmendids; taken by Barbarossa in 1190, and temporarily occupied by Leon II in 1210, who offered it to the Hospitallers. It became the capital of the Karamanids in 1265. *Guide Bleu* (1965), pp. 618–19.

Karamurt, River: In the Amanus mountains, flowing past Baghras to the plain of Antioch.

Karataş: 49 km. south of Adana, close to the ancient port of Megarsus; on Cape Karataş are some medieval ruins. At one time this was the main mouth of the Pyramus river. *Guide Bleu* (1965), p. 522; Beaufort, *Karamania*, p. 229.

Kayseri, v. Caesarea

Kesoun, v. Crasson

Kharput, Harput, Quartapiert, Elaziq: North-east of Melitene. The fortress, of which there are considerable remains, was originally Byzantine. Occupied by Philaretus, and taken by Malik-Shah in 1090. It was used as a prison for Baldwin and Joscelin, and in 1124 passed into the hands of the Artukids. Tozer, *Turkish Armenia*, pp. 217–21; Percy, *Highlands of Asiatic Turkey*, pp. 110–18; *Guide Bleu* (1965), p. 663.

Kilissa Kale: On a precipitous hill, SW. of Gösne, a hermitage church with a long Armenian inscription stating that it was built in 1241 by Constantine, father of Hetoum I. Davies, *Life in Asiatic Turkey*, pp. 45–7; Gottwald, *BZ.* XLI (1941), pp. 97–103.

Kiz Kale: (1) v. Dorak; (2) the island of Corycus, q.v.

Kum Kale: On right bank of Pyramus, N. of Bodrum; a small fortress-like tower of fine rustic masonry. Schaffer, *Cilicia*, p. 92. (Kozan, G–IX; 90, It.)

Lamas: A river that descends from the Taurus through a steep gorge, never more than half a mile across, on which there are many Roman and Byzantine ruins. After Pompey's destruction of the pirates at Coracesium in 67 B.C. this area seems to have been very thickly populated. The river marks the boundary between Rough and Plain Cilicia. A Roman paved road in the plain heads towards the first practicable ford upstream, in which vicinity there are fortified sites on or near both banks; one may have been the castle taken by Manuel Comnenus in 1155. The fortress named to Langlois as Lamas Kale, west of the river and near the coast, may have been Ak Kale, q.v.

Lamus, Adanda Kale, Lamos: In the hills north of Antiochetta, presumably the Lamos of the Coronation list, held with Manion, Germanicae and Anamur. Considerable remains of the Byzantine citadel. Bean and Mitford, *Journeys*, pp. 172–3.

Lampron, Lambro, Namrun (Pl. 6): 1072. Occupied by Oshin of the Hetoumids; it became the seat of that family, and controlled one of the routes from the Cilician Gates. It was unsuccessfully besieged by Mleh in 1171–2 and again in 1182 by Roupen III. Leon II secured it by treachery in 1186. Seat of an archbishopric. Langlois, *Voyage*, pl. XXIII; Robinson and Hughes, *AS.* XIX (1969), pp. 183–207; J. Thomson in *Geog. Mag.* XXIII (1951), p. 570.

Laranda, v. **Karaman**

Lausada, Lavsa: Fortified by Shahenshah in 1195 and surrendered in 1218 along with Loulon. In 1198 it was held with Timidouplos. There is a medieval fortress on the acropolis of the classical town. Bean and Mitford, *Journeys*, p. 210.

Liman Kale at Aga Liman: In the bay west of the Saleph delta, below Cape Cavalieri. Beaufort (*Karamania*, p. 220) describes it as a small castle, 'an irregular polygon of 8 sides, the walls of which are thick, with a footway and parapet near the top, and flanked by towers at each angle.'

Loulon, Loulou, Loulva, Luluah, Lolon, ?Leve: The name occurs from the ninth century; it constantly changed hands between Byzantines and Arabs and was regarded as 'a very strong fortress' of great importance 'on the frontiers of Cappadocia', and as controlling the approach to the Cilician Gates. The treaty between Alexius Comnenus and Bohemond in 1108 stipulated that it should depend on Antioch. In 1195 it was re-fortified by the Hetoumid, Shahenshah. Nerses of Lampron, his brother, states that it was at that time 'falling to ruins', and was rebuilt, making more solid and habitable the fortress built by the Greeks and destroyed by the Ishmaelites, 'so the power of Leon increased and he was able to extend his rule to the second Cappadocia'. Later, in 1218, Leon II sur-rendered the fortress to the Sultan of Iconium, as ransom for the constable Constantine, lord of Babaron and Partzapert, Constantine of Lampron, Kyr Isaac of Sigh, and other barons captured in 1216 when attempting to relieve the besieged castle of Gaban.

Its site has never been definitely fixed, but almost certainly it was on the northern side of the Cilician Gates. Bertrandon de la Broquière (ed. Dulaurier, p. 104) passed a castle on a mountain called Leve between the pass and Heraclea. (Loulon is written Loulva in the 1198 list.) This would place it at Ulukişla, wrongly identified by Ramsay as Faustinopolis. He describes a great mass of rock projecting from the plain; he could from a distance see no traces of walls, but was told that there were some on the further side. This seems the most possible site, but it has never been closely examined, and the identification remains hypothetical.

Ramsay, *Geographical Journal*, XXII (1903), p. 401 and *Historical Geography of Asia Minor*, pp. 351–54; Alishan, *Sissouan*, p. 117; Forrer, *Klio* XXX (1937). (Ulukişla, G–VIII; 74, İş.)

Maghva, Mavga Kale, Manga: The castle is built on an isolated pinnacle of rock in the Pirincsuru gorge, below the road from Mut to Dağ Pazari. The only approach is by a shelf of limestone rock, narrowing to a width of about 5 m. At the narrowest point of the approach a gap has been cut some 2 m. across and 2.5 m. deep. On either side of the shelf at this point are sheer drops of 245 m. Nine m. below the entrance are remains of outer walls. The entrance consisted of a tower commanding the approach and a bent entrance into a vaulted room. The arched doorway has rosettes carved on either side. The citadel was built on a limestone rock pinnacle, reached by steps cut in the characteristic limestone ledges. Rooms were cut into the rock, some of which still retain signs of coloured plastering. An inscription in Arabic refers to Ala'-ad-Din Kai-Qobad (1220–37). (Information from notes made by Mr A. Harrison and Mr Guthrie on a visit in August 1962.)

In the coronation list Maghva was held with Sig and Paleopolis by Kyr Sag. There is a description of the castle in Davis, *Asiatic Turkey*, pp. 327–9.

Maidzar: Site in the Gouglag area; where Hetoum I, his father Constantine and the constable Sempad inflicted a defeat on Kai Khusrau in 1245 (*RHC.Arm.* I, p. 649). Possibly the same as Medzbar, where there was an abbey and a bishopric.

Mamistra, Mopsuestria, Massisah, Msis, Misis: Taken by Tancred. See H. Hagenmeyer, ed., *Anonymi Gesta Francorum* (Heidelberg, 1899), I, p. 224. Occupied *c.* 1134 by Leon I, but brought under Byzantine control by John Comnenus. It was here that Manuel Comnenus in 1158 received the surrender of Reginald of Châtillon and Thoros II. From 1173 (Mleh's defeat of the Byzantine force under Constantine Coloman) Mamistra was in Armenian hands. (Its forced cession to Antioch by Rupen II probably never took effect.) It became an important centre, and the Genoese had a considerable depot there.

Manache, Manash, Convent of the Saviour at or near Babaron: Founded by the Regent Constantine. Drawing of triple round arches in Alishan, *Sissouan*, pp. 77–8. The holding of Manash in the 1298 list should probably be identified with this district.

Manakir: Imad Abu Charna (*RHC.Or.*, p. 212) mentions a castle burnt by the Armenians before the threat of Saladin's presence on the Göksu near Marash. See Cahen, *Syrie*, p. 149 n. 4.

Manion, Manioun: Lordship held with Anamur, Lamos and Germanica in 1198. It should lie somewhere on the Anamur–Laranda route. In 1259 Oshin of Corycus was lord of Manioun and of Gantschi, presumably not the Gantchi of the Andirin area.

Manoughade, Manavgat: Held with Alara in 1198. At the mouth of the river of the same name, 47 km. north-west of Alanya. Whether this was ever more than a titular occupation seems doubtful, but it is possible that Leon II pushed his frontier to the river Manavgat and that it was held there until Kai-Qobad's conquest of Alanya in 1221. (Antalya, H–V; 47, IIc.)

Maraba: Described by Matthew of Edessa (ed. Dulaurier, p. 216) as the district in which Gobidara is situated, and again as adjoining the territory of Anavarza (p. 274).

Marash, Germanica, Maraş: At the foot of the Anti-Taurus, and a town of some importance throughout the Middle Ages. It was the capital of Philaretus, passed to the Selchukids and was taken by the crusaders in 1097, but ceded by them to Alexius Comnenus, who installed the Armenian Tatoul as governor. In 1104 Baldwin incorporated it in the county of Edessa. It was held from 1136(?) to 1146 by Count Baldwin, who appears at times to have acted independently of both Edessa and Antioch; occupied by Nur-ad-din in 1152, who seems to have ceded it to his Armenian ally, Mleh. Until the Mamluk invasions it remained, with some interruptions, under Armenian control. Nerses of Lampron states that the Franks built a large church here. The citadel seems to have been little changed from its original tenth century Arab work. *RHC.Arm.* I, p. xlv n. 2; Humann and Puchstein, *Reisen*, pp. 197–20; Cahen, *Syrie*, p. 137.

Marra, Marrim, Forest of; v. **Sarvantikar**

Mazod-Khatche: In list of 1299 between Schoghagan and Til-Hamdun; possibly one of the castles of the Andirin route.

Megarse, Cape; Megarsi promontorium: The western point of the Gulf of Alexandretta; **v. Karataş.**

Melitene, Malatya: The ancient town was abandoned after being destroyed by Cimmerians in the seventh century B.C. The second town was a Roman creation. Justinian fortified and enlarged it, but from the Arab conquest onwards it was a border town, constantly changing hands. Occupied by the Byzantines in 972, it remained in their control until taken by the Selchukids in 1057. Philaretus held it for a period after 1070, and in 1090 it was in the hands of another Armenian, Gabriel. In 1103 he was over-thrown and killed by the Danishmendids. The present Malatya is on a third site, and little remains of the medieval city. *Guide Bleu* (1965), pp. 657–8.

Merkez: The small river Merkez (Cersos) flows from the Amanus mountains into the gulf between Alexandretta and Payas, above the Pillars of Jonah. The castle is sometimes identified with Sari-Saki (q.v.), but Edib (*Itinerary,*

p. 104) in 1682 distinguishes between a castle on the shore at 'Sakal-touton' and a castle in the hills called Merkez. Jacquot, *Antioche*, p. 150.

Michel-cla, Mikhailaq (Castle of Michael): Armenian fortress held in 1307 by Raymond; site unknown (Galanus, *Concilatio* I, p. 504). In 1198 a baron Michel held Pertiq, in the neighbourhood of Bragana, and it is possible that his name was transferred to the castle.

Molevon, Mauleon, Mons Leonis, Mons Livonis, ? Melanos: Mentioned by Byzantine sources in association with Loulon. In Sempad's list it comes between Gobidara and Gouglag, but that is only a very rough geographical indication. Molevan was besieged by Leon II during the revolt of Levon of Molevon and Vardan of Hamus (der Nersessian in *REA.* IV, pp. 103–4). It was here that Hetoum II was imprisoned and blinded by his brother Sempad in 1299. It was held by Alinakh (*d.* 1310), brother of Hetoum II and Oshin, along with Lampron, Gouglag and Roisso (? Anasha Kalesi). The monastery of Kemer, nearby, was the seat of the bishop of Molevon. Alishan, *Sissouan*, pp. 150–6.

Mountas, Mintas Kale: Taken in 1259 by Oshin (probably Oshin of Corycus, who was lord of Manioun and Gantschi). The sultan, Kilij-Arslan IV, sent a force to regain it, but was defeated by Hetoum I. Mountas was however evacuated. Alishan (*Sissouan*, p. 191) identifies it with a ruin south of Kara-Yusuf on north slopes of the Taurus not far from Ivriz (but v. **Asgouras**).

Mut, Claudiopolis: On the route from Silifke to Laranda. Considerable remains of the citadel with a round keep; probably Selchukid or Kara-manian work of the fourteenth century. It must for a time have been in Armenian occupation.

Muthakkab, el- (The Pierced): A name given by Arab geographers to an Omayyad fort or its site, the last halting-place on the route from Alex-andretta to Til Hamdoun. Probably identical with a Roman archway afterwards known as Demir Kapi (Iron Gate); this spanned the road, which retained the Roman paving into recent times (Bartlett, *Syria* III, pl. 58). There seems no explicit mention in crusader or Armenian writings; the comparable Roman gateway at Jonah's Pillar was called a Portella, and the word may conceivably refer on occasion to this counterpart.

Neghir: Lordship held with Partzapert (Rüdt-Collenberg, p. 65 n. 113, and p. 68 n. 136). Rüdt-Collenberg on his map places it on the northern slopes of the Amanus mountains, near the present village of Dortyol, south-west of Til Hamdoun but gives no evidence. This seems an improbable locality to be held in conjunction with Partzapert, and the site of Neghir must be regarded as uncertain.

Niğde: South-west of Kayseri, with an important group of Selchukid, Mongol and Karamanid monuments. The polygonal tower of the citadel above the town dates from the Ottoman period, after they had dispossessed the Karamanids in 1467. *Guide Bleu* (1965), p. 608.

Norpert, Castellum Novum: In 1198 held by the Sebastos Henry along with Goumardias (Camardias); his son Constantine held Silifke and Bounard, another son Baldwin held Antchouzeda and Gouba, and a third, Joscelin, Sinida. Henry was married to a sister of the Catholicos John, and he and his sons were imprisoned by Leon in 1207; in 1210 Leon transferred Norpert, Camardias and Silifke to the Hospitallers. Langlois, *Cartulaire*, p. 113.

Osmaniye: 12 km. east of Til Hamdoun, at the western foot of the Amanus Gates, a road junction for the route via Bodrum to Kadirli, and for that via the Bahce Pass and Sarvantikar. No Armenian name can be associated with it, and there are no remains of fortifications. The new road on which it stands was built 1885–90 and continues towards Yarpuz, and from there by a caravan track to Islahiye. Janke, *Alexanders Pfaden*, pp. 35–49.

Paleopolis, Pallopoli: Held in 1198 by Kyr Isaac along with Maghva and Siq; on Guglielmo Soleri's map of 1380 (reproduced Deschamps, *Crac des Chevaliers* Album, pl. 1). Pallopoli is shown on the coast west of Porto Cavaler, but the names here are very vaguely placed, and Porto Cavaler could be Taşucu not Cape Cavalieri. Possibly to be identified with Palaea, where Bean and Mitford report considerable ruins of Byzantine fortifications (*Journeys*, p. 195).

Paqsimat: Monastery destroyed in 1275 by Arabs raiding as far as Sis and Corycus, and again in 1279 or 1280 (Bar Hebraeus, pp. 453, 462).

Partzapert, Partrspert, Barsbirt (High Castle): Held by Thoros I; about two days journey north of Sis. Vartan writing soon after 1271 (St Martin,

Mémoire II, p. 437) states it was near Molevon. Abulfida (p. 29) calls it: 'A strong citadel on a high mountain, where the king of Little Armenia keeps his treasure and passes the summer . . . it is seen from afar.' Possibly John Mandeville's Castle of the Sparrowhawk above the town of Pharsipée or Persipée (M. Letts, *Mandeville's Travels* (London, 1953) II, p. 311). Alishan (*Sissouan*, p. 157) places it in the Zamanti valley, but possibly it is the Kale marked east of the Göksu, a tributary of the Zamanti. (Kozan, G–IX; 84, Ir.)

Payas, Pegae: On bay of Alexandretta, 21 km. north of Iskanderun. The present fortifications are Ottoman, built by Ibrahim Khan-Zadek under Sulaiman II; restored in nineteenth century by Ibrahim Pasha. Ainsworth, *Travels* II, p. 91; Humann and Puchstein, *Reisen*, p. 161; Bell in *Revue Archéologique* VI, pp. 1–29. (Adana, H–IX; 90, IIa.)

Pertiq, v. Michel-cla

Pertounk, Pertoud, Pertouce, Pertous: It was here that Kogh-Vasil had a victory over the Selchukids in 1107. It was captured by Stephen, brother of Thoros II, in 1156 as a base from which he planned to reconquer the lands of the county of Marash. With the population of Behesni he plotted a rising against their Moslem governor, but the plot was betrayed. Thoros became suspicious of his brother and for a time imprisoned him, and handed over Pertounk to the Selchukids to ameliorate the lot of the Christian communities in Commagene. Under Leon II it was once more in Armenian hands and was taken by Kai-Khusrau I in 1208, when its lord, Gregory, was captured. Seat of a bishopric. It is stated to be 15 miles north-west of Marash (Gazetteer, Wolf and Hazard, *History of the Crusades* II, p. 795). This would place it at the point where the main route to Coxon crosses the Pyramus river, but no ruins have been identified. v. Çinçin Kale.

Pinarbaşi: Town at junction of the Caesarea-Melitene road with that to Coxon and Marash. Possibly the Plastencia (? Comana) of the first crusade, where Peter 'de Alfibus' was left as governor, the first piece of crusading settlement. Peter appears to have taken service with Alexis. See Hagenmeyer, *Anonymi Gesta Francorum* (Heidelberg, 1890), p. 229 nn. 10 and 12.

Platanistus: Ruins of a fortress some 5 km. north of Anamur.

Podandus: The classical and medieval town lay to the north of the present Pozanti on the Cakit Su, north of the Cilician Gates. R. H. Harper, *AS.* XX, pp. 149–53.

PLATE 48

YILAN KALE

*Semicircular towers and main entrance in
south-west face of upper castle, walls of the
lower court in the foreground*

The approach was safeguarded by a lower court, enclosed within a double
line of walls. The gatehouse, projecting between the towers is entered through
the arch, enforcing another turn at right angles to reach the interior, most of
which was left as empty space; probably the local peasantry took refuge there.
A chapel and a cistern are isolated within but only three buildings remain
attached to the back of the circuit. Precisely similar masonry and a similar
design are found at Sis; Yilan can therefore be dated to the thirteenth century (see also Pl. 47).   A. W. L.

Port Bonnel: A short way north of the Ras al-Khanser, the promontory at the end of the Amanus mountains. It is to be identified either with Arsuz or with the small port 15 km. south of Arsuz, still known as Port des Francs, above which are the ruins of a medieval castle. Port Bonnel was in the possession of the Templars and was abandoned by them at the loss of Antioch in 1268. Cahen, *Syrie*, p. 141. Jacquot, *Antioche*, pp. 141, 142 (identifying the castle, wrongly, with Roche de Roissol. The *Guide Bleu*, p. 632, follows Jacquot).

Portella: On the narrow stretch of coast north of Alexandretta, between the mountains and the sea; v. Jonah's Pillar, Muthakkab.

Port Provençal, Portus Prodensalium, Pityusa Island: South-west of Silifke. 'A citadel stands on the summit of the highest peak; and the whole island presents such means of natural and artificial defence as to make it probable that it was once a station of great military strength' (Beaufort, *Karamania*, p. 214). Heyd, *Commerce* I, p. 303.

Portus Pallorum, Port de Paus, Port de Plas, Kaghertik: A harbour between Ayas and the mouth of the Pyramus. A crusading pamphlet by a Franciscan, Fidenzio of Padua (G. Golubovich, *Biblioteca biobibliografica della Terra Santa*, 5 vol. (Quaracchi, 1906–23), II, pp. 9–60), described it as 'one of the world's best harbours and all the world's ships could winter there'. The whole estuary of the Pyramus has silted up and changed course, though no such splendid harbour can ever have existed. It was here that the entrails of John Comnenus were buried, and a monument erected to him. Rey, *AOL.* II, p. 333; Atiya, *Crusade in Later Middle Ages*, p. 42; Brochard, Directorium ad Passagium Faciendum, *RHC.Arm.* II, pp. 500, 501; Heyd, *Commerce* II, p. 74 n. 3.

Pylae Amanides, v. Amanus Gates

Pyramus, Chahan, Ceyhan, Jeyhan: River flowing from the Taurus mountains, passing Marash and Mamistra and entering the sea by Ayas (Lajazzo). Its main tributaries flowing from the north are: Sumbas, Savrun, Andirin, Korsulu. Strabo (lib. XII) thought the delta would eventually reach Cyprus. Ainsworth, *Travels* II, p. 89.

Raban, Altountach Kale: Between Hromgla and Crasson. Cahen, *Syrie*, p. 119.

Rabban Qawma: Monastery burnt in 1275 and again in 1280. Bar Hebraeus, p. 462.

Ravendel, Ruwandan: Occupied by Baldwin in his advance on Edessa; considerable remains of citadel, partially rebuilt by Saladin. Cahen, *Syrie*, p. 117.

Rhegma: Lagoon at mouth of the Cydnus; at one time port of Tarsus.

Rocca Guillelmi, Roche Guillaume: Preceptory and house of the Templars lost in 1299. It was attacked by Saladin after he had taken Darbsak in 1188, and is therefore on the eastern side of the Amanus mountains. It could well be the fortress whose ruins can still be seen near Bektasli on the eastern approach to the Hadjar Shoglan Pass. Cahen, *Syrie*, pp. 143, 144; *Guide Bleu* (1965), p. 648.

Roche de Roissol, Roche Roussel: Cahen (*Syrie*, p. 143) identifies it with Chilvan Kale (q.v.). v. also **Port Bonnel.**

Sagrou, Our Lady of: Convent in the Taurus mountains above the river Jeragne; frequented by St Nerses of Lampron. *RHC.Arm.* I, p. 560.

Saleph, Calycadnus, Göksu: River flowing from the central Taurus mountains south-east past Silifke and forming a large delta below Cape Sarpedon.

Samosata, Samsat: On the Euphrates. Occupied for a time by the Franks. Some of the enceinte is still standing but the acropolis is completely ruined. Humann and Puchstein, *Reisen*, pp. 181–4; Ainsworth, *Travels* I, p. 844.

Sari-Saki, Saqaltutan, Merkez?, Castrum Puellarum?, Castle of Godfrey of Lortet?: Castle by the Pillars of Jonah. Most of the extant work is Turkish, but there is a ruined tower of earlier, possibly crusading, masonry within the Turkish entrance. Jacquot (*Antioche*, p. 150) wrongly identifies it with Gaston, but also suggests Merkez (q.v.) and 'castle of Godfrey of Lortet', a very uncertain designation. Cahen (*Syrie*, p. 149) identifies it with the Castrum Puellarum mentioned by Albert of Aix. (Adana, H–IX; 90, IIb.)

Saruj, Sororgia: South-east of Edessa; occupied by Baldwin I in 1101.

Sarus, Sahan, Seyhan: River flowing past Adana and reaching the sea at the eastern point of the Gulf of Mersin. North of Adana it forms a lake, the

Seyhan Gölü. Further north it splits into two branches, the Göksu and the Zamanti.

Sarvantikar, Savaran, Servantikar (Pl. 40): On the south side of the Amanus Gates. Abulfida (p. 34) calls it a strong citadel, naturally fortified by rocks and surrounded by a forest of pines 'incomparable for height and thickness'. This is the forest of Marra or Marrim. It was by this route that Baldwin III led the refugees from Edessa in 1150, and it was here that in 1266 Baybars inflicted a crushing defeat on the Armenians, in which the prince Thoros was killed, and his brother Leon captured.

Sarvantikar was occupied by Leon I in 1135, but after his capture by Raymond of Poitou he was forced to restore it to Antioch. Retaken by the Armenians it was again surrendered in 1185, as part of the ransom of Rupen II. Leon II re-established the Armenian garrison. In 1269 the castle was much damaged by an earthquake. It was finally lost to the Egyptians in 1337.

P. Deschamps, 'Le Château de Servantikar en Cilicie', *Syrie* XVIII (1937), pp. 379–88; Cahen, *Syrie*, p. 145; J. Thomson, *Geog. Mag.* XXIII (April, 1951), p. 572.

Schoghagan, Chogagan, Izdi, ?Yczidler: Scene of the battle in 1209 at the foot of the mountain, when the relieving force marching to Gaban was defeated by the Sultan of Iconium. It was held by a certain Geoffrey at the time of Leon's coronation, possibly the same man who as Geoffrey, lord of Sarvantikar, was suitor for the hand of Leon's widow. It seems possible that this place is the castle of Geoffrey or Jofre Cla (q.v.) listed in 1316. Its exact locality has not been identified, but it may well be one of the castles on the Andirin route. Alishan, *Sissouan*, p. 211.

Seleucia, Seleucia-in-Pieria, Soueidiyeh: Port of Antioch at mouth of the Orontes, with a rock-cut tunnel made by Vespasian. *Guide Bleu* (1965), pp. 641–3.

Selinus, Selinunte, Selinti, Gazipaşa: Some remains of classical and Selchukid buildings, on the coast between Alanya and Antiochetta. About 5 km. to the south-east there is another field of ruins, probably the ancient Cestrus, now known as Macav Kale. Heberdey and Wilhelm, *Reisen*, p. 149. Bean and Mitford, *Journeys*, pp. 155–6; Beaufort, *Karamania*, pp. 186–93; Alishan, *Sissouan*, p. 375.

Sempada-gla (Sempad's Castle): Near Babaron; built by Sempad the Constable in *c.* 1265, who, in his *Introduction to Aristotle's Works*, writes:

> Je jetai sur un pan naturel,
> Un château imprenable, inexpugnable,
> Et je lui donnai mon nom:
> Sempad-gla, puissante forteresse.

It belonged in 1320 to his grandson, another Sempad and also Constable. The description suggests that this may be another name for Babaron. Alishan, *Sissouan*, p. 79.

Seyhan River, v. Sarus

Shakad: Behram was lord both of Corycus and of Shakad in 1221 (Barhebraeus, p. 380). At the time of Raymond-Rupen's attempt to seize the throne in 1220 it was held by the Marshal, Volram of Corycus, probably the same man. The site is not identified.

Shalan Kale, v. Chilvan Kale

Shughr: Armenian monastery on the Black Mountain, two days' journey from Marash on the route to Sis. In Indjidi's time (*c.* 1805) the church was still standing.

Silifke, Seleph, Saleph, Seleucia (Frontispiece and Pl. 2): On a ridge overlooking the river Saleph and the bridge crossing it. The castle is approximately oval in shape with eight semicircular towers, a double enceinte, protected in places by a rock-cut ditch.

Silifke frequently changed hands in the twelfth-century border wars between Armenia and Byzantium. Taken by Leon II in 1188 and given to Shahinshah of Sassoun, the husband of Leon's niece. Shahinshah was however assassinated in 1193, and Silifke was given to Constantine, son of the Sebastos Henry. From 1210 to 1226 it was ceded to the Hospitallers. In 1216/17 it was attacked by Kai-Kaus I but the knights repulsed him. In 1224 they sold Silifke back to the Armenian kingdom. An inscription records Hethoum I's enlargement of the castle in 1236.

J. Keil and A. Wilhelm in *MAMA.* III (1931), p. 238, pl. 4; Beaufort, *Karamania*, p. 221; Langlois, *Voyage*, p. 53, pl. II; W. Müller-Wiener, *Castles*, p. 80, 2 pls.; J. J. Langendorf and G. Zimmermann in *Genova* XII (1964), pp. 155–65; Fedden and Thomson, *Castles*, pp. 103–5; pls. 24–5 (the authors identify the castle as Camardesium (q.v.), using the name

Silifke only for the town); Riley-Smith, *Knights of St John*, pp. 132, 157–60, 432. The data used in the caption to Pl. 2 were supplied by the late M. R. E. Gough.

Simana-gla (Fortress of Simon): Castle in the Cilician plain near Amouda. Occupied by Thoros II *c.* 1145. Held by Sirouhi in 1198. In Golden Bull of April 1212 is held with Amouda (Langlois, *Cartulaire*, p. 118). Nerses of Lampron described it as near Anavarza. It must have been situated between the two castles Amouda and Anavarza.

Sinap Kale, Oş Kale: Square tower near Babaron. Gottwald, *BZ.* XLI, p. 96 (photograph). There is a similar tower, known by the same name, near Lampron. Both were probably built by the Hetoumids.

Sine Kale: Medieval ruins on a pyramidal hill some 300 m. above Sindirfe, east of Gündogmuş in the Alana valley. There is no Armenian identification. Bean and Mitford, *Journeys*, p. 121.

Sinapaç, v. **Sivile**

Siq, Sechin, Siquinium, Softa Kale, Eski Anamur: On a height some 12 km. east of Anamur. Described by Beaufort with sketch (*Karamania*, pp. 181, 195, 207) as having flat pointed arches to the gateways, similar to Anamur. Part of the outer enceinte with round towers still survives. In 1198 and in 1216 its holder was Kyr Isaac; Rüdt-Collenberg (*Rupenides...*, p. 60) thinks that he was the son of Adam of Baghras. His brother, Kir Vartan, held Alanya and Galaros, but *c.* 1222 married his daughter to Ala-'ad-Din Kai-Qobad, when presumably these holdings changed hands. Offered in 1332 along with Antiochetta to the Hospitallers. Alishan, *Sissouan*, pp. 380–3; Fedden and Thomson, *Castles*, p. 39; Stark, *Alexander's Path*, pp. 36–8. (Silifke ve Mersin, I–VII; 62, IIi.)

Sis, Sisium, Kozan (Pl. 3): Taken by Thoros I from Byzantium; retaken by John Commenus; it became from 1162 the Armenian capital. In 1294 Ailors of Hromgla the Armenian Catholicos moved there. In 1309–10 (*RHC.Arm.* I, p. 466) there was a persecution at Sis by Oshin of heretics who 'refused to accept water in the chalice and other innovations'. In 1375 it was taken and largely destroyed by the Mamluks. Considerable remains of citadel on the spur of the hill above the town; one of the few Armenian castles with continuous rows of machicolations. The outer shell of the cathedral and two towers of the Armenian palace were until

N

recently identifiable; in the Armenian church the throne of Leon II carved with a double eagle was seen by Lohmann in 1901, but is no longer there. E. Lohmann, *Im Kloster zu Sis*; Langlois, *Voyage*, pl. IV; Alishan, *Sissouan*, pp. 241–65; Favre and Mandrot, *Voyage*, pp. 245–8 (with photographs); Müller-Wiener, *Castles*, p. 77, pl. 109; Fedden and Thomson, *Castles*, pp. 97–100; Thompson, *Geog. Mag.*, XXIII (April, 1951), p. 574. Deschamps, *Crac*, Album, pl. VI. Information from Dr Cleave.

Sissouan: The name used for the Armenian Kingdom in the rhyming chronicle of Gregory Dgha. Alishan, *Sissouan*, p. 40.

Sivile, Sevila, Sibelia: Captured by Kilij Arslan in 1156; on Barbarossa's route from Karaman, Ramsay (*Historical Geography*, p. 369) suggests it may equal Coropissus between Karaman and Mut. Another possibility is the acropolis on the circular hill of Sinapiç, in the gorge north-west of Maghva (q.v.). Bean and Mitford, *Journeys*, p. 224.

Skevra, Sghevra: The Hetoumid monastery near Lampron – the exact site is unidentified. The reliquary, dated 1293, and made at Skevra, with Christ on the Cross and the Annunciation on the wings (in the Hermitage Museum) is the most important surviving work of Armenian silversmiths. The main church was built by Hetoum, brother of Nerses, in 1110. There were two other churches. Der Nersessian, *The Armenians*, p. 134; Alishan, *Sissouan*, pp. 103–15.

Sumbas: River flowing past Anavarza to join the Pyramus.

Syrian Gates, Pylae Syriae: Name given to the Beylan Pass on the route from Antioch to Alexandretta, but also sometimes applied to the pass on the coast road round the bay of Alexandretta, where it cuts across the Gebel Missis at Kourd Kulak to reach Mamistra.

Tarsus: A town of ancient history, and already of importance under the Hittite domination. Under the Seleucids it became a prosperous and cultured centre, particularly noted for its Stoic philosophers. Annexed to Rome in 64 B.C. it became the capital of the Roman province of Cilicia. With the acceptance of Christianity, Tarsus, the birthplace of St Paul, became an important bishopric. Occupied by the Arabs in 831, it was regained by Nicephorus Phocas in 965. Shortly before the first crusade it was taken by the Selchukids. In the twelfth century it remained debatable between Byzantium, Antioch and the Armenians, but, from 1173, after the defeat of Constantine Coloman by Mleh, the Armenians had control, and

Bohemond III in 1183 formally ceded it to Rupen II. The mouth of the Cydnus was by then silting up, and Tarsus, a viable port in Roman times, was losing its trading importance to Lajazzo. It was, however, the chief city of the area. There seems to have been considerable building activity under King Oshin (1308–20). The Armenian church of the Virgin has a displaced inscription (1319) referring to a castle built by him, and the church of St Paul (Kilisse Cami) has two inscriptions referring to work done by him. Little remains of its ancient fortifications. The castle was used as a powder store by Ibrahim Pasha, and was eventually blown up (Langlois, *Voyage*, pp. 286–331).

Three medieval churches partially survive. The church of St Paul (now Kilisse Cami), the Latin cathedral, is a simple romanesque building, probably crusading work. Hugh of Vermandois was buried here in 1101. Part of the medieval church of St Peter is incorporated in the Ulu Cami.

C. Enlart, *Les Monuments des Croisés dans le royaume de Jérusalem*, 4 vols. (Paris, 1925–8), pp. 375–80; Langlois, *Voyage*, pp. 315–38; Davies, *Life in Asiatic Turkey*, pp. 152–7.

Taublur, Khurman: The seat of the Armenian patriarchate in the early twelfth century, midway between Marash and Caesarea, north of Göksun; substantial remains. King, *Asiatic Review*, XXXVI (1940), pp. 375–80.

Tchelganotz: Site unknown but near Lampron. Only mentioned when its lords Hetoum and Constantine fell in battle against the Egyptians in 1322. Alishan, *Sissouan*, p. 117.

Teghenkar, Terenkhar (Yellow Rock): Castle held in 1319 by the Constable Constantine under the reign of Oshin, according to an inscription used as an altar stone in the Armenian church at Tarsus. The site is unidentified. Langlois, *Inscriptions*, p. 28 and *Voyage*, p. 317.

Termel Kale: Ruins east of Mersin. Gottwald, *BZ*. XLI, p. 94.

Til Hamdoun, Thila, Tell Hamdun, Toprakkale (Pls. 45, 46): At the point where the route from Marash joined that from Alexandretta. This position made it the most important of the south-east Armenian castles. It was in the possession of Thoros in 1151, taken by Manuel in 1158, ceded to Bohemond of Antioch in 1185 and regained by Leon II. After the battle of Darbsa in 1266 it passed into Mamluk hands, but it was later again under Armenian control. Surrendered as one of five fortresses east of the Pyramus by Leon IV in 1337 and does not seem to have been re-occupied. A double rectangular enceinte encloses a platform of approximately 100 by 70 m.; between the two walls is a small ditch; the inner wall is of two storeys, the upper being occupied by a gallery with meutrieres. Large rooms at south-west corner and in north wall. A cistern occupied part of the platform, which was reached on the north by a ramp defended by outworks, and which penetrated to north-east of the castle by a vaulted hall. The ruins are of black basalt and may be largely Byzantine work. Anavarza, and on a clear day even Sis, are visible from Til Hamdoun. Cahen, *Syrie*, p. 147. Gottwald, *BZ*. XL, pp. 89–103 with plans and photographs; Alishan, *Sissouan*, pp. 323–6; Müller-Wiener, *Castles*, p. 75 (plan and 3 plates). (Kozan, G–IX; 89, Iv.)

Trapesac, v. Darbsak

Trazarg, Tres Arcus, Tres Arces, Monastery of: Near Sis. The site is not identified. Restored by Thoros I, it became the burial place, known as 'the Tomb of Saints', for many of the distinguished theologians of Cilicia. It was here that both Rupen III and Hetoum of Lampron became monks, and the latter eventually became abbot. Matthew of Edessa, ed. Dulaurier, pp. 291, 320, 455.

Tumlu: Small castle on a ridge east of the Seyhan, between Sis and Yilan; its mediaeval name has not yet been identified. G. R. Youngs, *AS*. XV, pp. 112–18.

Turbessel, Tell-Bashir, Tell Beşir, Tilbechar: Given by Baldwin to Joscelin of Courtenay in 1102. After the loss of Edessa in 1144 it became the capital of the county. Finally lost in 1150. Hardly any remains of citadel. Cahen, *Syrie*, p. 116.

Ulukişla, v. Loulon

Vahka, Vagha, Bahga, Feke (Pl. 4): Captured from its Byzantine garrison by Constantine, son of Rupen, *c*. 1090; besieged and taken by John Comnenus in 1137; in 1139 taken by Mohammed ibn Ghazi of Danishmend; recaptured *c*. 1145 by Thoros. From that time it remained one of the chief Armenian strongholds; the date of its loss to the Mamluks is uncertain, but an Armenian community survived in the village below till the displacements of 1927. Two building periods, the latter showing similarities with Tumlu, Yilan and Anavarza. J. Thomson, *Geog. Mag.* XXIII (April, 1951), p. 572; Dunbar and Boal, *AS*, XIV, pp 175–84..

Vaner, Varan: Castle *in territory of Meloun,* apparently in between Til Ham-doun and Partzapert. Held in 1198 by the Marshal Basil; in 1214, pre-sumably on Basil's death, Leon ceded the castle to the Hospitallers in return for 10,000 Saracen *bezants* given by the order for the dowry of Leon's daughter. Langlois, *Cartulaire,* p. 122.

Yilan Kale [*Castle of the Snakes*]**, Shah-Meran Kale** (Pls. 47, 48): A huge castle above the east bank of the Ceyhan; the mediaeval name is unidentified. Edib (*Itinerary,* pp. 100–2) describes a castle called 'Shah-Meran' between Adana and Mamistra, said to be full of snakes, but the name (which survived into the nineteenth century as an alternative to Yilan) is the Kurdish for 'King of Snakes' and probably referred to a carving which remains over the gateway. Gottwald, *BZ.* XLI, pp. 89–93 (with plan and photographs); Youngs, *AS.* XV, pp. 125–33; Müller-Wiener, *Castles,* pp. 78–9 (plan and photograph); J. Thomson, *Geog. Mag.* XXIII (April, 1951), p. 574. (Adana, H–IX; 85, Iz.)

Zamanti River: Flowing from the Taurus to join the Sarus north-east of Sis.

Zephyrion, Cape, v. **Cape Cavalieri**

Zeytin: Village on the river Fornos, east of Coxon.

Appendix

THE RULERS OF CILICIAN ARMENIA

The numbering of the Armenian rulers in Cilicia shares in the general confusion of nomenclature. The authoritative work is by W. H. Rüdt-Collenberg, *The Rupenides, Hethumides and Lusignans* (Paris, 1963), who makes a division at the crowning of Leon and entitles him Leon I, while retaining the same title for his predecessor, Leon I (1129–39). The Wisconsin *History of the Crusades* (ed. K. M. Setton) uses the simpler method of disregarding a break at the coronation and of calling the first King Leon II. I have also followed their use of Leon rather than Leo.

The list therefore of rulers as numbered here runs as follows:

Rupen I d. 1095	Thoros III 1293–8
Constantine I 1095–1102	Hetoum II[1] 1294–7
Thoros I 1102–29	Sempad 1297–9
Constantine II 1129	Constantine III 1299
Leon I 1129–40	Hetoum II 1299–1307
Thoros II 1144–69	Leon IV (joint ruler) 1301–7
Rupen II 1169–70	Oshin 1307–20
Mleh 1170–5	Leon V 1320–41
Rupen III 1175–87	Constantine IV[2] 1342–4
Leon II 1187–1219	Constantine V 1344–62
Zabel 1219–52	Leon VI[3] 1363–4
m. (1) Philip 1223–5	Constantine VI 1367–73
(2) Hetoum I 1226–70	(Peter I of Cyprus 1367/8–69)
Leon III 1270–89	Leon VI 1374–5
Hetoum II 1289–93	

[1] The various resignations and re-accessions of Hetoum II explain the vicissitudes of the crown at this period.

[2] Guy of Lusignan took the name of Constantine on his accession.

[3] The most probable explanation of the confused accounts of this period is that Leon, an illegitimate nephew of Guy, obtained the throne for a year and was then displaced by Constantine VI, cousin of Constantine V. He was regarded by some of the baronage as a usurper, and the crown was certainly offered and accepted by Peter of Cyprus, though he never came to claim it. Leon returned to the throne in 1374.

BIBLIOGRAPHY

Crusading and Arab historians make frequent reference to Armenian affairs, as, particularly in the thirteenth and fourteenth centuries, do the papal registers. The main chronicles and documents directly concerned with Cilician Armenia are printed in the two volumes of the *Recueil des historiens des croisades; Documents arméniens.* The secondary authorities on the crusading movement, such as Grousset, Runciman and Prawer, all deal incidentally with the Armenian kingdom. General histories of the Armenian people also deal, at varying length, with Cilicia. There is, however, no full-scale history of the Cilician settlement and kingdom. The most recent accounts are chapters by Sirapie der Nersessian in volume II of *A History of the Crusades,* ed. R. L. Wolff and H. W. Hazard and in *The Armenians.* A further chapter dealing with the kingdom after 1311 is planned for volume V of the *History.* Cahen (*Syrie du Nord*) and Segal (*Edessa*) are of first importance for the Antioch–Edessa area.

SOURCES

Chronicles. For the settlement in Cilicia and Edessa the most important Armenian source is the *Chronicle* of Matthew of Edessa. The author was born in Edessa and spent most of his life there, though there are indications that in his later years he was in Crasson and he refers to Baldwin of Marash as 'our count' (*RHC.Arm.* I and *Chronique de Matthieu d'Edessa,* ed. E. Dulaurier (Paris, 1858)). The crusading chronicles all have some reference to the passage of the first crusade through Armenian areas, but the *Historia Iherosolymitana* of Baldwin I's chaplain Fulcher of Chartres, ending in 1127 (ed. H. Hagenmeyer (Heidelberg, 1913)) and the *Gesta Tancredi* of Raoul of Caen, ending in 1105 (*RHC.Occ.* III) are of particular importance. Of Arab chronicles the most relevant is the Damascus Chronicle of Ibn al-Qalānisi (extracts trs. and ed. by H. A. R. Gibb (London, 1932), and in French by R. Le Tourneau, *Damas de 1075 à 1154* (Paris, 1952)). The Syriac chronicle of the Jacobite patriarch, Michael, extends to the beginning of the reign of Hetoum I (1226), but as Michael is known to have died in 1199 the concluding passage must be the work of a continuator (*RHC.Arm.* I; ed. and trs. by J.-B. Chabot, 3 vols. (Paris, 1899–1905)). The Syriac tradition is carried on by Bar Hebraeus (*The Chronography of Gregory Abu'l Faraj . . . commonly known as Bar Hebraeus* (trs. and ed. E. A. Wallis Budge (Oxford, 1932)). Bar Hebraeus was born in Melitene 1225/6 and died as bishop of Aleppo in 1286. See also 'The First and Second Crusades from an Anonymous Syriac Chronicle', trs. A. S. Tritton and H. A. R. Gibb, *JRAS.* (1933), pp. 69–101 and 273–305. The Armenian chronicle of Matthew is continued by that of Gregory the Priest. Little is known of his life but he was at Crasson in 1137 and his chronicle ends in 1162. The funeral oration for Baldwin, count of Marash, by the count's friend and chaplain Basil, 'a man worthy of all praise' Gregory calls him, fills out in a more personal way our knowledge of this period, and adds to the general impression that under Baldwin Crasson had become a place of some learning and culture. The poems by the Catholicos (1166–72) Nerses Schnorhali and his successor Gregory Dgha (1172–89) respectively on the loss of Edessa and the loss of Jerusalem are examples of another Armenian literary form. The writings and letters of St Nerses of Lampron (d. 1198) throw considerable light on both the ecclesiastical and political problems of the time.

In the thirteenth century three learned Armenian writers contributed historical works. Vartan, known as the Great, was born at Partzapert early in the century. He summarised the chronicles of Matthew of Edessa and Gregory the Priest, and for the Mongols made use of a work by John Vanagan, no longer extant. He himself visited the court of Hulagu, and seems to have made a deep impression there. (Extracts covering 1163–1221 in *RHC.Arm.* I; the full text is available in a Russian edition by N. O. Emin (Moscow, 1861); for embassy to Hulagu see *JA.* (1860).) Guragos (Kirakos) of Kantzoy in Greater Armenia was born *c.* 1200 and his *History* ends in 1269. He was particularly well informed on the ecclesiastical problems of Cilicia, and must almost certainly have visited it; there is a French translation by M. F. Brosset (St Petersburg, 1870). Most outstanding of all was the Constable Sempad (see *supra*, pp. 25–2). The problems of the various versions are examined by S. der Nersessian in *DOP.* XIII (1959), pp. 143–168. The account of his mission to the Mongols in 1247 is printed in William of Nangis, *Vie de saint Louis, Recueil des historiens des Gaules et de la France* XX, pp. 361–3. Vahram of Edessa wrote his rhymed chronicle of the kings of Armenia at the request of Leon III, a ruler for whom he had the greatest admiration, and ends it with Leon still on the throne *c.* 1280.

The fourteenth century brings us to the important if somewhat enigmatic figure of Hetoum the historian (see *supra*, pp. 28–30). The *Chronology* (*RHC.Or.* I, pp. 488–90) is assigned by a recent editor (V. A. Hakopian) to Hetoum II. For a discussion of the life of the historian see Ch. Schefer in *RHC.Arm.* II, pp. xxiii–lxxxiv. The *Chronique d'Arménie* of Jean Dardel is the main if prejudiced source for the second half of the fourteenth century. Dardel became Leon VI's chaplain in Cairo in 1377, was despatched by him to Europe in 1379, and returned in 1382 with the letters from the kings of Castille and Aragon that secured Leon's release. He died in 1384 and was buried at Étampes. (See *RHC.Arm.* II, pp. v–xxii, and U. Robert, 'La Chronique d'Arménie de Jean Dardel', *AOL.* II (1884), pp. 332–54.)

SOURCES

Armenian, Syriac and Latin Sources

Recueil des historiens des croisades: Documents arméniens, 2 vols. (Paris, 1869, 1906), re-published (Farnborough, 1967).

S. Akelian, *Chronicle of the General Sempad* (in Armenian) (S. Lazzaro, Venice, 1956).

F. Amadi and D. Strambaldi, *Chroniques de Chypre*, ed. R. de Mas Latrie (Paris, 1891).

Bar Hebraeus, *Chronography of Gregory Abu 'l Faraj . . . commonly known as Bar Hebraeus*, trs. E. A. Wallis Budge (Oxford, 1932).

R. P. Blake and R. N. Frye, *History of the Nation of Archers (the Mongols) by Grigor of Akanc'* (Cambridge, Mass., 1954).

S. der Nersessian, 'The Armenian Chronicle of the Constable Smpad', *DOP*. XIII (1959), pp. 141–68.

V. A. Hakopian, *Short Chronicles: XIII–XIV Centuries* (in Armenian), 2 vols. (Erevan, 1951–6).

G. I. Hovsepian, *Colophons of Manuscripts* (in Armenian) (Antilias, 1951).

L. S. Khachikian, *Colophons of Armenian Manuscripts of the XIVth Century* (in Armenian) (Erevan, 1950).

Kirakos of Ganzag, *History*; French trs. M. F. Brosset (St Petersburg, 1870).

W. Long, *Flor de las ystorias de Orient by Hayton, Prince of Gorigos* (Chicago, 1934).

A. Lüders, 'Die Kreuzzüge im Urteil syrischer und armenischer Quellen', *Berliner Byzantinistische Arbeiten*, 29 (Berlin, 1964).

Matthew of Edessa, ed. E. Dulaurier (Paris, 1858).

Michael the Syrian, *Chronique*, ed. J.-B. Chabot, 4 vols. (Louvain-Paris, 1899–1905).

—— Armenian version, trs. V. Langlois (Venice, 1868).

J. Muyldermans, *La Domination arabe en Arménie* (trs. of Vardan) (Paris, 1927).

G. Raynaud ed., *Les Gestes des Chiprois* (Geneva, 1887).

U. Robert, 'La Chronique d'Arménie de Jean Dardel', *AOL*. II (1884), pp. 331–54.

Samuel of Ani, *Chronological Tables* (to 1179 with anonymous continuation to 1358); French trs. M. F. Brosset in *Collection d'historiens arméniens*, II (St Petersburg, 1879).

A. K. Sanjian, *Colophons of Armenian Manuscripts: 1301–1480* (Cambridge, Mass., 1969).

Marino Sanudo, *Secreta Fidelium Crucis* in G. Bongars, *Gesta Dei per Francos*, vol. II (Hanover, 1611). (Eng. trs. by A. Stewart in *Palestine Pilgrims Text Society*.)

Sempad, *Chronicle from 952–1274* (with continuation to 1335); French trs. by V. Langlois (St Petersburg, 1862).

A. S. Tritton and H. A. R. Gibb, 'The First and Second Crusade from an Anonymous Syriac Chronicle', *JRAS*. (1933), pp. 69–101, 273–305.

Greek Sources

Michael Attaliates, *Historia*, ed. I. Bekker, *CSHB*. (Bonn, 1853).

Cedrenus-Skylitzes, *Historia Compendium* II, *CSHB*. (Bonn, 1839); also in *PG*. CXXI.

Nicetas Choniates, *Historia*, *CSHB*. ed. I. Bekker (Bonn, 1935); also in *PG*. CXXIX.

John Cinnamus, *Epitome rerum ab Ioanne et Alexio Comnenis gestarum*, *CSHB*. ed. A. Meinecke (Bonn, 1836); also in *PG*. CXXXIII.

Anna Comnena, *Alexiad*, ed. and trs. B. Leib, 3 vols. (Paris, 1937–45); Engl. trs. E. A. S. Dawes (London, 1928).

Joannes Zonaras, *Epitome Historiarum* III, ed. M. Pinder and T. Büttner-Wobst, *CSHB*. (Bonn, 1897); also in *PG*. CXXXIV.

Arab and Persian Sources

Recueil des historiens des croisades: Historiens orientaux, 5 vols. (Paris, 1872–1906, republished (Farnborough, 1967).

Abū Al-Fida, *Géographie*; French trs. J. T. Reinaud and M. S. Guyard (Paris, 1848).

al-Baladhuri, *Futuh al-Buldan*. Translated by P. K. Hitti in *Origins of the Islamic State* (New York, 1915).

Baha' al-Din, *Kitāb al-nawādir al-sultānīya wa'l mahāsin al-Yūsufīya*. Translated by C. W. Wilson, *Life of Saladin* (London, 1897).

Chèref-ou'ddine, *Chèref-Nâmeh*; trs. by F. B. Charmoy, 2 vols. (St Petersburg, 1873).

Ibn Baṭṭūta, *Travels in Asia and Africa 1325–1354*, selected and translated by H. A. R. Gibb, 3 vols. (London, 1958–71), and by C. Defrémery and B. R. Sanguinetti, 4 vols. (Paris, 1853–59).

Ibn Bibi, *Seldjouq-nâmeh*. Translated by H. W. Duda, *Die Seltschukengeschichte des Ibn Bibi* (Copenhagen, 1959) and extracts by H. Massé, 'Le Sultan Seldjoukide Keykobad Iᵉʳ et l'Armènie', *REA* IX (1929), pp. 113–29.

Ibn al-Furat, *Tarikh al-duwal wa'l mulūk*. Selections translated by U. and M. C. Lyons in *Ayyubids, Mamlukes and Crusaders* (Introduction and notes by J. S. C. Riley-Smith), 2 vols. (Cambridge, 1971).

Ibn-al-Qualānisī, *Dhail ta'rikh Dimashq*. Extracts translated by E. Blochet, *Histoire d'Alep de Kamal-ad-Din*, *ROL* II–VI (1894–98), and H. A. R. Gibb, *The Damascus Chronicle of the Crusades* (London, 1932).

al-Jazarī, *Hawādith az-zamān*. Extracts and summaries in J. Sauvaget, *La Chronique de Damas* (Paris, 1949).

al-Maqrīzī, *Kitāb al-sulūk li-ma'rifat duwal al-mulūk*. Extracts translated by E. M. Quatremère, 2 vols. (Paris, 1837–54).

Mehemmed Edib, *Itinéraire de Constantinople à la Mecque* in *Recueil de voyages et de mémoires publié par la Société de Géographie*, translated by Bianchi (Paris, 1825).

Charters, Letters and other Documents

Marquis d'Albon, *Cartulaire générale de l'Ordre du Temple*, ?*1119–50* (Paris, 1913).

L. M. Alishan, *Assizes d'Antioche* (Venice, 1876).

—— *L'Arméno-Veneto*, 2 vols. (Venice-San Lazzaro, 1893).

H. de Curzon ed., *La Règle du Temple* (Paris, 1886).

J. Delaville Le Roulx, *Cartulaire générale de l'ordre des Hospitaliers de St. Jean de Jérusalem (1100–1310)*, 4 vols. (Paris, 1894–1906).

E. Déprez and G. Mollat, *Clément VI: Lettres closes, patentes et curiales intéressant les pays autres que la France* (Paris, 1960).

C. Desimoni, 'Actes passés en 1271, 1274 et 1279 à l'Aïas (Petite Arménie) et à Beyrouth par devant des notaires génois', *AOL*. I (1881).

C. Galanus, *Conciliationis ecclesiae Armeniae cum Romana ex ipsis armenorum patrum et doctorum testimoniis, in duas partes*, 3 vols. (Rome, 1650–61).

Innocent III, *Epistolae*, J. P. Migne, *PL*. vols. CCXIV–CCXVII (1855): J. B. Pearson, *Tabular index to letters* (1911).

C. Kohler, 'Lettres pontificales concernant l'histoire de la Petite Arménie au XIVe siècle', *Florilegium . . . Melchior de Vogüé* (Paris, 1909).

—— 'Deux Projets de Croisade en Terre-Sainte composés à la fin du XIIIe siècle et au début du XIVe', *ROL*. X (1903–4).

V. Langlois, *Inscriptions grecques, romaines, byzantines et arméniennes de la Cilicie* (Paris, 1854).

—— 'Documents pour servir à l'histoire des Lusignans de la Petite Arménie 1342–1375', *RA*. XVI (1859), pp. 109–16, 143–66, 216–34.

—— *Le Trésor des Chartes d'Arménie ou Cartulaire de la Chancellerie royale des Roupéniens* (Venice, 1863).

S. Pauli, *Codice diplomatico del sacro ordine militare Gerosolimitano oggi di Malta*, 2 vols. (Lucca, 1733–7).

F. B. Pegolotti, 'La pratica della mercatura' in G. F. Pagnini della Ventura, *Della Decima et di varie altre gravesse imposte dal Comune di Firenze*, II, Bologna, 1967 (reprint); (first printed Lisbon and Lucca, 1765, 1766).

J. Richard, *Chypre sous les Lusignans; Documents chypriotes des Archives du Vatican (XIVe et XVe siècles)*, Inst. français d'Archéologie de Beyrouth, Bibl. arch. et hist. LXXIX (Paris, 1962).

R. Röhricht, *Regesta regni Hierosolymitani* (Innsbruck, 1893–1904).

E. Strehlke, *Tabulae ordinis Theutonici* (Berlin, 1869).

Travels and Guides

M. N. Adler, *The Itinerary of Benjamin of Tudela* (Oxford, 1907).

W. F. Ainsworth, *Travels and Researches in Asia Minor* II (London, 1842).

—— 'Notes upon the Comparative Geography of the Cilician and Syrian Gates', *JRGS*. (1833).

G. E. Bean, *Turkey's Southern Shore: An Archaeological Guide* (London, 1968).

G. E. Bean and T. B. Mitford, 'Sites old and new in Rough Cilicia', *AS*. XII (1962), pp. 185–287, and in *Denkschriften der Österreichischen Akademie* LXXXV (1965), pp. 1–44.

—— *Journeys in Rough Cilicia 1964–68*, Ergänzungsbande zu den Tituli Asiae Minoris, Nr. 3, Austrian Academy (Vienna, 1970).

F. Beaufort, *Karamania, a description of the south coast of Asia Minor* (London, 1817).

J. Becquet and L. Hambis, *Histoire des Mongols, J. de Plan Carpin* (Paris, 1965).

Gertrude L. Bell, 'Notes on a Journey through Cilicia', *RA*. N.S. VI (1906), pp. 1–29.

J. T. Bent, 'A Journey in Cilicia Tracheia', *JHS*. XII (1891), pp. 206–24.

—— 'Recent Discoveries in Eastern Cilicia', *JHS*. XI (1890), pp. 231–35.

P. Bergeron ed., 'Observations du Moine Bacon', *Voyages faits principalement en Asie dans les XII, XIII, XIV et XV siècles* (Paris, 1735).

Bertrandon de la Broquière, *Le Voyage d'outremer*, ed. Ch. Schefer (Paris, 1892).

A. Chauvet and E. Isambert, *Itinéraire de l'Orient* III, Collection des Guides Jaunes (Paris, 1881).

O. Dapper, *Asia* (Amsterdam, 1692).

E. J. Davis, *Life in Asiatic Turkey* (London, 1879).

J. C. Dewdney, *Turkey* (London, 1971).

C. Favre and B. Mandrot, 'Voyage en Cilicie, 1874', *Bulletin de la Société de Géographie de Paris* (1878).

——— 'Cilicie' in A. Chauvet and E. Isambert, *Itinéraire descriptif de l'Orient* III (Paris, 1882), pp. 754–78.

G. H. Forsyth, 'Architectural Notes on Cilicia', *DOP.* XI (1957), pp. 223–36.

Mary Gough, *The Plain and the Rough Places* (London, 1954).

M. R. Gough, 'Anazarbus', *AS.* II (1952), pp. 85–150.

Guide Bleu, Turquie (Paris, 1965) (the historical notes by R. Boulanger are excellent).

R. Hartman, *Im neuen Anatolien* (Leipzig, 1928).

M. Hartmann, 'Das Liwa Halep', *Zeitschrift der Gesellschaft für Erdkunde zu Berlin* XXIX (1894), pp. 142–88, 475–550.

R. Heberdey and A. Wilhelm, 'Reisen in Kilikien', *Denkschrift der Kaiserlichen Akademie* XLIV (Vienna, 1896), pp. 1–168.

E. Herzfeld, 'Eine Reise durch das westliche Kilikien im Frühjahr 1907', *Petermanns Mitteilungen* LV (1909), pp. 25–34.

D. G. Hogarth and J. A. Monro, 'Modern and Ancient Roads in Eastern Asia Minor', *Royal Geographical Society Supp. Papers* III, pt. 5 (1893).

K. Humann and O. Puchstein, *Reisen in Kleinasien und Nordsyrien* (Berlin, 1890).

L. Indjidian, *Description de l'Arménie moderne* (Venice, 1806).

P. Jacquot, *Antioche*, 3 vols. (Antioch, 1931).

A. Janke, *Auf Alexanders des Grossen Pfaden* (Berlin, 1904).

J. M. Kinneir, *Journey through Asia Minor, Armenia and Koordistan* (London, 1818).

T. Kotschy, *Reise in den cilicschen Taurus über Tarsus* (Gotha, 1858).

V. Langlois, *Voyage dans la Cilicie, 1852–1853* (Paris, 1861).

J. M. C. Laurent, *Peregrinatores medii aevi quattuor* (Leipzig, 1864).

W. M. Leake, *Journal of a Tour in Asia Minor* (London, 1824).

Macarius, Patriarch of Antioch, *Travels*, trs. F. C. Belfour (London, 1836).

N. Maggiore, *Adana* (Palermo, 1842).

Metheny, 'Road Notes from Cilicia and North Syria', *Journal of American Oriental Society* XXVIII, pp. 155–67.

U. Monneret de Villard, *Liber Peregrinationis di Jacopo da Verona* (Rome, 1950).

A. Nöldeke, 'Der Euphrat von Gerger bis Djerebus', *Petermanns Mitteilungen* LXVI (1920), pp. 15, 53.

H. A. G. Paul, *Journal de voyage Italie-Égypte-Judée-Samarie*, 2nd ed. (Paris, 1865).

E. Percy, *Highlands of Asiatic Turkey* (London, 1901).

Marco Polo, *La Description du monde*, trs. L. Hambis (Paris, 1955).

B. Poujoulat, *Voyage dans l'Asie Mineure*, 2 vols. (Paris, 1840–41).

G. Pullè, *Historia Mongolorum: Viaggio de F. Giovanni da Pian del Carpe 1245–47* (Florence, 1913).

W. M. Ramsay, 'The Historical Geography of Asia Minor', *Royal Geographical Society Supp. Papers* IV (1890).

R. Röhricht and H. Meisner, *Deutsche Pilgerreisen nach dem Heiligen Lande* (Berlin, 1880).

E. Rosenbaum, G. Huber and S. Onurkan, *A Survey of Coastal Cities in Western Cilicia*, Turkish Historical Society (Ankara, 1967).

F. Sarre, *Reise in Kleinasien, Sommer 1895* (Berlin, 1896).

F. X. Schaffer, 'Cilicia', *Petermanns Mitteilungen*, Ergänzungsheft, N. 141 (1903).

P. de Tchihatchef, *Asie Mineure. Description physique, statistique et archéologique*, 4 pts. and atlas (Paris, 1853–69).

C. Texier, *Description de l'Asie Mineure* II (Paris, 1849).

W. Tomaschek, 'Zur historischen Topographie von Kleinasien in Mittelalter', *Sitzungsberichte der Kaiserlichen Akademie der Wissenschaften*, philos.-hist. Classe, CXXIV, Abt. VIII (Vienna, 1891), pp. 1–106.

H. F. Tozer, *Turkish Armenia* (London, 1881).

Wilbrand of Oldenburg; see Laurent, *Peregrinatores*.

M. V. Seton Williams, 'Cilician Survey', *AS.* IV (1954), pp. 121–74.

Castles and Sites

M. H. Ballance, 'Derbe and Faustinopolis', *AS.* XIV (1964), pp. 139–45.

P. Deschamps, 'Le Château de Servantikar en Cilicie', *Syria* XVIII (1937), pp. 379–88.

—— *Le Crac des Chevaliers* (Paris, 1934), text and album.

J. G. Dunbar and W. W. M. Boal, 'The Castle of Vahga', *AS.* XIV (1964), pp. 175–84.

R. Dussaud, *Topographie historique de la Syrie antique et médiévale* (Paris, 1927).

R. Fedden and J. Thomson, *Crusader Castles* (London, 1957).

J. Gottwald, 'Die Kirche und das Schloss Paperan in Kilikisch-Armenien', *BZ.* XXXVI (1936), pp. 86–100.

—— 'Die Burg Til im Südöstlichen Kilikien', *BZ.* XL (1940), pp. 89–104.

—— 'Burgen und Kirchen im mittleren Kilikien', *BZ.* XLI (1941), pp. 82–103.

R. P. Harper, 'Podandus and the Via Tauri', *AS.* XX (1970), pp. 149–53.

E. Herzfeld and S. Guyer, 'Meriamlik und Korykos', *MAMA.* II (1930).

J. J. Langendorf and G. Zimmermann, 'Trois Monuments inconnus des Croisés', *Genava* XII (1964), pp. 155–65.

Seton Lloyd and Rice D. Storm, *Alanya* (British Institute at Ankara, 1958).

J. F. E. Lohmann, *Im Kloster zu Sis* (Striegau, 1905).

W. Müller-Wiener, *Castles of the Crusaders* (London, 1966).

F. C. R. Robinson and P. C. Hughes, 'Lampron, Castle of Armenian Cilicia', *AS.* XIX (1969), pp. 183–207.

F. M. Stark, *Alexander's Path from Caria to Cilicia* (London, 1958).

—— 'From Tarsus to Lake Van', *RCAJ.* XLIII (1956), pp. 7–19.

J. Thomson, 'Castles in Cilicia', *Geographical Magazine* XXIII (April, 1951), pp. 569–77.

G. R. Youngs, 'Three Cilician Castles', *AS.* XV (1965), pp. 113–34.

Secondary Historical Works

N. Adontz, 'Notes arméno-byzantines, IV, l'aïeul des Roubéniens', *Byzantion* X (1935), pp. 185–203.

N. Akinian, 'Hetoum Heghi, Lord of Lampron 1151–1218(?)' (in Armenian), *Handes Amsorya* LXIX (1955), pp. 397–405.

L. M. Alishan, *Léon le Magnifique, premier roi de Sissouan ou de l'Arméno-Cilicie*, trs. G. Bayan (Venice, 1888).

—— *Sissouan ou l'Arméno-Cilicie* (Venice, 1899).

A. S. Atiya, *The Crusade in the Later Middle Ages* (London, 1938).

K. J. Basmadjean, 'Jacques II, roi d'Aragon et Oschen, roi de la Petite Arménie', *ROL.* XI (1905–8), pp. 1–6.

C. Cahen, *La Syrie du Nord à l'époque des Croisades et la principauté franque d'Antioche* (Paris, 1940).

Cambridge History of Islam, 2 vols. ed. P. M. Holt, A. K. S. Lambton and B. Lewis (Cambridge, 1970).

Cambridge Medieval History, ed. J. M. Hussey, vol. iv, pt. i (Cambridge, 1966), vol. iv, pt. ii (Cambridge, 1967).

M. Canard, 'Les Relations entre les Mérénides et les Mamelouks au XIVᵉ siècle', *Annales de l'Institut d'Études orientales: Université d'Alger* V (1939–41), pp. 53 ff.

—— 'Le Royaume d'Arménie-Cilicie et les Mamelouks jusqu'au traité de 1285', *REA.* N.S. IV (1967), pp. 216–59.

G. Cappelletti, *L'Armenia*, 3 vols. (Florence, 1841).

A. Carrière, 'La Rose d'or du roi d'Arménie Léon V', *ROL.* IX (1902), pp. 1–5.

J.-B. Chabot, 'Un Épisode de l'histoire des Croisades', *Mélanges offerts à G. Schlumberger* (Paris, 1924), pp. 159–68.

F. Chalandon, *Jean II Comnène (1118–1143) et Manuel Comnène (1143–1180)* (Paris, 1912).

P. Charanis, *The Armenians in the Byzantine Empire* (Lisbon, 1964).

R. W. Crawford, 'Ridwan the Maligned', *Studies in Honour of P. K. Hitti* (London, 1960), pp. 135–44.

J. Delaville le Roulx, *La France en Orient au XIVᵉ siècle*, 2 vols. (Paris, 1886).

S. der Nersessian, *Manuscrits arméniens illustrés des XIIᵉ, XIIIᵉ et XIVᵉ siècles*, 2 vols. (Paris, 1936, 1937).

—— *Armenia and the Byzantine Empire* (Cambridge, Mass., 1945).

—— *The Armenians* (London, 1969).

—— 'Le Reliquaire de Skevra et l'orfèvrerie cilicienne aux XIIIᵉ et XIVᵉ siècles', *REA.* N.S. I (1964), pp. 121–47.

—— 'Un Évangile cilicien du 13ᵉ siècle', *REA.* IV N.S. (1967), pp. 103–19.

—— 'The Kingdom of Cilician Armenian', *History of the Crusades* II, ed. R. L. Wolff and H. W. Hazard (University of Wisconsin Press, 1969).

E. Dulaurier, *Histoire, dogmes, traditions et liturgie de l'Église arménienne orientale* (Paris, 1859).

—— 'Les Mongols d'après les historiens arméniens', *JA.* Series 5, XI (1858).

R. Dussaud, *Topographie historique de la Syrie antique et médiévale* (Paris, 1927).

S. M. Fadil, *The Decline of the Saljûquid Empire* (Calcutta, 1938).

K. Forstreuter, *Der Deutsche Orden am Mittelmeer* (Bonn, 1967).

M. Gaudefroy-Demombynes, *La Syrie à l'époque des Mamelouks d'après les auteurs arabes* (Paris, 1923).

J. Gay, *Le pape Clément VI et les affaires d'Orient 1342–52* (Paris, 1904).

R. Grousset, *Histoire des Croisades et du royaume franc de Jérusalem*, 3 vols. (Paris, 1934–1936).

W. Hecht, 'Byzanz und die Armenier nach dem Tode Kaiser Manuels I 1180–1196', *Byzantion* XXXVII (1967), pp. 60–74.

W. Heyd, *Histoire du commerce du Levant*, trs. F. Raynaud, 2 vols. 2nd ed. (Leipzig, 1923).

G. Hill, *A History of Cyprus* II (Cambridge, 1948).

H. H. Howorth, *History of the Mongols*, 3 vols. (London, 1876–88).

N. Iorga, *Brève Histoire de la Petite Arménie: l'Arménie Cilicienne* (Paris, 1930).

D. M. Lang, *Armenia: Cradle of Civilization* (London, 1970).

V. Langlois, *Numismatique de l'Arménie au moyen âge* (Paris, 1855).

J. Laurent, 'Des Grecs aux Croisés', *Byzantion* I (1924), pp. 366–449.

—— 'Arméniens de Cilicie: Aspiétès, Oschin, Ursinus', *Mélanges offerts à G. Schlumberger* I (Paris, 1924), pp. 159–68.

—— 'Byzance et Antioche sous le curopalate Philarète', *REA*. IX (1929), pp. 61–72.

T. E. Lawrence, *Oriental Assembly* (London, 1939).

G. Le Strange, *Palestine under the Moslems* (Cambridge, 1890).

—— *The Land of the Eastern Caliphate* (Cambridge, 1905).

A. Luttrell, 'The Crusade in the fourteenth century', *Europe in the Late Middle Ages*, ed. J. Hale *et al.* (London, 1965).

Marco Polo, *The Description of the World*, ed. A. C. Moule and P. Pelliot (London, 1938).

L. de Mas Latrie, *L'Ile de Chypre* (Paris, 1879).

G. Millet and S. der Nersessian, 'Le Psautier arménien illustré', *REA*. IX (1929), pp. 137–81.

J. de Morgan, *Histoire du peuple arménien* (Nancy-Paris, 1919).

Sir W. Muir, *The Mameluke or Slave Dynasty of Egypt 1260–1517* (London, 1896).

M. Sáez Pomés, 'La ayuda de Valencia a León V de Armenia, I de Madrid', *Estudios de Edad Media de la Corona de Aragón* III (1947–8), pp. 413 ff.

J. Prawer, *The Latin Kingdom of Jerusalem* (London, 1972).

J. S. C. Riley-Smith, *The Knights of St. John in Jerusalem and Cyprus c. 1050–1310* (London, 1967).

W. H. Rüdt-Collenberg, *The Rupenides, Hethumides and Lusignans* (Paris, 1963).

S. Runciman, *A History of the Crusades*, 3 vols. (London, 1952–54).

A.-J. St-Martin, *Mémoires historiques et géographiques sur l'Arménie*, 2 vols. (Paris, 1818–1819).

J. J. Saunders, *The History of the Mongol Conquests* (London, 1971).

G. Schlumberger, 'Bulles d'or et sceau des rois Léon II (I) et Léon VI (V) d'Arménie', *ROL*. I (1893), pp. 161–7.

—— *L'Épopée byzantine à la fin du dixième siècle*, 3 vols. (Paris, 1896–1905).

—— 'Les Arméniens au Moyen Age', *Récits de Byzance et des Croisades* (Paris, 1917).

J. B. Segal, *Edessa, the Blessed City* (Oxford, 1970).

K. M. Setton (ed.), *A History of the Crusades*. I, *The First Hundred Years*, ed. M. W. Baldwin, 2nd ed. (Madison, Milwaukee and London, 1969); II, *The Later Crusades, 1189–1311*, ed. R. L. Wolff and H. W. Hazard, 2nd ed. (Madison, Milwaukee and London, 1969); III, *The Fourteenth and Fifteenth Centuries*, ed. H. W. Hazard (Madison, Milwaukee and London, 1975).

G. Soulier, 'Le Moine arménien Hethoum et les apports d'Extrême-Orient', *REA* IX (1929), pp. 249–54.

B. Spuler, *History of the Mongols Based on Eastern and Western Accounts of the Thirteenth and Fourteenth Centuries*, trs. H. and S. Drummond (London, 1972).

G. Tabacco, *La casa di Francia nell'azione politica di Papa Giovanni XXII* (Rome, 1953).

T. Talbot Rice, *The Seljuks in Asia Minor* (London, 1961).

M. Tchamtchian, *History of the Armenians* (in Armenian), 3 vols. (Venice, 1784–6).

P. Tekeyan, 'Controverses christologiques en Arménie-Cilicie', *Orientalia Analecta Christiana* CXXIV (1939).

R. W. Thomson, 'The influence of their environment on the Armenians in exile in the eleventh century', *Proceedings of XIII Congress of Byzantine Studies* (Oxford, 1967).

C. Toumanoff, 'Armenia and Georgia', *Cam. Med. Hist.*, ed. J. M. Hussey, IV (Cambridge, 1966), pp. 629–38.

—— 'The Background to Manzikert', *Proceedings of the XIII Congress of Byzantine Studies* (Oxford, 1967), pp. 411–26.

H. F. Tournebize, 'Les Cent dix-sept Accusations présentées à Benoît XII contre les Arméniens', *Revue de l'Orient Chrétien*, N.S. I (1906), pp. 163–81, 274–300, 352–70.

—— *Histoire politique et religieuse de l'Arménie* (Paris, 1910).

C. Trasselli, 'Sugli Europei in Armenia', *Archivio Storico Italiano* CXXII (1964), pp. 471–91.

Previous publications relating to Baghras

A view of the castle and surroundings, engraved after a sketch by W. H. Bartlett, was included in John Carne, *Syria, The Holy Land, Asia Minor etc.* III (Fisher's Views, 1838), facing p. 56; since, as the text implies, Bartlett saw the ruins only from a distance, he misunderstood various details.

L. M. Alishan, *Sissouan ou l'Arméno-Cilicie* (Venice, 1899), p. 506, crude over-dramatic re-engraving of Bartlett's view.

G. Schlumberger, *Un Empereur byzantin* (Paris, 1890), p. 708, view from SE., apparently after a photograph.

Paul Jacquot, *Antioche* (?Antioch, 1931), pt. 2, reproduces (from indistinct blocks) photographs of the south side (facing p. 192) and from the air (facing p. 196).

Mgr Ardavazd Surmeyan, *Le Château de Baghras* (Aleppo, 1937), in Armenian; photograph from west, p. 32.

Illustrated London News (26th Aug. 1939), p. 339, reproductions of photographs by A. W. Lawrence, lost in the war.

W. Müller-Wiener, *Castles of the Crusaders* (London, 1966), pp. 48–9 (with plan, unreliable in detail), pls. 28–31 (4 photographs).

T. S. R. Boase, *Castles and Churches of the Crusading Kingdom* (London, 1967), pp. 58 (photograph), 80.

INDEX

Page numbers are given in roman, and plate numbers in italic, type. Armenian rulers are numbered according to the list on page 186. Place names are indexed where they occur in the main text, or within an entry in the Gazetteer. Entries in the Gazetteer are not indexed since these are already in alphabetical order; the Gazetteer should therefore be consulted separately.

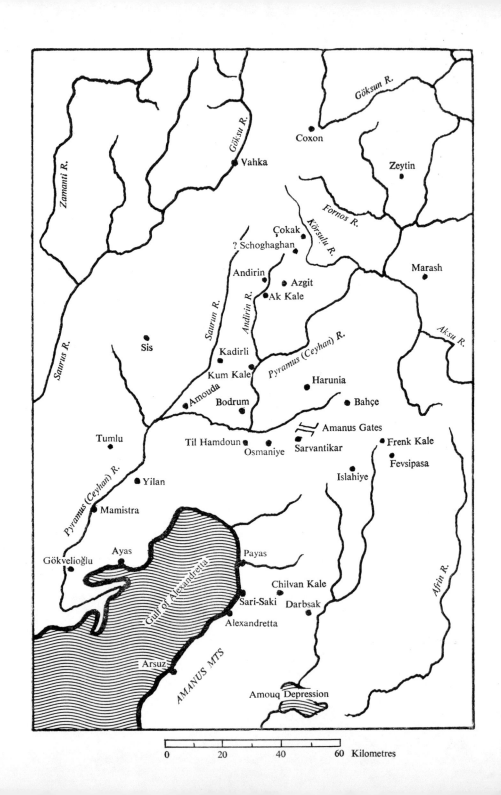

Göksun R.

Göksu R.

Zamanti R.

Coxon

Zeytin

Vahka

Fornos R.

Çokak

Köïrsulu R.

? Schoghaghan

Marash

Andirin

Azgit

Ak Kale

Saurun R.

Andirin R.

Saurus R.

Aksu R.

Sis

Kadirli

Pyramus (Ceyhan) R.

Kum Kale

Harunia

Amouda

Bahçe

Bodrum

Amanus Gates

Tumlu

Til Hamdoun

Frenk Kale

Osmaniye

Sarvantikar

Fevsipasa

Islahiye

Yilan

Pyramus (Ceyhan) R.

Mamistra

Afrin R.

Ayas

Payas

Gökvelioğlu

Chilvan Kale

Gulf of Alexandretta

Sari-Saki

Darbsak

Alexandretta

Arsuz

AMANUS MTS

Amouq Depression

0   20   40   60   Kilometres